A Guide to the Management of Curriculum Materials Centers for the 21st Century: The Promise and the Challenge

Prepared by

The Ad Hoc Management of Curriculum
Materials Committee
Education and Behavioral Sciences Section
Association of College and Research Libraries

Edited by

Jo Ann Carr

Association of College and Research Libraries
A Division of the American Library Association
Chicago, 2001

The paper used in this publication meets the minimum requirements of American National Standard for Information Sciences—Permanence of Paper for Printed Library Materials, ANSI Z39.48—1992.∞

Library of Congress Cataloging-in-Publication Data
A guide to the management of curriculum materials centers for the 21st century : the promise and the challenge / edited by Jo Ann Carr ; prepared by the Ad Hoc Management of Curriculum Materials Committee, Education and Behavioral Sciences Section, Association of College and Research Libraries.
    p. cm.
Includes bibliographical references.
  ISBN 0-8389-8175-5
  1. Education libraries--United States--Administration. 2. Instructional materials centers--United States--Administration. I. Carr, Jo Ann. II. Association of College and Research Libraries. Ad Hoc Management of Curriculum Materials Committee.
  Z675.P3 G85 2001
  025.1'977--dc21
                              2001007464

Printed in the United States of America.

05 04 03 02 01   5 4 3 2 1

Table of Contents

Introduction   viii
Jo Ann Carr

Professional Education   1
Scott Walter
One of the major issues regarding professional education for librarianship is of particular significance to librarians working in the curriculum materials center (CMC) of an academic library system: the persistent difficulty that library and information science programs have had in preparing would-be specialists for work either in specific types of libraries or in specific subject fields. An outline of the core competencies for CMC librarians and suggestions on how to provide a relevant professional education program to CMC librarians is provided in this chapter.

Curriculum Materials Centers Budgets   25
Mike Tillman
Many CMCs are heavily used and under funded. At the same time, materials and services offered by CMCs are rapidly evolving. To successfully manage a CMC budget, one must possess a keen understanding of allocation trends, budget preparation, and budget submission. The importance of efficient use of the budget and excellent advocacy skills is also discussed.

Paying the Piper and Retaining a Tune Worth Dancing To: 34
Balancing Funding Sources and the Collection Development Process
Judith M. Hildebrandt and Peggie Partello
How does "he who pays the piper" call the tune on issues of collection development? And how does a CMC funded by a number of separate "pipers" develop cohesive and meaningful collections to meet the needs of various and discrete constituencies, while at the same time, fulfilling obligations to each "piper"? Keene State College's Curriculum Materials Library (CML) has danced to numerous "tunes" during the past 10 years. This chapter addresses the needs of budgeting wisely while meeting the needs of diverse constituents.

K–12 Textbooks Series Sets in CMCs: Collection Development   42
and Management Issues
Lorene R. Sisson and Allison G. Kaplan
Collection development and management issues related to K–12 textbooks have become increasingly complex. The acquisition and organization of textbooks are challenging activities that require awareness
about the unique characteristics of the materials. Issues such as physical
size, cost, components of a series, requisite supporting equipment, and
bibliographic identification and access problems are discussed. This
chapter reviews those issues related to the specific needs of CMCs. A
definition of a textbook series along with elements for describing a
textbook series is given as well as suggestions for acquiring and organizing PK–12 textbook series materials.

Criteria for Selection and Deselection of CMC Materials,   57
Both New and Donated
John Hickok
CMCs have the responsibility of acquiring materials through purchases and donations. What should be the guiding criteria to determine whether a new or donated item should be added or not? This
chapter discusses four recommended criteria to be used in making
material selection decisions for a CMC: Duplication vs. Deficiency,
Condition/Format, Authority/Content, and Relevance/Currency.
These principles are also discussed in the equally important task of
deselecting (weeding) existing materials.

Providing Effective and Efficient Access to Curriculum Materials   69
Gary Lare
Managing a CMC collection involves many activities, not the least of
which is the provision of effective and efficient physical and intellectual access. Physical access to the collection includes such areas as organization of the collection, the processing of materials, location of
the CMC, staffing, and hours of availability. Intellectual access to the
collection involves the online catalog, pathfinders, and guides. Physical and intellectual access are concerned with access to the local CMC
collection; however, access to curriculum materials can also involve
access to materials outside the CMC.

Management Tools for Maintaining a CMC Virtual Collection 81
Patricia O'Brien Libutti
The last five years presented curriculum materials center staff with exponential expansion of resources on the World Wide Web, which then needed the same evaluation, personnel, and service decisions as earlier information formats demanded. This chapter explores the parameters of choices facing CMCs and outlines a process to make decisions about a virtual collection. Existing CMC sites are used in a description of collection scope and provide examples of reflecting upon past decisions. The development of a CMC Virtual Collection Management Plan is explored by examining broadly defined Management Tools. These tools include: 1) Using information audit strategies in the present situation; 2) Exploring available capital to implement a plan; 3) Preparing a virtual collection plan; 4) Developing continual exploration of education Web sites for review; and 5) Setting in place a systematic review process. The chapter concludes with categories and examples of sites for a Virtual Collection of Curriculum Materials.

Collection Development for CMC Reference Materials 101
Peter Cupery, Lori Delaney, and Bernie Foulk
Collection development for reference materials in a CMC should be based upon a written policy and should address the needs of its clients: students, staff, faculty, and education professionals in the community. Communications between CMC staff and teacher educators is necessary to improve pertinence of the reference materials to the clients, the larger collection, and the needs of the future.

Information and Instruction Services in CMCs 109
Adelaide Phelps and Jeneen LaSee-Willemssen
The variation in information and instructional services in CMCs can be traced back to the early evolution of the CMC from laboratory to library. Even though CMCs provide a wide-ranging variety of instructional services, there is one service —assisting users in selecting materials—that is universal. This service is explored extensively, specifically in terms of the specific instructional and informational services of: reference; library user education; tours and orientations; workshops and in-services; bibliographies and pathfinders. Finally, the future of CMC instructional services is pondered, with particular attention paid to educational technologies and information literacy.

The CMC Librarian: Collaborative Activities with Faculty: 128
Grant Writing, Action Research, and Scholarly Activities
Martha Henderson
>   Collaboration, defined as a cooperative endeavor in which profession-
>   als identify common goals, coordinate efforts to achieve objectives,
>   and share responsibilities for achieving outcomes, is not a new con-
>   cept. Faculty sometimes view the role of the CMC librarian only in
>   the context of service and are not fully cognizant of the librarian's
>   multidisciplinary strengths and research knowledge and skills. Because
>   of this, the librarian must take an active role in extending collabora-
>   tion between the librarian and faculty members. This chapter explores
>   three collaboration areas: grant writing, action research, and scholar-
>   ship. The chapter defines and describes each area, provides a brief
>   literature review, suggests topics for investigation, and profiles examples
>   of collaborative activities. It also includes URLs for Web-based re-
>   sources (including CMCs), bibliographies of print resources, and lists
>   of additional sites and resources.

Outreach and Public Relations in CMCs   137
Harriet Hagenbruch
>   Directors of CMCs have developed a variety of strategies for reaching
>   out to the various people with whom they interact on campus and in
>   the community at large. This chapter examines many of these strate-
>   gies as well as the opportunities that exist to form meaningful part-
>   nerships with faculty and other librarians. The author also points out
>   that while a CMC's lack of size and its specialized nature may have
>   certain drawbacks, both of these characteristics can serve to enhance
>   a close working relationship with education students and other pa-
>   trons who use the CMC.

Technology and the CMC   148
Judith Walker
>   A wide variety of technological advances in the twentieth century have
>   impacted education. However, none have been quite as enormous as
>   electronic technologies, particularly the personal computer. Curricu-
>   lum Materials Centers have existed most of the 20th century, but have
>   they kept pace with the technological advances in instruction? This

chapter discusses why Curriculum Materials Center must keep pace with the changing face of instructional technology and provides some suggestions about how they can accomplish the task.

A Selective Annotated Bibliography   164
Ann E. Brownson

Contributing Authors   187

Contributors of Profiles   192

Index   194

INTRODUCTION

Jo Ann Carr

A Guide to the Management of Curriculum Materials Centers for the 21st Century: The Promise and the Challenge is designed to assist teacher education programs in meeting the information and technology literacy needs of teachers and teacher educators. This work was initiated by the ACRL Education and Behavioral Sciences Section Curriculum Materials Committee and builds upon the past work of the Ad Hoc Curriculum Materials Management Committee, chaired by Ronald Edwards. The members of the Ad Hoc Management of Curriculum Materials Committee who finalized this publication were Beth Anderson, Jo Ann Carr, Allison Kaplan, Gary Lare, Jeneen LaSee-Willemssen, and Michael Tillman.

Curriculum Materials Center (CMC) is the generic name for resource centers that support teacher education programs. CMCs may contain a variety of materials, including textbooks, juvenile materials, videos, academic library resources, media production areas, and computing centers. CMCs have also been referred to by a wide variety of names, as indicated in a review of the *Directory of Curriculum Materials Centers* (ALA, 1996). Among the names listed in that volume are Computer and Curriculum Inquiry Center, Curricular Library, Curriculum and Materials Center, Curriculum and Technology Center, Curriculum Center, Curriculum Collection, Curriculum Laboratory, Curriculum Library, Curriculum Materials Library, Curriculum Resource Center, Educational Media Center, Educational Resources Center, Instructional Materials Center, Instructional Media Center, Instructional Resources Center, Learning Resource Center, and Teacher Materials Center. Whatever the name, this publication will demonstrate that CMCs are poised to play a critical role in meeting the challenges of educating teachers for the 21st century.

The chapters in this volume reflect not only the perspectives and experiences of their authors but also reflect the contributions of 26 curriculum materials librarians who completed profiles describing their centers. The authors of the chapters and the profiles were selected to address the diverse needs of CMCs that vary in size of user populations, collections, services, and staffing. These profiles will be included in a complementary electronic publication being developed by EBSS.

The volume begins with a chapter by Scott Walter, Head of Brain Education Library at Washington State University, which explores the need for professional education that prepares the CMC librarian to focus on a specific subject matter and to

Professional Education

Scott Walter

Within the library-information profession there is little doubt
that the whole question of professional education and training is
the one most likely to arouse interest and passions (Cronin, 1982, 2).

Introduction

The question of how best to prepare preservice librarians for their professional responsibilities is a vexing one. Concerns about the structure of professional education in the 21st century have been so great in recent years, in fact, that the American
Library Association (ALA) sponsored a Congress on Professional Education in
1999 that brought together practitioners, professors, and pundits from across the
country to discuss such pressing issues for the field as accreditation, the place of
core competencies in library and information science (LIS) education, and the problems faced by preservice librarians hoping to serve specific user groups (Haycock,
1999; ALA, 2000). As Sullivan (1999) noted in her review of the Congress, this
latest effort was simply the most recent in a series of such programs through
which practicing librarians and LIS educators have come together to periodi-
cally reconsider the efficacy of prevailing norms in the professional education
of librarians.

Carroll's (1970) historical overview of the profession's attempts to regulate
and improve LIS education throughout the 20th century cites a number of endur-
ing concerns relevant to the professional education of librarians that have yet to be

adequately addressed either by practitioners or by professors. Several such issues were discussed once again at the Congress on Professional Education, including one of particular import to librarians working in CMCs: the persistent difficulty that LIS programs have had in preparing would-be specialists for work either in specific types of libraries or in specific subject fields.[1]

For librarians working in CMCs, the issue of specialization has particular significance. As other chapters in this collection shall demonstrate, CMC librarians are required by the nature of their collections to focus on a specific subject matter and to acquire, organize, and manage materials of specific (often unusual) types. Moreover, CMC librarians, even when part of an academic library system, are required by the interests of their primary user groups to address information needs aligned more toward practice than toward research. To meet those needs, the CMC librarian often must collaborate with information professionals housed not in the academic library but in one of a number of related organizations (e.g., school libraries). Finally, CMC librarians are required by the composition of their primary user groups to consider how to meet the information needs of a variety of nontraditional academic library users, including adult learners, community members not otherwise affiliated with the college or university, and even school children. Undoubtedly, the CMC librarian must possess the professional skills common to work in all libraries, but the unique nature of his or her work also demands expertise in a variety of fields specifically related to teacher education.[2]

Perhaps the key to understanding and addressing the professional education needs of the CMC librarian can be found in the definition of the CMC provided by Buttlar and Tipton (1992). CMCs, they write, are special library collections in academic settings (370). Dana (1910) defined a special library as any library devoted to a special purpose and serving a limited clientele (1), and, while Skinner (1980) questioned the applicability of this term to subject-oriented academic collections, works such as Clark (1982) clearly demonstrate that this is a definition that fits the CMC. Historically designed as a laboratory in which preservice teachers might study, experiment with, and construct curriculum materials for use in their K–12 classrooms, the CMC has evolved into a multifaceted service point that houses unusual material types (including instructional materials, multimedia, and juvenile literature), serves a diverse, but well-defined, clientele not typically served by academic library services (including in-service teachers, parents, and school children), and enters into collaborative work with allied agencies not often identified with academic library work (including local school districts, public libraries, and state boards of education). To address the professional education needs of the CMC librarian, one must understand the nature of this special library collection and the characteristic information needs of its community of users.

Given that other chapters in this collection will describe in greater detail the nature of familiar professional responsibilities such as acquisitions, administration, collection management, information services, and technology services within the CMC context, further discussion of such issues in this chapter will be limited to the ways in which professional education programs (either preservice or in-service) might better prepare the CMC librarian for the issues that he or she will face in working with this special collection and its primary user groups. This chapter will focus instead on the debate over specialization in the professional education of librarians and on the ways in which existing patterns of educational opportunity might be adapted or enhanced to better meet the needs of the CMC librarian.

Educating the CMC Librarian—Lessons from the Literature

Special libraries dedicated to collecting in a single subject area have been a distinctive feature on the landscape of American librarianship at least since the late 19th century (Hausdorfer, 1970; Williams and Zachert, 1986). Among the earliest of these subject-oriented collections were those in the field of education. Familiar watersheds in the development of the education library include the establishment by Henry Barnard during the last quarter of the 19th century of the collection that would eventually become the National Library of Education, and the incorporation of the Teachers College collection into the Columbia University Libraries in 1899 (Morrill, 1981; Floyd, 1996). By the 1920s, the CMC had become a recognized feature of the academic library collection in the field of education (Clark, 1982). The development of the CMC was facilitated both by the rise of the scientific study of curriculum, which became an important part both of teacher training and of advanced study in the field of education during these years (James, 1963; Morrill, 1981; Kliebard, 1992; Pinar, et al., 1995), and by the contemporaneous movement within academic librarianship toward the establishment of departmental libraries focused on discrete subject areas (Hausdorfer, 1970; Baughman, 1984). Today, the work of the CMC librarian is closely linked to the work of professionals in a variety of related organizations, including those working in school libraries, government libraries, special libraries, and other education collections within the academic library system (Baughman, 1984). Any attempt to address the professional education needs of the CMC librarian must take into account not only the unique characteristics of his or her work in the CMC, but also the broad areas of overlap between that work and the work of the like-minded professionals found in these complementary institutions.

The position that the CMC librarian holds in this constellation of education information professionals is suggested by Edwards (1996), who referred to the CMC as the vital link between the library system of a college or university and its teacher education programs; and by Pohlman (1979), who described the CMC as a unique amalgam of the school media center and the college library (43). Given this context, it is perhaps understandable that our conception of the appropriate professional education for the CMC librarian has long been informed by the standards promoted by accrediting bodies such as the American Association of Colleges for Teacher Education (AACTE) and the National Council for Accreditation of Teacher Education (NCATE).

Unfortunately, as several studies of the CMC have noted, these standards have always been extremely vague (Ellis, 1969; Houlihan, 1978; Pohlman, 1979; Ho, 1985; Toifel, 1992). The influential AACTE (1967) standard, for example, requires only that the CMCs in accredited institutions be headed by a faculty member well informed in the various instructional media and materials at different grade levels (118). In comparison with the standards associated with other aspects of teacher education programs, the standards guiding the view of the appropriate professional education for the CMC librarian are lacking in terms of both specificity and definition (Pohlman, 1979). This lack of specificity has led to a situation in which the CMC may be governed by myriad administrative structures and headed by professionals boasting a variety of educational backgrounds—a situation which McGiverin (1988), Buttlar and Tipton (1992), and others have noted makes it difficult to effectively compare the services provided by CMCs found in different institutions. Perhaps because the CMC has historically been characterized by such a wide array of organizational structures, no one has felt comfortable attempting to prescribe the professional education appropriate for its librarian.

Certain basic educational requirements, however, can be identified in the literature. Clark (1982), for example, provides a useful discussion of the educational background typically identified with the CMC librarian. As she writes:

The person preparing for this specialized library service needs to have a knowledge of the field of professional education and familiarity with the needs of children ... [The CMC librarian] needs to understand the methods of elementary and secondary teaching and have knowledge of curriculum development (30).

In addition to this broad familiarity with the methods, materials, and professional concerns associated with teacher education, the CMC librarian may be required to have a background in related fields such as juvenile literature and educational technology, depending on the scope of the individual CMC collection and on the services provided therein. In short, the specialized services with which the CMC has historically been associated may require specialized education and experience of the CMC librarian.

The provision of information services to nontraditional academic library users, for example, may have a significant impact on the professional education needs of the CMC librarian. As later chapters in this volume illustrate, information services in CMCs are often used by in-service teachers as well as directly by children. Learning to meet the information needs of nontraditional user groups such as these is a concern that can and should be addressed as part of the professional education of the CMC librarian.

The challenges that the provision of information services to children may present to the CMC librarian have already been briefly noted above, but teachers and other professionals present similar concerns (Hammond and Mitchell, 1997). James (1985), for example, describes the difference between the academic approach to information seeking familiar to most college and university librarians and the practice-oriented use of information that characterizes the needs of preservice teachers. Baran (1984) demonstrates how this practice-oriented approach to information seeking and evaluation is carried forward into the teacher's in-service career and how the lack of attention to the practitioner's information needs may have a negative impact on the in-service teacher's ability to effectively transfer information skills acquired in the academic context to the professional one. O'Hanlon (1987) describes how the perceived distance between research-oriented information skills and practice-oriented information skills influences the attitude of both teacher education faculty and students toward bibliographic instruction. Finally, Carr and Zeichner (1988) note the challenges that these practice-oriented users of information present to the CMC librarian when they return to the academic library, either to make use of the professional resources held by the CMC or to pursue an advanced academic degree. Echoing Baughman's (1984) description of a network of information professionals in the field of education, they conclude that there must be partnerships among academic librarians, school library media specialists, and practicing teachers to ensure that preservice teachers learn to apply those information access skills learned as part of their education courses in a meaningful way in the [PK–12] classroom (Carr and Zeichner, 1988, 88). Just as the professional education of the CMC librarian must incorporate some knowledge of the information needs of children and how these may best be met, so must it incorporate some knowledge of the information needs of practitioners and the approach to information seeking, evaluation, and use that they take as part of their own professional work.

In the end, as Smith and Gardner (1956), MacVean (1958), Ellis (1969), Nevil (1975), Clark (1982), and others have argued, an academic and professional background in the field of education is highly useful to anyone providing the information services typically offered by CMC librarians. Moreover, the lack of such experience can have a significant impact on the ability of the CMC as an organization to provide the specialized services with which it has long been associated (Ho, 1985). As Cook and Heimers (1945) wrote over 50 years ago, education and experience in librarianship are useful to the CMC librarian, but equally important (if not more so) is experience in the field of education "long enough to make one aware of the problems which teachers face" (203).

A recent announcement by the State University of New York at Buffalo, for example, requires the successful candidate for its CMC position to possess not only the MLS (or an equivalent degree in a related field), but also coursework in instructional methods. Moreover, the successful candidate should demonstrate not only basic skills in information retrieval and database searching, but also a familiarity with finding educational resources and teacher materials (lesson plans, etc.) on the World Wide Web. Finally, the successful candidate should have experience with teaching methods and curriculum materials ... [and experience] working with teachers (State University of New York at Buffalo, 2000). Similarly, a position description from Bowling Green State University requires not only the MLS degree, but also experience in education, curriculum, multimedia, children's literature, and electronic resources (Curriculum Resource Center Head Librarian, 2000). These brief examples suggest, again, that the specialized services historically provided through the CMC require of its librarian a thorough knowledge of the field of education and of the characteristic information needs of its primary user groups (especially practicing teachers).

The educational and professional requirements outlined in position descriptions in the CMC field dovetail, then, with the requirements suggested to be useful by the relevant literature. Despite this fact, however, and despite the fact that various surveys of CMC librarians conducted over the years have requested data on their educational backgrounds (e.g., MacVean, 1958; Pohlman, 1979; Ho, 1985; McGiverin, 1988), no significant attempt has ever been made to elaborate on the appropriate professional education for the CMC librarian. There is no document for CMC librarians comparable to the Medical Library Association's *Platform for Change: The Educational Policy Statement of the Medical Library Association* (2000), or the American Association of Law Libraries *Core Competencies of Law Librarianship* (2000). Typically, the conclusions drawn by earlier studies of CMC librarians have been highly generalized: e.g., that CMC librarians, as a group, exhibit a broad and varied educational background (Pohlman, 1979, 104); and, following the literature, that the CMC librarian should have a background both in librarianship and in the field of education.

Why, one might ask, is it important for the CMC librarian to have academic and professional experience related to teacher education? Moreover, given the fact that many CMC librarians enter the field without this preservice background, how might a CMC librarian without experience in teacher education become better prepared for the professional responsibilities associated with the field?[3] The resources described above provide some answers to the first question, as well as some clues to the general outline of the educational experience that may be of use to the CMC librarian. Additional ideas about the reasons why specialized education is required of the CMC librarian may be discovered in the disparate library literature related to the education of other subject specialists.

Educating the Subject Specialist—Lessons from Related Literature

As should be clear from the preceding discussion, the CMC librarian is a subject specialist. The professional work associated with the CMC librarian's provision of information services, development and maintenance of collections, and management of resources is closely tied to the nature of the curriculum field and is in many ways distinct from the work conducted by other academic librarians. The predominant mode of preservice professional education for librarians, however, aims at producing a generalist rather than a specialist.

There are a number of very practical reasons why this is the case. Chief among these are the following: the relatively small number of LIS programs in the United States; the relatively short time during which preservice professional education may be effected under the current system; and the fact that many preservice librarians do not discover the specialty which they wish to pursue until late in their academic program. Surveys of government documents librarians (Cross and Richardson, 1989) and business librarians (Kendrick, 1990), in fact, have found that many subject specialists do not decide to specialize in a particular area until long after they have entered the profession. Regarding the professional education of subject specialists in the academic library, then, it would appear that the conclusion drawn by Conant (1980) continues to apply, "The development of specialists is more likely to be accidental than arranged as part of professional training" (99).

The effective provision of specialized professional services, however, requires more than just a serendipitous placement into a specialist position. Williams (1991) has contended that any motivated individual may quickly acquire the basic knowledge of a field that is required of a novice bibliographer, but others have suggested that there is more to consider in preparing a subject specialist than just a working familiarity with the literature of a field. Hay (1990), for example, enumerates a variety of professional responsibilities with which the subject specialist has been identified in addition to bibliography, including information services such as reference and instruction, technical services such as cataloging and classification, and liaison work with academic departments. It is not unusual, in fact, as Stebelman (1989) has noted, for the subject specialist to take his or her association with a specific field so far as to actually teach in the academic department. To identify the work of the subject specialist purely with the bibliographic work associated with collection development and management is to provide support for Hay's charge that, as a profession, U. S. librarians have no clear conception of what constitutes a subject specialist (11).

Contrary to Hay's opinion, though, a number of authors have made persuasive arguments over the years that demonstrate a clear understanding both of the multiple professional roles which the subject specialist is regularly called upon to play, and of the value of specialized education for those librarians hoping to serve in specialist positions. Smardo (1980) advocated for the specialized education needs of the preservice children's librarian. Her arguments suggest that the subject specialist must possess not only a thorough understanding of the literature of his or her chosen field, but also an understanding of the information needs of his or her primary user groups, of the unique materials that his or her users may require for their use in the library, and of the allied organizations that share the library's responsibility for meeting those information needs. Professional associations of law librarians and health sciences librarians, among others, have identified a similar array of professional responsibilities and have developed relevant educational programs at both the preservice and in-service levels (Williams and Zachert, 1986).[4]

Smardo's suggestion for one effective means of meeting this challenge of educating the would-be specialist across a variety of professional responsibilities was to develop a cross-disciplinary course of study between schools of library science and the colleges of education that would allow preservice children's librarians to study alongside their future counterparts—PK–12 teachers and school librarians (278). As Conant (1980), and Marchant and Wilson (1983) have noted, this approach to providing for the needs of would-be specialists through the creation of joint degree options has been in use for some time by a number of LIS programs.[5] Cherubini (1998), for example, provides a thorough overview of such programs available to preservice music librarians. Unfortunately, few (if any) of these joint programs, as they currently stand, successfully address the range of academic knowledge and professional skills required of the well-prepared CMC librarian.[6] Useful overviews of the substantive debates on the question of specialized education over the past half century, especially in the academic library context, are provided by Haskell (1984), Williams and Zachert (1986), Hay (1990), and Jones (1998).

Collection development is the professional responsibility most commonly discussed in the literature related to the education of the subject specialist (Haskell,

1984). Byrd (1966) provides one of the seminal discussions of this topic in his description of the subject specialist program in the Main Library of Indiana University. While Indiana's subject specialists provided a number of user services, including reference assistance and bibliographic instruction, the majority of their time was taken up by issues related to collection development. Danton (1967) also focused on the specialist's role in collection development in his comparative study of national and university libraries. More recently, Stebelman (1989) described the role that subject specialists can play in building and maintaining a reference collection. In each case, the argument is advanced that the library collection benefits greatly from the focused attention which the subject specialist can pay to his or her work in this area, and by the knowledge that the specialist brings to that work in terms of familiarity with trends in the research, avenues of scholarly communication in the field, etc.

Williams (1991) argues that a basic familiarity with the literature of a field will allow a newly appointed specialist to meet his or her responsibilities in this collection development area, and this is the approach most commonly taken in the subject bibliography courses that are presently a common feature of preservice professional education for librarians (Hopkins, 1987). Unlike recognized specialties such as law, health sciences, and music, however, there are no subject courses in the field of education. Given the unique considerations described above in terms of the distinctive information needs of CMC user groups and the challenges related to collecting CMC materials such as curriculum guidelines, textbooks, unit plans, and realia (Clark, 1982; Thurston, 1987; Lare, 1997), there can be no question that the CMC librarian, novice or not, requires considerably more than a passing acquaintance with the field of education if he or she is to effectively develop and maintain this special collection. At the very least, the professional education model already adopted by specialties such as government documents librarianship, business librarianship, science librarianship, and others, should be extended to the field of education librarianship and a separate subject course developed as an option for preservice librarians considering specializing in this field.

Closely related to the specialist's responsibility for collection development is his or her role as liaison between the library and the classroom faculty. It has been recognized for decades that the specialist can play an important role in facilitating communication between the classroom faculty and the academic library (Byrd, 1966), but this responsibility has become increasingly important as the common commitment to the use of information technology in the classroom brings the work of the classroom faculty progressively further into the professional realm of the academic librarian (Jayne and Vander Meer, 1997; Smalley, 1998; Raspa and Ward, 2000).

Budd (1984), Holley (1985), and Herubel (1991) have described the distinctive organizational culture of higher education and the ways in which it can affect the professional work of the academic librarian. Nowhere is this more the case than in liaison work, where specialized education is the pre-eminent means of identifying one's colleagues on campus. Liaison work is made doubly difficult for the CMC librarian by the fact that he or she must not only collaborate effectively with researchers among the academic faculty, but also with the practitioners and student teachers participating in the teacher education programs field components. The CMC librarian is the library's liaison not only to faculty, but also to teachers, administrators, and community members who make use of the professional collection. Again, it is clear that this responsibility requires the CMC librarian to have a command not only of the literature of his or her field, but also of its professional practice.

As is the case with both collection development and liaison work, the ability of the subject specialist to meet his or her professional responsibilities in the area of information services is tied to his or her familiarity both with the subject field and with the characteristics of those users most often associated with the field. As one observer wrote almost 50 years ago, "the subject specialist must be equipped to speak the language of the person requiring information and serve as the interpreter for the general librarian who may lack knowledge of the terminology and technicalities of the special field" (Subcommittee on Special Library Education, 1954, 18). As Stuart and Drake (1992) concluded: "[the] quality of information services provided to scientists and engineers is less effective when the librarians serving them have little or no experience in these disciplines" (79).

While every subject specialist must face this challenge of serving as the resident expert both on the literature of a specific field and on the information services associated with that field (e.g., specific databases, scholarly networks, and government and professional organizations), the CMC librarian's responsibility in this area is made more difficult, again, by the nature of the curriculum field. The CMC librarian must serve not only as a specialist in the academic field of education, but also as a specialist in the information sources and professional expertise relevant to working with practicing teachers. As noted in the chapter on information services "Information and Instruction Services in CMCs," many such resources are more typically associated with public and school librarianship than with academic librarianship. We are reminded at this point of Smardo's (1980) suggestion of an interdisciplinary course of preservice professional education that would bring children's librarians into greater contact with their counterparts in preservice teacher education programs. The CMC librarian would likewise be well served by a preservice course of study that recognizes his or her place in the network of information professionals concerned with the field of education.

The final area of professional responsibility that marks the work of the CMC librarian as distinctive is his or her work as the manager of a specialized collection containing materials of many unusual types. The Music Library Association (2000) has published a variety of manuals dedicated to preparing the music librarian to meet his or her responsibilities in this area, as has the Society of American Archivists (2000b). Nemchek (1980) wrote that the materials which generally make up theater archives are uniquely related to the profession and do not have their counterparts in standard print collections (50). Theater posters, scripts, props, and programs are all mentioned as materials that are not only atypical of most academic library collections, but that require special attention in terms of technical services such as cataloging, access, and storage. The same could certainly be said of music library materials such as scores and sound recordings, as well as of materials typically found in a CMC, including test banks, textbooks, multimedia, juvenile literature curriculum sets, realia, games, models, and manipulatives.

For all these reasons, then, it may be concluded that the library literature related to the question of the appropriate professional education for the subject specialist reiterates the need for a specialized professional education for those librarians who are working with specific user groups, or who are responsible for collections that include unusual material types. Specialized education is even more important when the primary users of a subject-specific collection are also professionals who may demonstrate a set of information needs substantially different from those typically associated with the academic library user. From this review of the relevant literature, both general and specific to CMCs, we may distill certain key features of the appropriate professional education for the CMC librarian.

Core Competencies for the CMC Librarian

In his survey of the field of academic librarianship, Budd (1998) notes that one of the distinguishing characteristics of any library is its community of users. In some cases, this means that there is a qualitative difference in the nature of the librarian's professional work depending on the type of librarianship in which he or she is engaged. The work of an academic librarian is often substantially different from that of a public librarian or a school librarian, for example, and these are distinctions with which we become familiar from the earliest days of our preservice professional education. Sometimes, however, type-of-library designations are so artificial that they cease to be helpful. For example, a specific academic library might conceivably have more in common with a specific special library than it does with other academic libraries (3). This is the case with CMCs.

As Baughman (1984) has noted, the CMC exists within a network of complementary professional collections, including those found in school libraries, special libraries, government libraries, and other education libraries within the academic library system. The professional work conducted in the CMC bears a strong resemblance to that which is conducted in these complementary collections. Consider, for example, the distinctions that Skinner (1980) enumerated between the academic library's subject collections and the special library:

• The mission of the special library is real world rather than learning oriented;

• The special library collection contains unusual material types, e.g., clipping files, archival materials, and graphic materials; and,

• The purpose to which special library users plan to put the information they find therein is practical, rather than academic (294–96).

Not all of these distinctions hold true for the CMC, which supports the work of users whose information needs may be simultaneously academic and practical, and which provides real-world–oriented users with a wide variety of materials not typically associated with the academic library collection. Obviously, the CMC's mission is, as Skinner puts it, learning oriented, but the nature of its collections and the composition of its primary user groups defy the facile distinctions between types of libraries that Skinner outlines. The CMC is one part academic library, but it is also one part special library, and one part school library. It is, as Pohlman (1979) wrote, a unique amalgam of the distinct library types with which we are familiar.

The recommendations for professional education that follow, then, are aimed not only at the librarian employed in the academic CMC, but at any professional who finds himself or herself responsible for a collection of materials that support research and practice in PK–12 instruction. This professional may answer to any of a number of titles and may be employed in any of a number of venues. The professional education outlined below will be relevant to each of them (albeit to different degrees), and the methods suggested for delivering the content may facilitate the collaboration across types of CMC collections that Carr and Zeichner (1988), among others, suggest is critical to the effective provision of services to our distinctive user groups.

What follows is not meant to be comprehensive, however, or to limit future discussion of professional education opportunities for the CMC librarian in any way. Rather, it is meant to synthesize the lessons learned from the literature described above and to open the way for further discussion of our mutual educational needs and the best way to work toward meeting them in the professional environment of the 21st century.[7]

✳ ✳ ✳ ✳ ✳

I. Core Competencies for the CMC Librarian

The American Association of Law Libraries opens its discussion of the Core Competencies of Law Librarianship (American Association of Law Libraries, 2000b) by noting that a profession can be defined by the skills and practical knowledge its members apply to the shared environment in which they work (1). Like CMC librarians, law librarians may find employment in a variety of professional venues, including academic law libraries, government law libraries, corporate law libraries, and special libraries, but are bound together by the common characteristics of their special collections and their users. Their listing of core competencies includes both the general competencies applicable to the work of all law librarians, and the specialized competencies that may be required by one arena of law librarianship more than another. Rather than attempt to address the general competencies that CMC librarians share with other academic librarians, the focus here will be on some of the specialized competencies required for effective professional work in the CMC that have been identified through the preceding review of the literature. Many of these competencies will be applicable, in different degrees, to all education librarians, including those who do not work directly with CMC materials.

The Education Environment

CMC librarians must understand the social, cultural, and political contexts within which education information is created and disseminated, and within which the profession of teaching is practiced. The CMC librarian:

• demonstrates a thorough familiarity with the American system of education and, in particular, with the profession of teaching;

• keeps abreast of local, state, and federal government initiatives in regard to education, especially those germane to curriculum development (e.g., subject-specific standards for academic achievement, standardized assessments);

• remains informed about local issues in education that may have an impact on user information needs (e.g., court decisions regarding desegregation or school funding);

• recognizes the impact that educational reform movements may have on CMC users (e.g., the rise of home schooling as a mainstream option for alternative education);

• develops collaborative relations with state bodies such as the textbook review board or the State Board of Education; and

• is familiar with accreditation requirements specific to the education field (e.g., NCATE) and works to ensure that the CMC meets the required standards.

Information Services

CMC librarians apply LIS principles to the handling of education information resources. The CMC librarian:

• demonstrates a thorough knowledge of information resources and bibliographic tools relevant to the field of education, and the ability to match those resources to specific information needs;

• demonstrates a thorough knowledge of information resources and bibliographic tools relevant to juvenile literature, instructional materials, and any other categories of material related to the specialized collections housed in the CMC;

• is able to assess the information needs of distinct CMC user groups, including practicing teachers, children and young adults, and other nontraditional user groups (e.g., adult students returning to an academic environment), and to provide professional services such as reference and instruction appropriate to those needs; and

• is able to assist nonprofessionals in accessing and evaluating education information (e.g., parents and other community members).

Instructional Services

The CMC librarian is a teacher. The CMC librarian:

• assesses the instructional needs of CMC user groups and develops programming designed to meet those needs at a variety of levels (e.g., professional vs. scholarly);

• develops instructional materials, pathfinders, and other bibliographic tools to assist CMC users in the location of professional materials available both in the CMC and through electronic resources such as ERIC and the World Wide Web; and

• assists CMC users in curriculum design, development, and evaluation.

Collection Care and Management

CMC librarians are responsible for the care and management of a variety of unusual collections, including instructional materials, test banks, multimedia materials (including instructional technology), and realia. The CMC librarian:

• demonstrates a thorough familiarity with the professional resources necessary for the identification, evaluation, and acquisition of CMC materials;

• is able to apply appropriate classification schemes to CMC materials;

• makes decisions about accessioning and deaccessioning CMC materials that are consistent with the needs of its primary user groups for historical and current information and instructional resources; and

• makes decisions about space allocation in the CMC that take into account the unique challenge of providing serviceable access to a variety of instructional materials, including print, multimedia, manipulatives, etc.

Information Systems and Information Technology

CMC librarians provide access both to information retrieval systems such as ERIC and to information technology relevant to curriculum development. The CMC librarian:

• is able to make expert use of information retrieval systems relevant to the field of education, and to assist CMC users in doing the same, especially in regard to the location and retrieval of professional materials such as lesson plans;

• is familiar with educational technology and is able to assist CMC users wishing to incorporate technology into their classroom plans; and

• provides access to current information technologies and computer-based instructional resources in the CMC, and can help resolve user problems.

Scholarly and Professional Communication

CMC librarians recognize the complexity of the education information environment and the avenues by which education information, both research-oriented and practitioner-oriented, is disseminated. The CMC librarian:

• recognizes that the CMC is part of a network of related information organizations and actively promotes collaborative efforts among education information professionals (e.g., school librarians);

• is familiar with relevant professional organizations in education (e.g., the National Council of Teachers of English);

• is familiar with relevant scholarly organizations in education (e.g., the American Educational Research Association);

• is familiar with relevant professional organizations in librarianship (e.g., the American Association of School Librarians); and

• Is familiar with and utilizes awareness services such as those provided by professional publications such as *Education Week* (Ed Week Update) and by government bodies such as the United States Department of Education (*ED Initiatives*).

II. Methods of Providing Professional Education to Meet the Core Competencies

There are a variety of methods through which preservice and in-service CMC librarians might prepare themselves to meet the core competencies outlined above. As before, the following suggestions are based on the preceding review of the literature and on a study of the work being done in this area by professional organizations such as the American Association of Law Libraries, the Medical Library Association, and the Music Library Association. The easiest method of meeting the professional education needs of the CMC librarian would be to institute a subject course in education librarianship as part of the preservice LIS curriculum. Several specialized branches of library service have followed this model, including government documents librarianship, business librarianship, science librarianship, and music librarianship. Other specialized fields have attempted to develop subject coursework, only to see it fail to become established in the curriculum. Nemchek (1980), for example, reported that coursework in theater librarianship had been developed at two LIS programs during the 1970s. For all the reasons described both in this essay and in the others found in this collection, there can be little doubt that the theory and practice of education librarianship is sufficiently complex to warrant its own course offering in a comprehensive program of LIS education. Although practicing specialists have questioned the utility of these relatively brief overviews of their subject areas (e.g., Cross and Richardson, 1989; Stuart and Drake, 1992), such an approach would be a useful start for a field that has been uncomfortably folded for too long into the broader subject of social sciences librarianship. A course such as this should be designed to appeal not only to future academic librarians with an interest in the field of education, but to all preservice librarians considering a career within the network of education information professionals, including school librarians, children's and young adult librarians, and special librarians.

A more ambitious approach to providing preservice education to aspiring CMC librarians would be to develop an interdisciplinary program along the lines suggested by Smardo (1980) as potentially useful to preservice children's librarians. A program that brought future academic librarians together with future children's librarians, school librarians, and school teachers would allow the preservice CMC librarian to more fully appreciate the network of education information professionals who are responsible for helping to meet the information needs of CMC user groups such as practicing teachers and school children. Moreover, the provision of such a program would foster future collaboration between these hitherto distinct groups of preservice librarians—a goal which, as Carr and Zeichner (1988) noted, is crucial to the information profession's support of contemporary educational reform movements.

A number of specialized branches of library service have built on the single-subject course option to develop full-fledged interdisciplinary programs. Among the variety of such options currently offered at a single LIS program include joint degrees in library science and music, library science and art history, and library science and law. Specializations available within the standard LIS educational program offered at the same institution include area studies librarianship, chemistry librarianship, and music librarianship (Indiana University School of Library and Information Science, 2000).

Finally, there is the continuing education model provided by fields such as law librarianship and health sciences librarianship. Both of these fields routinely find subject coursework offered during preservice professional education, but neither has ever accepted such limited specialized education as sufficient to their professional needs. As Williams and Zachert (1983) wrote, "The health sciences librarians and law librarians [developed] their own certification programs designed to assure quality control and continuing education for the professionals who practiced in their fields" (228). In 1999 alone, the Medical Library Association offered continuing education coursework in areas such as information services, information retrieval systems, print and Web-based information resources, and teaching the adult learner (Medical Library Association 2000a). The American Association of Law Libraries offers continuing education coursework in areas including legal research, legal reference services, and space planning for law libraries (American Association of Law Libraries 2000a). The Society of American Archivists offers coursework in specialized cataloging, space planning for archival collections, and the administration of special collections (Society of American Archivists 2000a). While regional groups such as the CMC Interest Group of the Academic Library Association of Ohio offer workshops that provide a limited degree of continuing professional education, the development of an active continuing education program by professional organizations such as the Education and Behavioral Sciences Section of the Association of College and Research Libraries or the Education Division of the Special Libraries Association along the lines of the programs described above is perhaps the most ambitious possibility of them all.

Conclusions and Recommendations

This chapter has drawn on a variety of resources to develop an outline of the core competencies that mark the professional responsibilities of the CMC librarian, and has introduced a number of options through which professional education toward meeting those competencies might be developed. Numerous opportunities for further research remain. The American Association of Law Libraries' listing of core competencies for law librarianship, for example, was developed following a survey of all AALL members. The CMC core competencies listed above would undoubtedly be improved and expanded by a similar survey of CMC librarians. Additional information is also required on specialized services provided in CMCs, e.g., instructional services provided to distinctive user groups such as in-service teachers and school children. Finally, further information is needed on the continuing education programs already being conducted by regional organizations such as the Academic Library Association of Ohio so that any future efforts at developing professional education programs for CMC librarians may be informed by the lessons already learned in practice.

Almost half a century of research on the curriculum materials center shows that the CMC can play a vital role in teacher education. Not only can the CMC provide valuable instructional services that supplement those already provided to preservice teachers in other departments of the academic library, but it can lead the way in helping the student to transfer the information literacy skills that are increasingly important to professional practice in teaching from their preservice lives to their in-service lives. Moreover, it can serve as an information center through which researchers, practitioners, and community members may locate information and materials relevant to the study and practice of PK–12 instruction. Finally, the CMC can be an arena for outreach activities from institutions of higher education into the surrounding communities. The degree to which the CMC can play such an active role in the life of its parent institution and its local community, however, is closely tied to the degree to which its librarian is prepared to meet the unique challenges posed by this specialized professional position.

Notes

1. One example of the passionate and ongoing nature of this debate can be found in a pair of recent articles in *Library Journal*: Fallis and Fricke (1999) and "Not by Theory Alone: Replies to D. Fallis and M. Fricke" (2000). An outline of the major issues and a listing of the relevant resources can be found in Woodsworth, et al. (1994).

2. Throughout this chapter, I employ the term "CMC librarian" to refer to the individual charged with managing a curriculum materials collection. Various studies have shown that this person may hold one (or more) of a variety of professional titles, including "Director, Curriculum Materials Center," "Curriculum Materials Librarian," and "Education Librarian." Pohlman (1979), for example, reported 19 separate titles being used by respondents to his national survey of CMCs (102). Rather than allowing this lack of uniformity in titles to suggest that it is impossible to outline a professional education program likely to benefit this individual, I will argue, instead, that there are certain basics that are germane to the work of all CMC librarians, regardless of their title, administrative home in the college and university, or other educational background.

3. Pohlman (1979) reported that the most commonly held graduate degree among CMC librarians in NCATE-accredited institutions was the MLS. Ho (1985) and McGiverin (1988) likewise reported that the most commonly held graduate degree among the CMC librarians was the MLS. Moreover, only 56% of McGiverin's respondents reported having a degree in the field of education at any level. Although this is an improvement over the 19% reported in Johnson's earlier survey (Johnson, 1973), it is still cause for concern. A much smaller sample of CMC librarians surveyed by Althage and Stine (1992) reported statistics similar to McGiverin's.

4. For information on these programs, visit association Web sites such as those maintained by the American Association of Law Librarians (2000), Medical Library Association (2000b), Music Library Association (Cherubini, 1998) and Society of American Archivists (2000a).

5. According to statistics provided in the Association for Library and Information Science Education (ALISE) statistical reports, approximately 33% of ALA-accredited LIS programs had established joint degree programs in the early 1980s (Marchant and Wilson, 1983). By 1992, this number had increased to almost 50% (Sineath, 1992).

6. Of the 29 institutions reporting joint degree programs in the early 1990s, only four reported programs directly germane to the education of the CMC librarian, e.g., programs in fields such as education, higher education, or instructional technology (Sineath, 1992). "Education," in fact, was one of the joint programs deemed to be of least interest to ARL library directors involved in hiring subject specialists (Marchant and Wilson, 1983), The number cited above does not include the school library media programs that are commonplace at the majority of institutions, but which are typically categorized as "certificate" rather than as "joint degree" programs. For a representative example of the variety of joint degree options being offered at leading LIS programs, see Indiana University School of Library and Information Science (2000).

7. This outline borrows both from the AALL "Core Competencies" (American Association of Law Librarians, 2000b) and from the Medical Library Association's "Educational Policy Statement" (Medical Library Association, 2000c) for its structure.

References

Academic Library Association of Ohio. 2000. *ALAO Interest Groups.* Columbus, Ohio: Author. Accessed at http://www.alaoweb.org/comsigs/igs.html on June 12, 2000.

Althage, J., and D. Stine. 1992. "Curriculum Centers as Support to Education Programs in Illinois Academic Institutions." *Illinois Libraries* 74 (6): 516–23.

American Association of Colleges for Teacher Education. 1967. *American Association of Colleges for Teacher Education: A Source Book on Selected Issues.* Washington, D.C.: Author.

American Association of Law Libraries. 2000a. *AALL Professional Development.* Chicago, Ill.: Author. Accessed at http://www.aallnet.org/prodev/ on June 7, 2000.

American Association of Law Libraries. 2000b. *Core Competencies of Law Librarianship.* Chicago, Ill.: Author. Accessed at http://www.aallnet.org/prodev/comp.pdf on June 7, 2000.

American Association of School Librarians/Association of College and Research Libraries Task Force on the Educational Role of Libraries. 1999. *Blueprint for Collaboration.* Chicago, Ill.: Author. Accessed at http://www.fiu.edu/~iannuzzi/aasl/tfedrlib.html on June 12, 2000.

American Library Association. 2000. *Congress on Professional Education.* Chicago, Ill.: Author. Accessed at http://www.ala.org/congress/ on May 19, 2000.

Baran, F. A. 1984. *Study of the Assessments of Urban Public Secondary School Teachers with Regard to Sources of Information.* Unpublished doctoral dissertation, University of Massachusetts.

Baughman, S. S. 1984. "Education Libraries in the United States." *Education Libraries* 9 (3): 45–48.

Budd, J. 1984. "The Education of Academic Librarians." *College and Research Libraries* 45 (1): 15–24.

Budd, J. M. 1998. *The Academic Library: Its Context, Its Purpose, and Its Operation.* Englewood, Colo.: Libraries Unlimited.

Buttlar, L., and M. Tipton. 1992. "Library Use and Staff Training in Curriculum Materials Centers." *Journal of Academic Librarianship* 17 (6): 370–74.

Byrd, C. K. 1966. "Subject Specialists in a University Library." *College and Research Libraries* 27 (3): 191–93.

Carr, J. A., and K. Zeichner. 1988. "Academic Libraries and Teacher Education Reform: The Education of the Professional Teacher." In *Libraries and the Search for Academic Excellence,* eds. P. S. Breivik and R. Wedgeworth, 83–92. Metuchen, N.J.: Scarecrow Press.

Carroll, C. E. 1970. *The Professionalization of Education for Librarianship.* Metuchen, N.J.: Scarecrow Press.

Cherubini, T. J., ed. 1998. *Directory of Library School Offerings,* 7th ed. McLean, Va.: Music Library Association. Accessed at http://www.musiclibraryassoc.org/services/se_schoo.htm on June 7, 2000.

Church, J. G. 1957. The Development of Criteria for Evaluating Curriculum Laboratories in Teacher Education Institutions. Unpublished doctoral dissertation, University of Utah.

Clark, A. S. 1982. *Managing Curriculum Materials in the Academic Library.* Metuchen, N.J.: Scarecrow Press.

Conant, R. W. 1980. *The Conant Report: A Study of the Education of Librarians.* Cambridge, Mass.: MIT Press.

Cook, M. C., and L. Heimers. 1945. "Extended College Library Service to Teachers." *College and Research Libraries* 6 (3): 199–205+.

Cronin, B. 1982. *The Education of Library-Information Professionals: A Conflict of Objectives?* London: ASLIB.

Cross, B. M., and J. Richardson Jr. 1989. "The Educational Preparation of Government Information Specialists." *Journal of Education for Library and Information Science* 30 (1): 28–38.

"Curriculum Resource Center Head Librarian [advertisement]." 2000. *C&RL News* 61 (1): 73.

Dana, J. C. 1910. "Foreword." *Special Libraries* 1 (1): 1–2.

Danton, J. P. 1967. "The Subject Specialist in National and University Libraries, with Special Reference to Book Selection." *Libri* 17 (1): 42–58.

Detlefsen, E. G. 1992. "Specialists as Professionals in Research Libraries: An Overview of Trends and an Analysis of Job Announcements." *Library Trends* 41 (2): 187–97.

Edwards, R. G. 1996. "Curriculum Materials Centers: The Vital Link to Teacher Education Programs." *Ohio Media Spectrum* 48 (1): 13–15.

Ellis, E. V. 1969. *The Role of the Curriculum Laboratory in the Preparation of Quality Teachers.* Tallahassee, Fla.: Florida A&M University.

Fallis, D., and Fricke, M. 1999. "Not by Library School Alone." *Library Journal* 124 (17): 44–45.

Hammond, C., and E. Mitchell. 1997. "Library Instruction for the Professions: Information Needs and Libraries." *Reference Services Review* 25 (2): 79–86.

Haskell, J. D., Jr. 1984. "Subject Bibliographers in Academic Libraries: An Historical and Descriptive Review." In *Advances in Library Administration and Organization*, eds. G. B. McCabe and B. Kreissman, vol. 3, 73–84. Greenwich, Conn.: JAI Press.

Hausdorfer, W. 1970. "Professional School and Departmental Libraries." In *Reader in the Academic Library*, ed. M. M. Reynolds, 193–213. Washington, D.C.: Microcard Editions. [originally published, 1939].

Hay, F. J. 1990. "The Subject Specialist in the Academic Library: A Review of the Literature." *Journal of Academic Librarianship* 16 (1): 11–17.

Haycock, K. 1999. "The Congress on Graduate Professional Education: Issues, Process, and Recommendations." In *Library and Information Science Annual*, ed. B. S. Wyner, vol. 7, 12–22. Englewood, Colo.: Libraries Unlimited.

Herron, N., ed. 1996. *The Social Sciences: A Cross-disciplinary Guide to Selected Sources*, 2nd ed. Englewood, Colo.: Libraries Unlimited.

Herubel, J. B. P. V. M. 1991. "To Degree or Not to Degree: Academic Librarians and Subject Expertise." *Indiana Libraries*: 10 (2): 90–4.

Hill, J. A. 1992. The Qualifications Sought by Academic Library Employers: A Content Analysis of Job Advertisements. Unpublished master's thesis, University of North Carolina.

Ho, M. L. 1985. *Competencies of Curriculum Materials Center Directors in Teacher Education Institutions*. ERIC Document Reproduction Service No. ED 256 319.

Holley, E. G. 1985. "Refining the Academic Librarian." *College and Research Libraries* 46 (6): 462–68.

Hopkins, R. L. 1987. "Perspectives on Teaching Social Sciences and Humanities Literatures." *Journal of Education for Library and Information Science* 28 (2): 136–51.

Houlihan, B. 1978. "The University Curriculum Library: Evaluate, Update, Renovate." *Curriculum Review* 17 (5): 361–63

Indiana University School of Library and Information Science. 2000. *Joint Degree Programs*. Bloomington, Ind.: Author. Accessed at http://www.slis.indiana.edu/Degrees/joint.html on May 18, 2000.

James, M. L. 1963. The Curriculum Laboratory in Teacher Education Institutions: Its Essential Characteristics. Unpublished doctoral dissertation, University of Connecticut.

James, R. 1985. "Teacher Education Students—Different Needs, Different Solutions." In *Reader Services in Polytechnic Libraries*, ed. J. Fletcher, 140–58. Brookfield, Vt.: Gower.

Jayne, E. A., and P. F. Vander Meer. 1997. "The Library's Role in Academic Instructional Use of the World Wide Web." *Research Strategies* 15 (3): 123–50.

Johnson, H. R. 1973. *The Curriculum Materials Center: A Study of Policies and Practices in Selected Centers*. ERIC Document Reproduction Service No. ED 081 449.

Jones, P. J. 1998. "Academic Graduate Work in Academic Librarianship: Historicizing ACRL's Terminal Degree Statement." *Journal of Academic Librarianship* 24 (6): 437–43.

Kendrick, A. 1990. "The Educational Background and Work Experience of Academic Business Librarians." *RQ* 29 (3): 394–99.

Kliebard, H. M. 1992. "The Rise of Scientific Curriculum Making and Its Aftermath." In *Forging the American Curriculum: Essays in Curriculum History and Theory*, ed. H. M. Kliebard, 83–96. New York: Routledge. [originally published, 1975].

Kuhlthau, C. C. 1988. "Meeting the Information Needs of Children and Young Adults: Basing Library Media Programs on Developmental States." *Journal of Youth Services in Libraries* 2 (1): 51–57.

Lancaster, F. W. 1985. "Educating the Agricultural Information Specialist." *Revista AIBDA* 6: 101–24.

Lare, G. A. 1997. *Acquiring and Organizing Curriculum Materials.* Lanham, Md.: Scarecrow Press.

MacVean, D. S. 1958. A Study of Curriculum Laboratories in Midwestern Teacher-training Institutions. Unpublished doctoral dissertation, University of Michigan.

Marchant, M. P., and Wilson, C. F. 1983. "Developing Joint Graduate Programs for Librarians." *Journal of Education for Librarianship* 24 (1): 30–37.

McGiverin, R. 1988. "Curriculum Material Centers: A Descriptive Study." *Behavioral and Social Sciences Librarian* 6 (3/4): 119–28.

Medical Library Association. 2000a. *AM99: Continuing Education Courses.* Chicago, Ill.: Author. Accessed at http://www.mlanet.org/am/am1999/ce/index.html on June 12, 2000.

Medical Library Association. 2000b. *Education.* Chicago, Ill.: Author. Accessed at http://www.mlanet.org/education/index.html on June 7, 2000.

Medical Library Association. 2000c. *Platform for Change: The Educational Policy Statement of the Medical Library Association.* Chicago, Ill.: Author. Accessed at http://www.mlanet.org/education/pfcindex.html on June 8, 2000.

Moore, P. A., and A. St. George. 1991. "Children as Information Seekers: The Cognitive Demands of Books and Library Systems." *School Library Media Quarterly* 19 (3): 161–68.

Morrill, R. L. 1981. "Library Service in Teacher Training Institutions." *Education Libraries* 6 (3): 64–66+.

Music Library Association. 2000. *Publications.* Chicago, Ill.: Author. Accessed at http://www.musiclibraryassoc.org/pub/pub.htm on June 7, 2000.

Nemchek, L. R. 1980. "Education for Theater Librarianship." *Journal of Education for Librarianship* 21 (1): 49–62.

Nevil, L. 1975. *A Survey of Curriculum Laboratories in Selected Colleges in Pennsylvania.* ERIC Document Reproduction Service No. ED 112 909.

"Not by Theory Alone: Replies to Fallis and Fricke." 2000. *Library Journal* 125 (3): 134–36.

O'Hanlon, N. 1987. "Library Skills, Critical Thinking, and the Teacher-training Curriculum." *College and Research Libraries* 48 (1): 17–26.

Pinar, W. F., W. M. Reynolds, P. Slattery, and P. M. Taubman. 1995. *Understanding Curriculum: An Introduction to the Study of the Historical and Contemporary Curriculum Discourses.* New York: Peter Lang.

Pohlman, J. P. 1979. A Description of Teacher Education Media Centers in Selected Institutions Preparing Teacher Candidates. Unpublished doctoral dissertation, Miami University.

Raspa, D., and D. Ward. 2000. *The Collaborative Imperative: Librarians and Faculty Working Together in the Information Universe.* Chicago: Association of College and Research Libraries.

Schillie, J. et al. 2000. "Outreach through the College Librarian Program at Virginia Tech." *The Reference Librarian* (71): 71–8 .

Sineath, T. W., ed. 1992. *Library and Information Science Education Statistical Report 1992*. Raleigh, N.C.: Association for Library and Information Science Education.

Skinner, A. 1980. "The Academic Departmental Library: Is It Special?" In *Special Librarianship: A New Reader*, ed. E. B. Jackson, 290–97. Metuchen, N.J.: Scarecrow Press.

Smalley, T. N. 1998. "Partnering with Faculty to Interweave Internet Instruction into College Coursework." *Reference Services Review* 26 (2): 19–27.

Smardo, F. A. 1980. "Are Librarians Prepared to Serve Young Children?" *Journal of Education for Librarianship* 20 (4): 274–84.

Smith, H. F., and C. A. Gardner. 1956. "Curriculum Materials in the Teachers College Library." *College and Research Libraries* 17 (4): 311–15.

Society of American Archivists. 2000a. *Continuing Professional Education*. Chicago, Ill. Author. Accessed at http://www.archivists.org/prof-education/index.html on June 7, 2000.

Society of American Archivists. 2000b. *Professional Resources Catalog*. Chicago, Ill.: Author. Accessed at http://www.archivists.org/catalog/catalog/index.html on June 7, 2000.

Starratt, J. A., R. P. Nash, and T. A. Tollman. 1985. "What Do They Want from Us?: Changes in Job Ads in Recent Years." In *Competencies for Librarians: Proceedings from the 1985 Spring Meeting of the Nebraska Library Association, College and University Section*, ed. V. I. Krzywkowski, 179–91. Omaha, Neb.: Nebraska Library Association.

State University of New York at Buffalo. 2000. *State University of New York at Buffalo Graduate School of Education: Position Opening: Coordinator, Curriculum Center (SL-4)*. Buffalo, N.Y.: Author. Accessed at http://webhost.bridgew.edu/snesbeitt/509.txt on May 19, 2000.

Stebelman, S. 1989. "The Role of the Subject Specialist in Reference Collection Development." *RQ* 29 (2): 266–73.

Stebelman, S., J. Siggins, D. Nutty, and C. Long. 1999. "Improving Library Relations with the Faculty and University Administrators: The Role of the Faculty Outreach Librarian." *College and Research Libraries* 60 (2): 121–30.

Stuart, C., and M. A. Drake. 1992. "Education and Recruitment of Science and Engineering Librarians." *Science and Technology Libraries* 12 (4): 79–89.

Subcommittee on Special Library Education of the Council of National Library Associations. 1954. "Education for Special Librarianship." *Library Quarterly* 24 (1): 1–20.

Sullivan, P. 1999. "The Congress on Professional Education: Lessons Learned from Library School, Past and Future." *American Libraries* 30 (7): 14–15.

Teclehaimanot, B. 1990. The Nature, Function and Value of the Curriculum Materials Center in Colleges of Education. Unpublished doctoral dissertation, University of Toledo.

Thurston, C. B. 1987. "Education." In *Selection of Library Materials in Applied and Interdisciplinary Fields*, eds. B. J. Shapiro and J. Whaley, 56–78. Chicago: American Library Association.

Toifel, R. C. 1992. *A Survey of Curriculum Materials Centers in Teacher Education Institutions*. ERIC Document Reproduction Service No. ED 343 904.

Walter, S. 2000. "Task Force Meets at ALA Midwinter to Discuss the Educational Role of Libraries." *EBSS Newsletter* 15 (1): 1.

Walter, V. A. 1994. "The Information Needs of Children." In *Advances in Librarianship*, ed. I. P. Godden, 111–29. San Diego, Calif.: Academic Press.

White, G. W. 1999. "Academic Subject Specialist positions in the United States: A Content Analysis of Announcements from 1990 through 1998." *Journal of Academic Librarianship*, 25 (5), 372–82.

Williams, L. B. 1991. "Subject Knowledge for Subject Specialists: What the Novice Bibliographer Needs to Know." *Collection Management* 14 (3/4): 31–47.

Williams, R. V., and M. J. K. Zachert. 1986. "Specialization in Library Education: A Review of Trends and Issues." *Journal of Education for Library and Information Science* 26 (4): 215–32.

Williamson, C. C. 1923. *Training for Library Service: A Report Prepared for the Carnegie Corporation of New York*. New York: Updike.

Woodsworth, A., R. Packard, M. J. Robinson, and J. Sabia. 1994. *The Future of Education for Librarianship: Looking Forward from the Past*. Washington, D.C.: Council on Library Resources.

Woodsworth, A., and M. Westerman. 1995. "Professional Education for Academic Librarians." In *Academic Libraries: Their Rationale and Role in American Higher Education*, eds. G. B. McCabe and R. J. Person, 49–69. Westport, Conn.: Greenwood Press.

Curriculum Materials Centers Budgets

Mike Tillman

CMCs' services and collections significantly impact teacher training; consequently, they influence the overall quality of education provided to PK–12 students. An increasing emphasis on an educator's ability to select and integrate media, primary materials, and computer software into the instructional process necessitates the purchase of an ever-expanding variety of curriculum materials. For example, *A New Compact for Learning*, developed by the New York Board of Regents (1991), calls on universities to prepare teachers who can teach with primary materials.

Generally, nonprint materials are more expensive than print materials and they often require specialized equipment. Staffing and facilities needs may also be affected. Complex materials and equipment require additional and better-trained staff. Housing models, kits, tape players, computers, etc., increase the demand for space and specialized/costly storage units.

At the same time, colleges and universities must deal with decreased purchasing power. Many college and university library systems have been forced to transfer funding from monographs to serials. Some have also transferred funding from ownership to access.

CMCs need more funds to provide and support a wider variety of increasingly expensive materials; colleges and universities have less to spend, especially for the types of materials teachers-in-training desire most. As a result, the significance and complexity of the budgeting process has increased. If CMCs are to continue to improve teacher education, CMC staff must become more adept at preparing, presenting, and promoting budgets that provide adequate funding.

According to Devlin (1988) "budgeting is the process by which necessary resources are determined, allocated, and funded" (20). CMC budgets should address collections, equipment, staff, and facilities located inside and outside of the CMC. However, creation of a list of budget needs is only the beginning. The budgets should document efficient use of the previous year's budget and articulate the CMC's impact on teacher training. To successfully administer a CMC budget, one must be able to demonstrate a thorough knowledge of teaching, curriculum materials, and teacher education. An awareness and understanding of allocation formulas, figures, and trends is also essential.

General Considerations

Before detailing the specifics of a CMC budget request, background information needs to be collected and formatted for easy digestion by those unfamiliar with CMC operations and/or PK–12 education. A comprehensive and prioritized listing of requested collections, equipment, staff, and facilities is a must. Clark (1982) states, "if the cost of the curriculum materials center is to be accurately identified and good fiscal management practiced, budget items should be specifically designated" (37). Items she believes should be designated include monographs; serials; standing orders; government publications; audiovisual materials; professional, support, and student personnel; equipment; supplies; services; and travel (37).

Guidelines for Curriculum Materials Centers developed by the Curriculum Materials Center Interest Group of the Academic Libraries Association of Ohio (1997) emphasizes the need to designate funding for the continuing education of the CMC director and a full-time support staff member. The guidelines recommend budgeting for an appropriate number of evening and weekend hours to provide service for students who are in PK–12 classrooms during the day. Facilities budget items are also addressed. Seating shall be provided for large group, small group, and independent activities; space shall be provided for equipment, repair work, storage, and processing. Funding for shelving units especially designed for curriculum materials may be required.

The National Council for the Accreditation of Teacher Education (NCATE) recognizes the importance of an identifiable and relevant media and materials collection. Proposed NCATE 2000 Unit Standards emphasize the importance of library and curricular resources. Decision makers (anyone who influences resource allocation) should be made aware of this fact and the role CMCs play in the preparation of teachers. They should also be made aware of dramatic changes within the field of education (e.g., the Internet, cross-curricular instruction) and the ways in which these changes have elevated the significance of curriculum selection, evaluation, and integration skills.

Statistics

Planning should precede budgeting, and data gathering should precede planning (Prentice, 1996, 30). Statistics for all meaningful CMC endeavors that impact budget needs should be compiled. Burgin & Hansel (1992) believe "you shouldn't spend a significant amount of time on an activity and fail to keep statistics on that activity" (74). Automated systems facilitate the collection of data. In a study conducted by Carrigan (1996), 43% of the libraries surveyed used data produced by automated circulation systems to make collection development decisions; 82% of the libraries that did not use the data planned on doing so in the future (432). This type of data could also be used to justify a satisfactory CMC budget due to the high rate of circulation at many CMCs. For example, at the California State University, Fresno, the circulation for a six-month period equals the number of items in the CMC collection. This type of information should be (and is) shared with decision makers.

When the university library provides the CMC budget, knowledge of an existing library allocation formula and the percentage of overall library funding the CMC receives for staff and collections can prove invaluable. CMCs generally provide a substantial amount of library user education and reference assistance. Statistics that demonstrate this should be collected and used to justify staff requests. If statistics such as scope of the literature, enrollment, number of courses offered, average price per item, etc., are part of the collections allocation formula, one should articulate statistics that identify CMC needs and contributions. Enrollment and course-offering tallies should include students and courses from all departments that make use of CMC materials. Some of the departments may be located outside of the College of Education. Nonprint curriculum materials such as videos, computer software, and realia should be taken into consideration when computing average price per item.

The CMC which receives all or part of its budget from the College of Education faces many unique challenges. Rather than educating a library director regarding the current state of teacher training, one may need to educate a dean regarding the current state of information delivery. CMC advocacy by education professors becomes even more essential. Distance education initiatives and technological infrastructure have consumed an ever-increasing percentage of College of Education funds. Holding on to one's piece of the pie is a challenge; getting a larger piece of the pie can be extremely difficult. When a CMC is funded through the university library, comparisons can be made with other library units. These comparisons are not so easily drawn when the CMC is not a part of the library. There may be a need to compare collection development dollar per circulation or the percentage of items requiring original cataloging to other campus libraries to maintain or increase the budget. Once the information is collected, an education dean may be more likely than a library director to adhere to the "benefits of a library can be measured through the use of a library" philosophy, a viewpoint that generally benefits CMCs.

Collection of data that demonstrates the high use and transitory nature of many CMC materials is a labor-intensive and worthwhile task. External circulation, in-house circulation, the number of items that disappear from the shelves without being checked out, and the number of items that need to be replaced or repaired because of heavy use should be noted. Not only do these statistics demonstrate the need for adequate collection funding, they justify the need for adequate staff funding. Materials that are used need to be reshelved. Materials that disappear need to be replaced.

The average CMC item costs more to order, catalog, and process than the average library item due to the multipart nature of many of these items and the special processing that may be required for audiovisual, electronic, and spiral-bound items. These items are seldom purchased at a discounted rate as they are not included in the materials offered by library book jobbers. Objective data that demonstrates CMC materials are more likely to require original cataloging may help secure additional cataloging resources.

Allocation and the CMC Budget

During the past decade, two budget allocation trends have disproportionately impacted CMCs. Astronomical serial price increases have forced libraries to transfer collection development funds from monographs to serials; however, the vast majority of curriculum materials are monographs rather than serials. An ever-increasing supply of full-text online resources and document delivery options has caused many libraries to transfer funds from ownership to access. Full-text academic journal articles and interlibrary loan are of minimal value to student teachers and practicum students, clientele heavily dependent upon CMC materials. If a student teacher or practicum student needs curriculum materials for a lesson she has to present in the near future, full-text academic journal articles are of little value and interlibrary loan is not a viable option. If the curriculum materials she needs are nonprint items interlibrary loan probably is not an option at all as many libraries do not make nonprint items available via interlibrary loan. Decision makers should be informed of the potential of these trends to have a negative impact on CMCs.

CMC Budget Efficiency

Successful CMC budget administration requires ongoing efforts to utilize the present budget allocation more efficiently. If the present facility cannot house the continuous influx of new materials without additional shelving and/or space, then CMC collections should be weeded to keep facility costs level unless the CMC has a mission and support to develop a historical as well as a current collection. Utilization of collections, staff, equipment, and facilities needs to be continually analyzed. If a particular part of the collection or piece of equipment is not being used, it may be appropriate to reallocate funds. It may also be appropriate to allocate funds for the purchase of new equipment rather than the repair of old equipment (Kalmback, 1990, 19). Staffing levels and hours of opening should be flexible and based on CMC usage.

CMC staff should also increase efficiency via utilization of resources beyond the walls of the CMC. There are many quality curriculum materials available for free on the Internet. These materials should be collected and organized (via the creation of substantive Web pages). They should be promoted during formal and informal library user education.

The staff at the reference desk in the principal library should be well versed regarding the variety of curriculum materials available and how to locate them. In effect, reference librarians who are well trained regarding curriculum materials increase the number of locations and hours where CMC assistance/service can be received, all without increasing the budget. If the CMC is located within the library, CMC materials may be more efficiently circulated from the main circulation desk. A decision to buy a new piece of equipment that supports curriculum materials may require knowledge regarding the availability of the equipment elsewhere in the library and/or College of Education.

Efforts must be made to obtain complementary materials. Potential donors include publishers, local school districts, and education professors. When soliciting materials, one should detail specific ways in which present and future teachers will gain exposure to the materials. College of Education enrollment, current budget constraints, and the pedagogical value of the materials should be noted. Whenever possible, written solicitations should be individualized.

Increasing the CMC Budget

Most CMC coordinators see their units as being underfunded. Toifel (1992) conducted an attitudinal survey of CMC coordinators that attempted to measure the desired and existing state of CMC personnel, collections, and facilities. Budget allocations for personnel and collections were considered "inadequate or mediocre at best" by a majority of those who completed the survey (20). In another study conducted by Teclehaimanot & Patterson (1992), college executives indicated that, although CMCs were not provided with adequate funding at that time, they believed CMCs would receive adequate funding in the future. CMC coordinators believed current levels of funding were inadequate; they also believed future levels of funding would continue to be inadequate.

Due to underfunding, an increasing emphasis on nontraditional curriculum formats, and ever-evolving teacher education programs, CMCs require more than just cost-of-living increases. While it is, or should be, obvious that media and computer software cost more than books, it might not be as obvious that new media requires new equipment, staff who know how to use the equipment, and a place to locate the equipment. Also, teacher education in particular often caters to nontraditional students. Classes are offered at night and on the weekends, and this has led to increased hours of operation and, in turn, increased staffing needs.

To increase the budget, one needs to have a keen understanding of what kind of budget allocation formula is in place, what statistics are taken into consideration, and whether or not the allocation formula is skewed toward economic efficiency or overall patron welfare. An understanding of historical and political budgeting considerations is also required. In many cases, CMCs are highly used, historically underfunded, and politically powerless. Therefore, CMC staff need to become adept at advocating for a budget allocation based on economic efficiency. According to Carrigan (1992), "allocation of the book budget is ultimately an economic problem, though political considerations may be present" (293). He further states, "the benefits of which libraries are capable and for which they exist are produced only through the use of library materials" (293). CMC staff should assert the importance of considering the materials-use numbers and other factors in economic efficiency in determining budget allocations.

CMC supportive allocation formulas such as proportional use (percentage of circulation divided by percentage of holdings) should be studied and promoted. One should also be aware of whether or not CMC collection development funds, equipment, staffing levels, and/or facilities are meager in comparison to CMCs at similar institutions. If so, decision makers should be made aware of the inadequacies. The Directory of Curriculum Materials Centers (Anderson, 1996) may provide useful statistical comparisons. Other sources, such as Guidelines for Curriculum Materials Centers (1997) developed by the Curriculum Materials Center Interest Group of the Academic Libraries Association of Ohio, provide suggested expenditures and collection quantities based on teacher education enrollment.

One should attempt to find and promote ways in which CMC services and collections are affecting the teaching-learning process. Relationships between CMC usage and specific courses should be analyzed and promoted. When the teaching-learning process for a particular course is significantly impacted by CMC services and collections, corresponding teaching faculty should be made aware of the relationship and encouraged to concretely support related CMC collections and staff requests. Outcome assessment data that provides proof of augmented value should be collected, analyzed, and shared with decision makers.

Finally, grant applications and advocacy for sufficient textbook funds are an important part of the strategy to increase the budget. Grants should be sought routinely. CMC staff should seek outside help when applying for grants. Universities, Colleges of Education, and libraries often employ development staff. These specialized staff can provide invaluable assistance with a task that is time consuming and complex. Outside help will allow CMC directors to focus on what is needed and why (McLaren, 1994, 15). While some grant applications will be rejected, others will be successful; and the ones that are successful increase the CMC budget. More important, decision makers will see that there is a need for more funds and that the CMC is working to secure those funds.

It is also very important that the CMC aggressively pursue increased regular library funding for textbooks. Many publishers no longer provide complimentary materials. Textbooks are among the most used and most expensive items in the CMC and are essential to the teacher education process. The CMC director must be able to communicate effectively the need for an increased budget to absorb the cost of purchasing textbooks that formerly were free.

Preparing and Submitting the CMC Budget

Appropriate information and data needs to be shared with decision makers via an efficiently worded and understandable budget. When preparing a budget, one should spend a little time looking back before looking forward. The budget request should highlight ways in which the CMC has become more efficient and effective during the past year. To maintain or even increase funding levels, one must demonstrate that the present budget is being used wisely.

While it important to use statistics that show the CMC in a positive light, it is even more important to use unbiased data to request and defend requests for funds. If biased or untrue data is used and exposed, future budget processes will be severely impeded. An attempt should be made to tie unbiased data to measurable goals and objectives and then to connect the goals and objectives to specific costs. The majority of goals and objectives and their corresponding costs should be tied directly to items of value to a wide variety of potential users.

The budget should enhance communication and planning as it facilitates the dissemination of a detailed overview of the past, present, and future. The budget not only serves as a request for current activities but also communicates how the CMC can continue to develop and meet future needs of the College of Education.

Conclusion

CMCs provide teachers-in-training with curriculum materials and skills needed to access curriculum materials. If teachers-in-training integrate a wide variety of curriculum materials into their lessons they will continue to do so when they are professional educators (Shoffner, 2000). Teachers who integrate a wide variety of curriculum materials into their lessons will provide a better education than teachers who do not.

Yet, most CMC directors struggle to obtain an adequate budget. CMC materials, services, and facilities are used far more than typical library materials, services, and facilities; but this does not necessarily transcend into large or even adequate budgets. It is not unusual for a CMC to account for 20% of a library's circulation and receive 1% of the materials budget. Because of the nature of CMC materials and assignments related to them, CMCs must also provide a substantial amount of library user education and reference assistance.

The importance of the CMC mission regarding the improvement of teacher education needs to be communicated to funding agencies to improve CMCs.

References

Anderson, B. 1996. *Directory of Curriculum Materials Centers*. Chicago: Association of College and Research Libraries.

Burgin, R., and P. Hansel. 1992. "Library Management: A Dialogue." *Wilson Library Bulletin* 66 (5): 73–75.

Carrigan, D. 1992. "Improving Return on Investment: A Proposal for Allocating the Book Budget." *The Journal of Academic Librarianship* 18 (5): 292–97.

Carrigan, D. 1996. "Data-guided Collection Development: A Promise Unfulfilled." *College & Research Libraries* 57 (8): 429–37.

Clark, A. 1982. *Managing Curriculum Materials in the Academic Library*. Metuchen, N.J.: Scarecrow Press.

Curriculum Materials Center Interest Group of the Academic Libraries Association of Ohio 1997. "Guidelines for Curriculum Materials Centers." In *Acquiring and Organizing Curriculum Materials: A Guide and Directory of Resources*, ed. G. Lare, 205–14. Lanham, Md.: Scarecrow Press.

Devlin, B. 1988. "Basic Budget Primer: Choosing the Best Budget for Your Library." *The Bottom Line* 2 (3): 20–24.

Kalmbach, J. 1990. "An Equipment Purchasing Tip: Expanding the Budget." *Ohio Media Spectrum* 42 (2): 18–19.

McLaren, M. 1994. "The Miracle of Money! Managing LRC Budgets, Funds and Fund Raising." *Tech Trends* 39 (4): 12–16.

National Council for Accreditation of Teacher Education. 2000. *Proposed NCATE 2000 Unit Standards.* Accessed at http://www.ncate.org/specfoc/feb2000stds.pdf on February 29, 2000.

Shoffner, Mary B. "Use of a Resource-based Learning Environment to Foster Self-directedness in Pre-service Teachers" in New York Board of Regents. 1991. *A New Compact for Learning.* Accessed at http://www.regents.nysed.gov/pol9193.html on February 29, 2000.

Prentice, A. 1996. *Financial Planning for Libraries.* Lanham: Scarecrow Press.

Teclehaimanot, B., and A. Patterson. 1992. "The Nature Function and Value of the Curriculum Materials Center on Colleges of Education." Paper presented at the Convention of the Association for Educational Communications and Technology. ERIC Document Reproduction Service No. ED 348 030.

Toifel, R. 1992. *A Survey of Curriculum Materials Centers in Teacher Education Institutions.* ERIC Document Reproduction Service No. ED 343 904.

Paying the Piper and Retaining a Tune Worth Dancing To: Balancing Funding Sources and the Collection Development Process

Judith M. Hildebrandt and Peggie Partello

"Success breeds success," but it can breed greater demand from an increasingly wider range of patrons who are not necessarily the targeted beneficiaries of the funding sources. This is a lesson learned in budget management at Keene State College's Curriculum Materials Library (CML). The CML was established to provide and manage curricular resources for disparate categories of classroom teachers and teachers-in-training, following the pattern of curriculum materials centers described by Alice S. Clark (1982). The CML is supported in part by Keene State College institutional dollars, but largely by various federal grants and other dollars flowing through the New Hampshire Department of Education. Through this unequal partnership, the CML responds to 1) the needs of the college's Education Department for PK–12 materials to support teachers in training, and 2) teachers throughout the state whom the grant(s) are designed to support. The needs of these two constituencies are not mutually exclusive; however, the CMC was frequently unable to meet the needs of either group.

History
The Curriculum Materials Library (CML) is incorporated as a branch collection

and service within the Keene State College library, and the CML Director reports to the Library Director. Policies parallel those of the college library, and all materials are fully cataloged in the college's online catalog.

The CML has been through various iterations over the past 30 years, called various names, housed in various locations, supported by an odd mix of long- and short-term funding sources. By 1990, it was a dusty, tired, dull-looking collection with a marginal reputation. Both service and collection development policies were ill-defined and lacking clear standards. The library was automating its catalog, and the bulk of CML titles had not been included in the retrospective conversion process. The two major funding sources (Keene State College and the New Hampshire Department of Education) let it be known that either the CML must become a credible collection/service point, or it would be dismantled altogether. This lack of standardization, as well as tensions between the parent institution and facility management, was a pattern noted earlier by Barbara A. Dullea (1978).

Over the past 10 years, the CML cleaned, weeded, expanded, and greatly improved its collection, marketed itself internally and externally. Currently it is viewed as "the" professional library for educators within the state, despite the fact that it is far removed from the state's population center, the state capitol, the state Department of Education, or the single state university.

It took the CML many years to develop credibility within the college's own Education Department. The CML had been seen as largely vocational, focusing on limited state needs, and marginally relevant to PK–12 teachers-in-training. Even as strong collections were being developed and marketing efforts were underway, faculty frequently failed to inform their students of the availability of the collections or to avail themselves of opportunities for library user education.

User Base

The CML's patron base includes 1) all members of the college community, and 2) all educators within New Hampshire, including school administrators, teachers, school psychologists, guidance counselors, school resource officers, and social workers. Other populations have access to the collection by virtue of membership in the following groups:

- alternative teacher certification programs;
- New Hampshire College and University Council—a consortium of 13 four-year, public and private institutions of higher education throughout the state;
- University System of New Hampshire—Plymouth State College, the University of New Hampshire, the University of New Hampshire at Manchester, and the College for Lifelong Learning;
- New Hampshire Automated Information System—the statewide auto-

mated system for libraries of all types that provides access to the holdings of approximately 300 libraries;

• Keene Public Library—the college has reciprocal borrowing privileges with the local public library; and

• OCLC Interlibrary Loan System—approximately 6,600 libraries worldwide.

Funding Sources

For CMCs, the budget process drives collections and services. Funding sources for CMCs vary from institution to institution. Many receive their funding solely through the parent institution, as described at Central Connecticut State University, Kansas State University, Kutztown University, University of Wisconsin-Stout, and Washburn University at Topeka. A number of curriculum materials centers, such as those located at Boston College, University of South Dakota, and Midwestern State University, engage in collaborative budget sharing through departmental funds. Brock University takes advantage of contractual relationships between the university and governmental agencies. Others supplement budgets through book fairs (University of Delaware), small grants (Central Connecticut State University), book fines (Silver Lake College), and copy machine revenues (University of Southern Mississippi). A broad range of creative fundraising strategies at the University of Tennessee at Martin represent one extreme but effective response to budget cuts.

Berthe Boudreau (1982) indicated the wide range of funding support available to curriculum materials centers in Canada. Berhane Teclehaimonot (1982) targeted the relationship between institutional support and accreditation standards. Overlooked in the curriculum center literature are those centers funded through state and federal vocational-technical dollars. A 1985 study by Becky Jon Hayward et al. (1985) examined the need for developing and maintaining vocational-technical curricular support at the state and regional levels. Judith O. Wagner (1990) presents a history of the National Network for Curriculum Coordination and the curriculum support provided for secondary school vocational educators. The network's 1995 directory identified six regional centers and 31 individual state centers. The CML at Keene State College has been one of those state centers.

For the last decade the CML has been supported, off and on, through five distinct funding streams with differing funding cycles. As with most institutions listed above, the College funds the CML largely to support certain aspects of its PK–12 teacher education program. Various federal and state grants, in support of "professional development" programs for specific categories of educators, have presented the greatest challenge. Such funding can be undependable and unpredictable. Developing and maintaining collections to support those targeted in the grants (e.g., AIDS/HIV educators, home economics teachers, geography teachers, and vocational-technical personnel) has required the staff to be alert to national and local trends, to engage in creative grant writing activities, and to advocate actively for the continuation of these funding sources.

Developing and Managing the Collection

CMCs appear to be uniform in supporting aspects of PK–12 education. Nearly all centers identify textbooks and curriculum guides as essential parts of the collection. A number of libraries identify specialties in children's literature (Boston College, Central Connecticut State University, Kansas State University, Midwestern State University, University of South Dakota, University of Southern Mississippi, University of Tennessee at Martin, Washburn University of Topeka). Materials supporting specific secondary education programs are identified at University of Wisconsin-Stout and North Carolina State University. Lucille F. Kerr (1979) identifies the range and variety of materials centers and services supporting preservice and in-service educators. Excellent coverage of collection development issues can be found in both Clark (1982) and the American Library Association's *Curriculum Materials Center Collection Development Policy* (1983).

The range and scope of Keene State College's CML collection fluctuates depending on the various activities occurring within the College's education curriculum, faculty needs in a particular year, educational trends within the state, and grant-driven teacher demands. The current collection includes K–8 textbooks in most academic areas and vocational-technical curricula corresponding with New Hampshire's high school vocational-technical programs.

Theodore Frank Yuhas (1952) recommends that the CMCs' planning "be in harmony with the development of the general university library and research facilities" and that the curriculum materials center maintain a "complementary, rather than competitive role" in the overall instructional program of the college or university. The CML has been fortunate in that both the former and current directors have been involved in the decision-making process for the main library and have been able to use the main library's systems when necessary. In this way, the CML has managed to achieve a complementary role in instruction and in collection development. Materials that are ordered by librarians or faculty and paid for by the main library's budget do not automatically end up as part of the main library's collection. If the material is deemed appropriate for the CML and has the potential to be useful to the state's educators, it is cataloged for the CML's collection. The rule of thumb is that materials of a theoretical nature belong in the main library and materials of an applied nature belong in the CML. This arrangement also has the advantage that students and professors know where to begin their quest depending on the nature of the research.

The CML receives the bulk of its support through Carl D. Perkins Vocational-Technical Education legislation to provide "professional development" support to educators working in various state vocational programs. Since Perkins dollars have provided over 90% of the materials budget, the CML has invested heavily in those kinds of materials that would support vocational-technical programs.

Earlier iterations of the Perkins grant had provided a sizable amount of money and supported a limited number of teachers. The CML had more than adequate dollars to support vocational-technical educators, but little opportunity to purchase materials outside that limited scope. It became clear that there was an entire population of educators whose needs were not served by the CML. As Perkins legislation was modified to acknowledge the overlap between the strictly vocational programs, their academic foundations, and workplace issues, the New Hampshire Department of Education provided additional funding for the purchase and duplication of a number of "applied academic" curricula developed by the Agency for Instructional Technology and the Center for Occupational Research and Development. As a result, the CML was able to expand its holdings to incorporate materials relating to mathematics, the sciences, the social sciences, career and personal guidance, and special needs. By combining Perkins and college dollars, the CML has been able to develop a strong PK–12 collection in each of those academic areas, while continuing to meet grant obligations.

Sometimes the constraints of grants prevented the purchase of items that were deemed essential to the educators. An example of this balance between the needs of educators and the constraints of grants played itself out in the Centers for Disease Control and Prevention (CDC) AIDS/HIV grant the CML received through the State of New Hampshire from 1992 to 1999. The purpose of the grant was to purchase materials suitable for the PK–12 audience, to be used by health educators, teachers, and parent groups. Materials purchased were limited to those previewed and approved by a statewide panel of experts and were restricted to specific topics: sexually transmitted diseases, prevention, and universal precautions. Initially the CML was precluded from purchasing materials on substance abuse, even though teachers and staff recognized that behavioral issues and attitudes play a part in the likelihood that an individual will be exposed to HIV. To round out the AIDS/HIV collection, CML staff looked to a combination of Perkins and college dollars. Materials were subsequently purchased in the areas of self-esteem, family relationships, substance abuse, sexual development, personal behaviors such as bullying and teasing, and other risky behaviors. All of these issues are related to the developing adult entering the workforce, therefore meeting Perkins grant mandates.

This combination of funds—from the CDC, Perkins, and Keene State College—along with a bit of thinking "outside the box," allowed CML to build a cohesive collection of materials about attitudes, belief systems, and behaviors that may lead an individual to contracting HIV.

Other Avenues

To build an adequate, useful, and timely collection, the CML increasingly is searching for additional grant opportunities. Fortunately, the CML's broad user base appeals to many foundations that want their money to go as far as it can. The CML has often been slow to respond to the latest "hot" topic, primarily because the dollars have not been available and staff have not had the luxury of purchasing materials in areas in which the emphasis may wax and wane. The CML has turned to foundations to support the acquisition of current materials in particular subject areas that will be of immediate use to teachers in the field.

One recent example was the need to have materials in the CML on the topic of safe schools. The National Center for Injury Prevention and Control, an agency of the Centers for Disease Control, has been working with federal agencies and other partners to find solutions to youth and school violence. Its preliminary research has revealed that effective strategies include school-based curricula that emphasize the development of problem-solving skills, anger management, and other strategies that help students develop better social skills. These are the areas identified as needing attention in the CML collection:

• Diversity—Celebrating and appreciating other cultures and rejecting stereotypes of minorities can potentially reduce the incidence of hate crimes.

• Conflict resolution—Juvenile delinquency and violence can be symptoms of a student's inability to manage conflict.

• Peer mediation—Many schools recognize the importance of directly involving youth in conflict resolution with their peers.

• Humane education—Children are often taught tolerance and kindness through interactions with animals, both at home and in the classrooms. In addition, there is a growing body of sociological and psychological literature that supports a connection between animal abuse and violence toward people, and suggesting that appropriate intervention with youthful animal abusers may derail the child's penchant for solving problems through violence.

• Social skills—Many children enter school lacking age-appropriate social skills and encounter problems in school and elsewhere in the community. Important skills for children to learn are self-control, healthy communication with others, and the ability to form and maintain friendships.

It was clear that the CML did not contain up-to-date materials that would help New Hampshire educators grapple with the issue of safe schools. To fill this need, which is outside the scope of the Perkins dollars, the CML turned to local foundations that have a stake in New Hampshire's schools and could respond in a timely fashion. The first foundation to realize the importance of such a collection was the D.D. Bean Foundation of Jaffrey, New Hampshire, which awarded the CML $2,500 for materials. The second was the Monadnock Community Foundation, which donated $5,000. It is hoped that this venture—the Safe Schools Media Collection— is the first of many as the CML continues to partner with the community to address local education issues.

Conclusion

CMCs grapple with numerous issues: location, space, staffing, funding, institutional support, patron base, collection development, and user services. The Keene State College Curriculum Materials Library has grappled with each during the past ten years. Of these, balancing tensions between funding sources and patron services has consumed most of the staff efforts. Several factors have been instrumental in maintaining the current level of stability:

1. Credibility. Curriculum Materials Library staff worked tirelessly over 10 years to bring in new collections, to piggyback on existing grant resources, to expand networks, and to deliver an excellent product. Teachers who were not connected to the college and who were not targeted by the various grants heard through the grapevine about the CML and have come to depend on its services.

2. Staffing changes. New, enthusiastic staff in key state education department offices has made it easier to exchange information and explore avenues for expansion. At the college level, two librarians switched positions, boosting the morale of each and bringing a fresh pair of eyes and renewed vigor to the CML.

3. Flexibility. The Curriculum Materials Library has been blessed with flexible persons on the staff—individuals who were willing to think creatively and explore possibilities.

Increasingly, the Curriculum Materials Library at Keene State College looks for ways to become its own piper and create its own tune—one, it is hoped, that will be sung by all New Hampshire educators.

References

American Library Association. 1993. *Curriculum Materials Center Collection Development Policy.* Chicago: Author.

Boudrea, B. 1982. Curriculum Materials Centers in Teacher Education Institutions in Canada. Unpublished Doctoral Dissertation, Indiana University-Bloomington.

Clark, A. 1982. *Managing Curriculum Materials in an Academic Library.* Metuchen, N.J.: Scarecrow.

Dullea, B. 1978. *Curriculum Materials Centers in Institutions of Higher Education in New York State and in Selected Midwestern Institutions.* ERIC Document Reproduction Service No. ED 175 798.

Hayward, B. et al. 1985. *An Assessment of the Impact and Effectiveness of the National Network for Curriculum Coordination in Vocational and Technical Education.* ERIC Document Reproduction Service No. ED 262 228.

Kerr, L. 1979. *Materials Centers: A Dream of the Future.* ERIC Document Reproduction Service No. ED 188 635.

National Network for Curriculum Coordination. 1995. *1995 Directory of State Vocational and Technical Curriculum Centers.* Washington, D.C.: Author.

Teclehaimonot, B. 1992. "Curriculum Materials Centers in Teacher Education: Trends for the 1990s." *Ohio Media Spectrum* 44: 38–41.

Wagner, J. 1990. *Locating Vocational Education Curricula.* ERIC Document Reproduction Service No. ED 318 915.

Yuhas, T. 1952. "The Curriculum Laboratory in the University." *Educational Administration and Supervision* 38: 241.

K-12 Textbooks Series Sets in CMCs: Collection Development and Management Issues

Lorene R. Sisson and Allison G. Kaplan

Introduction

In CMCs, textbook series materials often form the backbone of the collection. Students in teacher education programs use these materials for the purposes of evaluating curriculum materials and to assist in tutoring and student teaching coursework. Education faculty use these materials for evaluative as well as research purposes. Over time, the collection of textbook materials has become increasingly complex, as the materials have changed to reflect the current needs of classroom teachers and their students. It is no longer likely that a textbook series will consist of only a teacher's edition, student edition, and workbooks. Recent changes in educational practices, including acknowledgment of different learning styles and aptitudes, along with advances in educational technology, have changed the types of instructional materials likely to be selected for use in the classroom. To provide support for teacher education programs, curriculum materials centers must acquire these new types of materials and make them accessible.

Acquisition and organization of the materials offers many challenges that librarians must address. These challenges include the following: the enormous variety and number of component parts in a textbook series, the extreme expense of purchasing a full textbook series, the lack of availability of review copies of textbook series sets, the short lifespan of textbook series sets, lack of space in most libraries to house new and store older textbook series sets, the need for a large physical space to display and use the materials, acquiring additional technology required by newer sets, and the lack of standard cataloging procedures to organize the textbook series sets. Acquisition and organization policies for curriculum materials centers must take into account all of these challenges and issues related to textbook series sets. Decision making will involve knowledge of standard practices as well as the ability to adapt the standards to the unique requirements of the materials and their users.

Definition of a Textbook Series

Before acquisition and organization policies can be created, an agreement about what comprises a textbook series set must be established. In the past, a textbook series was easily definable. There was, usually, one student textbook and one teacher's guide for each grade level. Then publishers expanded the sets by including test booklets, books of black line masters, and similar supplementary teaching tools. Nevertheless, the basic design of the series was relatively constant.

Today a textbook series is not always easy to define because the textbook design has changed in response to changes in educational theory. Research has demonstrated the need for educators to adapt to different learning styles and aptitudes. According to Corno and Snow (1986), "The majority of students will need more aptitude support than conventional teaching provides, and different kinds of specialized support will likely be needed for different kinds of students." (625) In recognition of different learning styles, teachers are becoming mediators rather than controllers of information. In this situation, textbooks represent a starting point for student exploration into subject areas. Textbook publishers have responded to this practice by creating supplementary materials to the "traditional" textbook.

Thus, a textbook series may comprise a number of different items. Usually there is still some form of a teacher's guide, but it may be constructed for use across multiple grade or unit levels. Further, there may not be student textbooks as such; rather, the series may make use of previously published books, called trade books, in place of student texts. Or, one may find a combination of both, wherein a textbook series may include both student texts and previously published trade books. In the discipline of English Language Arts, short controlled vocabulary books are beginning to appear that supplement if not supplant the traditional single volume student text (see figure 1).

In addition to book materials, textbook series sets may now also include many component parts. These component parts allow teachers to apply strategies for individual student aptitudes. Some of the parts might be manipulative materials, calculators, cassette tapes, puppets, transparencies, computer disks, videodiscs, interactive CD-ROMs, etc. Given these considerations, the following definition of a textbook series is proposed: PK–12 textbook series sets are defined as a collection of materials distributed by a publisher as a set of instructional materials directed to a particular grade or unit level or levels and/or to a particular curricular subject. Components of these sets may include the following:

1. Materials for specific users; i.e., students, teachers, facilitators, etc.

2. Book as well as nonbook materials.

3. Previously published trade books or other materials.

4. Parts that have not been published simultaneously with the main part of the set (i.e., items with various publication dates or publishers such as alternate editions: e.g., Spanish, Vietnamese, or other languages, special editions for hearing impaired, etc.) and are packaged to accompany the set.

Figures 2 through 5 show examples of titles that will serve to illustrate each component of the definition.

Acquisition of Textbook Series Sets

The acquisition of textbook series sets can be a difficult process. Multipart sets are usually prohibitively expensive, take up a great deal of space, and require additional technology for full functionality. This section will examine the challenges of acquiring and housing textbook series sets.

Figure 1. The traditional teacher and student texts supplemented by controlled vocabulary reading books. *Scott Foresman Reading,* 2000.

Figure 2. The first component of a textbooks series set showing the text for specific users; in this case, teacher and student books. This example is from *Zaner-Bloser Handwriting Series*, 1996.

Figure 3. The second component of a textbook series showing book and nonbook items as part of the series. This example shows the book, video, and lab components from *Scott Foresman Science*, 2000.

As with any other library item, textbook series materials are acquired either through actual purchase or through donations. In the case of donations, some institutions have agreements with local school districts or with textbook publishers to house donated materials as a clearinghouse or examination center. Education faculty may also donate materials. Unfortunately, both of these donations seldom consist of complete or current sets.

The cost of purchasing a complete textbook series set (that is, all materials for all grade and/or unit levels) is almost always prohibitive. Although prices vary, an institution can expect to pay anywhere from a few hundred to several thousands of dollars to purchase a complete textbook series set. For example, the 1997 Prentice-Hall series, *The Nature of Science*, grades 6–9 (student text, teacher's edi-

Figure 4. The third component of a textbook series showing a previously published trade book reissued with the series. This example shows the *Houghton Mifflin Reading: The Language Experience* series (1991) with a teacher's text, student text, *The Glad Man* by Gloria Gonzalez (originally published 1975), *Julie of the Wolves* (originally published 1972), *Trial by Wilderness* (originally published 1985), *High Elk's Treasure* (originally published 1972), and *The Rocking Chair Rebellion* (originally published 1978), all reprinted for this series, 1991.

Figure 5. The fourth component of a textbook series showing multiple publication dates. This example is from the Houghton Mifflin series shown in Figure 4. The dates for these items are: 1991 copyrights, 1993 impression for the Teacher's Book; and 1991 copyright, 1993 impression for *Quick as a Cricket* and *First Day of School*. *I Like Me* has a Houghton Mifflin edition date of 1991. *On Monday When It Rained* has a 1989 copyright, no other Houghton Mifflin dates. The trade book *Quick as a Cricket* has a note on the title page which reads, "1993 Impression. Houghton Mifflin Edition, 1991. No part of this work may be reproduced... Houghton Mifflin is not authorized to grant permission for further uses of this work. Permission must be obtained from the individual copyright owner..." The videotape is also interesting because the package has a copyright date of 1992, the label on the tape reads 1993, and the date on the tape itself is 1991.

tion, activity book, laboratory manual, and resource package), is approximately $175. This is in comparison to another 1997 Prentice-Hall series, *Exploring Life Science*, also grades 6–9 (student text, teacher's edition, laboratory manuals, computer disks, videodiscs, and interactive CD-ROMs and videodiscs) that could cost well over $4,000. This astronomical price does not include the price of support technology to run the required programs. Prohibitive costs may lead to the decision to purchase set parts rather than the complete set. In this case, curriculum materials centers usually opt to purchase only a teacher handbook for each grade or unit level. Since the teacher's manual or handbook is a guide to using the whole set, it may give the user an understanding of the series but may not be sufficient for educational needs.

Publishers of large textbook series sets invest a great deal of effort and funds in producing new series, but they are unable to meet the demand for review copies or donations. Sending samples of these materials is difficult due to the enormous number of schools and school districts who might request them. In addition, because some textbook series sets contain hundreds of component parts, some of which may be very bulky and heavy, shipping is another burden that limits the ability of publishers to send donations. It is undeniably advantageous for publishers to promote purchase of their materials through sending review copies of textbooks and other instructional materials to schools and curriculum materials centers. However, publishing houses are businesses that must be fiscally responsible. Sending out numerous free materials, although beneficial to educators, may be detrimental to publishing budgets. Therefore, many publishers are often unable to satisfy the great demands for free review materials. Additionally, when free samples are given to CMCs, the items donated may be older editions and most often are incomplete sets.

One way of trying to acquire full textbook series sets that some CMCs might wish to attempt is by establishing a collaborative relationship with a school district or group of districts; in that relationship, the CMC serves as the preview and selection center that houses a number of textbook series sets. This would provide publishers greater exposure to their buying customers while limiting the number of preview materials they need to send out to a geographical area. It would also allow educators to preview textbook series sets in their complete form as they are meant to be used and preview many different publishers' products in one location. In some states, regional curriculum materials centers exist to assist teachers and teacher education programs by collecting textbook series sets and instructional materials. Nebraska has such a center, called the Regional Instructional Materials Review Center (RIMRC), located at the University of Nebraska at Kearney. RIMRC supports both the teacher preparation program and local school districts. One of the services mentioned in their brochure is hosting textbook selection and curriculum development committees. RIMRC actively solicits donations and review copies from publishers to assist local schools in acquiring the materials needed.

California has 26 such centers, called Learning Resources Display Centers. Most centers are housed in a regional county office of education. However, some are housed and managed by universities with teacher education programs. Publishers who wish to submit their textbook series or instructional materials for the California adoption cycle must send samples of the materials to these centers. The centers provide relief to beleaguered publishers who cannot meet demands for donations or samples to every school while providing opportunities for teachers, faculty in teacher education programs, teacher candidates, and the community to review the latest instructional materials available. Centers gain additional benefit from being in touch with their regional communities while supporting their campus teacher education programs. The wider array of materials available to review in the center encourages the purchase of better learning materials through the ability to select appropriate materials from a greater variety of publishers.

Other difficulties hampering collection development are the limited sources from which to acquire textbook series and the short life spans of the textbook series. There are no approval plans for PK–12 textbook series, and the expense of developing these sets has limited the field to very few publishers. In addition, most textbook series have a useful life of only five to ten years. In fact, the California Department of Education has a printed chart that represents the adoption cycle for all subject areas (see http://www.cde.ca.gov/cilbranch/eltdiv/adoptscheule.htm). Generally at the end of seven years an adopted item is no longer kept on the list of adopted instructional materials.

Because of their short life span, textbook series must be acquired soon after they are published if they are to be of maximum use. One potential source of assistance in this facet of curriculum materials center management is the *ENC Catalog of Curriculum Resources*, a database from the Eisenhower National Clearinghouse for Mathematics and Science Education. This resource provides educators with a tool for quickly locating and researching textbook series and other instructional materials in science and math. The Web site catalog describes the collection of K–12 materials in all formats, "including print, audio, video, multimedia, kits, and games." The detailed records include such information as an abstract, grade level, availability, and cost. (See http://www.enc.org.)

Next to financial resources, space availability is one of the greatest concerns for CMC librarians. Full textbook sets are notorious for taking up large amounts of shelving space. For example, the Curriculum Materials Center in the Clark Library at San Jose State University in San Jose, California, has a science textbook series set that occupies a wall of shelving 15 feet long and 8 feet high. In addition, the components of the textbook series sometimes require not only a huge amount of shelving but also physical space that is not easily accommodated by standard library shelving. Recently, many elementary grade level textbook series sets have started to incorporate poster books or "big books"; manipulative materials in boxes, bags, or tubs; games and game boards; supplies and samples of materials from the lessons or units; easels; and other bulky materials. Some CMC staff are overwhelmed by the need for physical space and actually store some components away from the center while displaying the more requested or more prominent components. Although this method is effective for conserving shelving space, this is not an optimal solution to the problem as it impedes examination of the full set.

The volume of space consumed by large textbook series sets requires careful planning to retain an orderly and logical arrangement of the CMC and thus make the materials accessible. Questions to be considered include:

• Are all the components necessary to represent the textbook series adequately?

• Are all the grade or unit levels necessary to represent the textbook series adequately?

• Can the flooring and shelving support the sometimes bulky and heavy materials?

• Are there any physical hazards from the materials (dangerous chemicals, breakable items, etc.)?

• Is theft protection necessary?

• Will there be space for later additions to a textbook series or revisions of a textbook series?

The final challenge of acquiring textbook series sets to be discussed is that of coping with the required technology. Many of the newer textbook series sets require supporting equipment that can be expensive to purchase and maintain. Equipment needed as integral to the instructional intent of the textbook series might include a videodisc player, videotape player, computer, camcorder, or electronic piano with MIDI device or multimedia component. The equipment may cost thousands of dollars to match the requirements listed in some textbook series sets. Some regional centers require that the publishers supply the equipment needed for the program or component that requires it. Some centers share the necessary equipment with other agencies such as the campus library or computer center. Some centers are able to acquire donations of equipment from the corporate world. The Learning Display Center at San Jose State University, for example, was given equipment from AT&T.

The expense and expertise required to support the equipment for the textbook series places an additional demand upon the CMC staff. The training necessary to adequately use and teach others to use the equipment associated with a textbook series can be very time-and-labor intensive. In 1996, in anticipation of the need for technology training and support for the 1996 English Language Arts/ English as a Second Language Adoption process, a full-day technology training for the California Learning Resources Display Center directors and their staff was provided. Training sessions such as these are essential to provide adequate support for the technology-based instructional materials managed by curriculum materials centers.

Organization of Textbook Series Sets

There has been periodic discussion in library literature, both in paper and electronic formats, regarding the unique nature of textbook series materials and the kinds of problems involved with cataloging these materials (EBSS, 1990; Stine, 1991; Varughese & Poirier, 1996). Often CMCs do not have their own cataloging staff; thus, responsibility for cataloging the materials falls to the cataloging department of the institution's main library. Textbook series materials are time consuming to catalog and often remain in the backlog of cataloging departments for extended periods of time. Additionally, some institutions have cited the "temporary" nature of these materials as a reason for not cataloging them at all. CMC staff must persuade their institutions to provide educators the same level of service as other disciplines through full cataloging of the very materials that comprise the core of the collection. Stine (1991) makes this argument for cataloging these materials: "Full cataloging encourages use of the materials, makes self-service easier, makes user instruction more consistent and shortens training for staff and makes it easier for users of the catalog to find information" (68). If these materials cannot be cataloged in a timely manner, it can affect research and teaching progress of the entire education faculty and student population. Communication between the CMC and the cataloging staff is essential, primarily because of the unique nature of these materials. Whether the collection is historic in nature or only contemporary, the materials must get from the cataloging department to the shelf as quickly, efficiently, and easily as possible.

As mentioned previously, it is often impossible for an institution to purchase (or even have donated) an entire textbook series set. The cataloging ramifications of owning an incomplete set are significant. Catalogers depend on having an entire set to work with. If the institution does not own the entire set, the cataloger must be informed about the conditions under which he or she is working. Under these conditions, it is entirely possible that the items in hand are not the main items of the set. Thus, the cataloger is either unable to make basic decisions regarding the description of the series or makes decisions based on the wrong part(s) of the series.

Standardized cataloging rules help the cataloger decide how each aspect of the series set will be included in the item record. The cataloging rules are based on the premise of a "chief source of information." The chief source of information is that part of the item from which most of the bibliographic data is taken. In describing a book, for example, the chief source of information is first and foremost the title page. In textbook materials the question has centered on which title page one should use for the chief source of information. Should one use the title page from the teacher's guide or from the student text? Often, these two pages have very different information. Decisions on the what part of the set determines the chief source of information will impact the bibliographic area with respect to title, edition statement, physical description, and added title tracings.

The way one decides to organize all the various types of materials included in a textbook series will affect the decision regarding which part of the series constitutes the chief source of information. With that in mind, the guidelines for cataloging interactive multimedia should be used. These guidelines state that the chief source of information is the item as a whole in its most perfect form. That is, rather than looking for a single title page or title screen from which to take the bibliographic information, the cataloger should make use of any and all information which applies to the item as a whole. This would include title pages from teacher's texts, student texts, title screens from included media, titles on containers, and even publisher's catalog information.

Title (MARC tag 245)

When we speak of the textbook series as a whole in its most perfect form, we are forced to consider what that form actually may be. Does one create a record according to the series title or according to the unit level title? Often these are not the same. Again, in earlier cataloging practice it would have been simple to catalog by series title with added title entries for individual level titles. Today it is not always as simple. Let us consider the positive and negative aspects of cataloging first by series title, then by unit level titles.

To catalog the set by series title conveys the idea that the series is a whole unit and should be treated accordingly. It may be faster to catalog the set by series title. The cataloger would have to deal with the series only one time, creating a single bibliographic record. However, cataloging by series title can lead to extremely long records. Even in a simple series consisting of one teacher's text and one student text for each grade level PK–12, no less than 26 ISBNs (twenty-six 020 tags in the MARC record) would be necessary. The possibility of including all ISBNs for a more complicated textbook series becomes staggering. Yet, for identification purposes, the ISBN is an important part of the bibliographic record; and, therefore, one must consider including each and every ISBN within the series set.

To catalog the series by each individual grade or unit title is to place the emphasis of the series on the parts rather than the whole. The decidedly negative aspect of this practice is the fact that a bibliographic record must be created for each individual title. While the resulting record may be shorter, it may take longer to catalog the series by virtue of having to create so many records. Additionally, the series becomes fragmented and no longer has the quality of being a whole unit. This fragmentation is magnified if one also has to deal with series items that cross grade or unit level. In which record, for example, should the grade 4–6 assessment book be placed, or is that book yet another separate bibliographic record?

Keeping in mind that the user can find the series as a whole unit by searching the series title, let us consider some positive aspects of cataloging by individual title. First, cataloging by individual title more closely follows the definition of a series according to the standard cataloging rules. Series is defined as "a group of separate items related to one another by the fact that each item bears, in addition to its own title proper, a collective title applying to the group as a whole" (*Anglo-American Cataloging Rules*, 622). The individual title would be recorded in the title area (245 MARC tag) and the series title would be recorded in the series area (4XX MARC tag). Second, using the individual title will dramatically decrease the number of items to be described in each record. Decreasing the sheer number of items will automatically make for a cleaner record. Third, using the individual title may make it easier for an institution to attach holdings to a record created by a different institution, thus eliminating the need and/or desire to create a new bibliographic record. Some series sets will easily lend themselves to cataloging by individual unit. Other sets, especially those containing materials that cross unit levels, will be more difficult to separate.

Edition (250 tag)

One of the most obvious variances between textbook series title pages is found in edition statements. According to MARC format rules, there can be only one edition statement in a given bibliographic record. Defining an edition statement for a textbook series becomes an exercise in splitting hairs. If one considers "teacher's edition" as an edition statement, what does one do with a teacher's edition that has another type of edition statement? If one opts to use the teacher's guide as the chief source of information and the statement "teacher's edition" appears on the title page, then the bibliographic record may reflect that statement in the edition area (250 MARC tag). However, if one selects the teacher's guide and there is the statement "teacher's edition" along with the statement "second edition," then one is in a quandary regarding which "edition" statement to record in the edition area. On the other hand, to reflect both "teacher's edition" and "second edition," one may include "teacher's edition" in the title statement (subfield p in the 245 MARC tag) and "second edition" in the edition statement (250 MARC tag). In some cases, textbook series sets are given nonnumerical edition designations. Such phrases as "award edition" and "sterling edition" are not uncommon, especially in the area of English Language Arts. It may be more reasonable to put these nonnumerical edition statements in the title, 245 subfield p area. In this way, one includes in the title information that should apply to the entire series. Using "teacher's edition" in the 245 results in the problem of creating a title statement that does not reflect the entire nature of the series as a whole.

The choice of using the student text as the chief source of information is also problematic. Although one would now be free to use the edition area for the edition statement (such as "second edition") another problem does arise. Now the quandary is what to do if one has only teacher's guides in hand. As mentioned previously, it is often the case that when receiving donations or when forced to purchase only selected items, the items received will be the teacher's texts because the center patrons (faculty researchers and preservice teachers) will have the benefit of having both student and teacher text in one item. Does the cataloger sometimes use the student text and sometimes use the teacher's text as the chief source of information? While there may be no easy answer to this question, the advisability of following the guidelines for cataloging interactive multimedia and using all available resources as chief sources of information is apparent (Interactive Media Guidelines Task Force, 1994).

Physical Description (260 tag)

Describing eight teacher's guides, six student books, three videotapes, and all the other component parts of a textbook series set can be a real challenge. The challenge only gets worse when the CMC does not own all of the parts of the set. Again, relying on the multimedia guidelines can help in the decision-making process. Use of notes (5XX) that describe what is actually owned by the center will also help in the process. For the sake of bibliographic standards, catalogers should, as much as possible, describe the item as a whole and make notes regarding actual institutional holdings.

Added Title Tracings

One final question in considering the series set as a whole is that of dealing with previously published items. As mentioned above, textbook publishers will often include with a series previously published media and/or trade books to supplement the textbook program or in substitution of student textbooks. The inclusion of trade books in textbook series presents a particular problem, both in cataloging and classifying the items. Trade books may be included in the series to replace student texts, as in the case of McMillan-McGraw Hill *Science Turns Minds On* series, or to enhance student texts and the curriculum, as in the case of the Houghton Mifflin reading series, *The Literature Experience* (see figures 4 and 5). These trade books are almost always reissues of previously published works. In the case of reissued trade books, the AACR2R rule 13.3 can be applied. This rule states that an item that is part of a monographic series with an independent title should be cataloged with an added series statement for the comprehensive title (AACR, 1998, 300). Thus, the item has a reference to the overall title of the textbook series. We further suggest the inclusion of a general note such as "This item is suggested for use with Houghton Mifflin reading series: *The Literature Experience, grade level X*" to further emphasize the relation of the trade book to the textbook series. Likewise, the record for the series itself would have a note linking the series to the separate titles, such as, "Trade books used with this series are *X, Y,* and *Z*." This kind of note reinforces the relationship of the trade book to the textbook.

We would like to touch briefly upon the topic of classification as it relates to trade books and the impact of classification on this topic. Once a record has been created, the item needs to be classified. Roughly defined, classification determines where the item will be placed on the shelf. One approach is to classify the trade book separately and put it on the shelf in children's literature or in another appropriate area. Another approach would be to classify the item with the textbook series. This keeps the trade book with the series but creates the possibility of multiple copies of the same item being located in two different places. The concern here is whether to break up a set of materials that are to be used together or putting like literatures in different places throughout the library.

Historically we find that it was not uncommon in school libraries for librarians to break up kits to keep like kinds of materials together in one place. For example, all filmstrips in one area and all books in another. This proved to be detrimental to the use of the kit as a whole, and current practice is to keep kits together. Using this argument, one might consider the utility of keeping trade books with their intended sets despite the problems of dispersing duplicate titles throughout the collection.

At this point, it is also necessary to discuss the practice of "copy cataloging" that takes place in most libraries. Today's catalogers have access to many cataloging aids through databases and information sites on the Internet. Copy cataloging, or using the cataloging others have produced to create one's own bibliographic record, is regular practice. Copy cataloging is accomplished through access to individual library catalogs and national databases. Catalogers look through other databases for a record of a specific item and copy that record, electronically or manually, into their own database. That new record is amended so that it reflects the nature of the item in the cataloger's hand. Some libraries contribute their own records to commercial- or consortium-based databases. The OCLC database is an example of one of the largest shared databases. For a fee, an institution can make use of the records found on OCLC and can add its own holdings to the OCLC database. This type of re-source sharing has been tremendously helpful in increasing the quality of bibliographic records around the world. With respect to cataloging textbook series sets, however, the lack of agreement on how to catalog these items decreases the value of shared cataloging.

Consider a cataloger from institution A who inputs a bibliographic record for a series set reflecting only its own holdings; for example, all teacher guides. Then, institution B's cataloger searches the database and finds that, although it shares some of the items held by institution A, it also has some different items; so institution B also enters a unique bibliographic record. This process continues, multiplying the number of bibliographic records for the same textbook series set. Eventually a cata-loger from institution X comes along and does not know which bibliographic record to use. Using the model of cataloging for the set as a whole, there may be a greater chance that institutions, regardless of the extent of their individual holdings, will add to an existing record rather than infuse national databases with multiple bibliographic records.

Conclusion

The nature of PK–12 textbook series sets will continue to change as educational theories on learning and advances in educational technology evolve. This paper has discussed some fundamental problems in collection development and organization of textbook series sets. We have proposed a definition of a textbook series, outlined some inherent challenges of these materials, and suggested some considerations for solving these problems. CMC managers must bear these issues and challenges in mind when making decisions and designing policy for their centers. Managing a CMC will require learning new technologies, seeking outside resources, and coop-erating with publishers and colleagues to maximize the effect of the curriculum materials center on teacher education programs.

Note

The authors wish to acknowledge an unpublished work on cataloging textbook series that comprise a major contribution to this chapter. This work was created by a joint subcommit-tee of the EBSS Problems of Access and Control of Education Materials Committee and the EBSS Curriculum Materials Committee, 1996–1998. Its members were Allison G.

Kaplan, University of Delaware; M. Suzanne Brown, University of Florida; Ting James, University of Alabama; Lorene R. Sisson, San Jose State University; Benita Strnad, University of Alabama; Lola Varughese, Louisiana State University; Karin Duran, California State University, Northridge; and Bee H. Gallegos, Arizona State University West.

References

Anglo-American Cataloging Rules. 1998. 2nd ed. Ottawa: Canadian Library Association. London: Library Association Publishing. Chicago: American Library Association.

Corno, L., and R. Snow. 1986. "Adapting Teaching to Individual Differences Among Learners." In *Handbook of Research on Teaching* 3rd ed. New York: Macmillan Publishing Co., 605–25.

EBSS Curriculum Materials in the Online Catalog Subcommittee, 1990. "Curriculum Materials in Online Catalogs," *College & Research Libraries News* 51 (6): 562–65.

The Interactive Multimedia Guidelines Review Task Force. 1994. *Guidelines for Bibliographic Description of Interactive Multimedia*. Chicago, Ill.: American Library Association.

Stine, D. 1991. "Suggested Standards for Cataloging Textbooks." *Cataloging and Classification Quarterly* 13 (2): 67–86.

USMARC Format for Bibliographic Data. (1994) Washington, D.C.: Library of Congress.

Varughese, L. and G. Poirier. (1996) "A Brief Survey of ARL Libraries' Cataloging of Instructional Materials," *Cataloging and Classification Quarterly* 18 (1): 125–34.

Criteria for Selection and Deselection of CMC Materials, Both New and Donated

John Hickok

Introduction

One of the most important responsibilities of managing CMCs is selecting materials to add to the collection. This typically occurs by purchasing new items from current educational booksellers and vendors, using a budget provided by the library or institution. However, with budgets often tight, donated materials can also be a source for supplementing the collection. These may be items such as examination textbooks from professors, lesson plans from retiring PK–12 teachers, kits/games from members of the community, or other items from other donors. Standard criteria should always be used in determining whether or not to add purchased or donated items to the CMC. This article will discuss four recommended criteria to use in making selection decisions, both for new and donated items: 1) Duplication vs. Deficiency, 2) Condition/Format, 3) Authority/Content, and 4) Relevance/Currency. Furthermore, these criteria will also be discussed in the equally important task of deselecting (weeding) existing materials.

Review of the Literature

Books and articles on general library collection development and new material acquisition are plentiful. They offer general principles on purchasing new materials and determining if existing materials should be added or removed from collections. A well-known example would be *Acquisitions Management and Collection Development in Libraries*, by Magrill & Corbin (1989). General works on establishing acquisition/collection development policies are also helpful, such as the ALA publication *Guide for Written Collection Policy Statements* (1996).

More specific are books and articles focusing on donations and gifts. Although 20 years old now, the most complete treatment available on all aspects of donation/gift operations in a library is Alred Lane's *Gifts and Exchange Manual* (1980). This work discusses establishing policy statements, gives sample forms, and mentions decision criteria. Looking at articles, a routine search of the *Library Literature* index/database using the subject headings "gifts, contributions, etc.—policy statements" and "gifts, contributions, etc.—administration" yields many useful articles. A few sample titles include: "Killing us with Kindness; or, What to Do with Those Gifts" (Buis, 1991); "LP donations: love them or leave them?" (Munstedt, 1995) and "How to Look a Gift Horse in the Mouth; or, How to Tell People You Can't Use their Old Junk in Your Library" (Strnad, 1995).

Literature searches on deselection (weeding), under the subject heading "Discarding of books, periodicals, etc." also yield useful books and articles. Some helpful titles include "On Writing a Deselection Policy; or, How to Toss Books Without PublicCcondemnation" (Pidgeon, 1999); "Weeding School Library Media Center Collections" (Livingston, 1999); and "See and Weed: Enlisting Teachers to Help Weed Outdated Filmstrips and Videos" (Editor, 1995).

While the above resources are valuable, none specifically focuses on CMCs. For works specifically on collection development in CMCs, there are three valuable resources. First is the ALA publication *Curriculum Materials Center Collection Development Policy* (1993). This work, developed by two subcommittees of the Educational and Behavioral Sciences Section of the Association of College & Research Libraries (division of ALA), is an excellent primer for all who deal with CMC collections. It discusses collection scope, criteria for material selection, criteria for deselection, and more. It also includes two sample collection development policies from actual university CMCs. Second is *Acquiring and Organizing Curriculum Materials* by Gary Lare (1997). This work offers detailed explanations of the different types of collections within a CMC—such as Curriculum Guides, Textbooks, and Teaching Activities—and offers sample scopes of each. Use of Lare's explanations can serve as a model for developing one's own CMC scope policy. Third is Alice Clark's *Managing Curriculum Materials in the Academic Library* (1982). This work was the first to address *all* aspects of running a CMC—including collection development. In the book, Clark discusses the importance of a collection development policy and gives several criteria for selecting and deselecting materials in accordance with the developed policy.

First Step: Establish a Written Collection Development/Selection Policy

One cannot begin to make a decision on whether to select an item or not if there is no written Collection Development/Selection Policy. A written policy is essential as it serves as the "recipe" for your collection. This policy should answer these questions:

• TYPES OF MATERIALS. What types of materials do you seek to maintain? Curriculum guides? PK–12 textbooks? Instructional media items and in what formats?

• SCOPE/DIVERSITY. What will be your scope/diversity? Materials reflecting what is used in local school districts? Or state-adopted and recommended materials? Or beyond?

• SIZE. How about the size of your overall collection? Are multiple copies a desired goal? Do you need earlier editions to support comparative analysis? The physical size of your CMC may dictate the answers to these questions.

• USERS. Who are your users? Primarily Education students? Faculty teaching Education courses? Or are you also open to teachers and the general public?

All of these questions can be answered by a written policy that reflects the goals of your particular CMC and Library/Institution. A model of such a policy can be found in *Curriculum Materials Center Collection Development Policy* (1993).

The Four Criteria Defined

Armed with your written collection development policy, you can now begin using criteria to evaluate items you are considering adding. These criteria should be used for both purchased and donated items, but they are especially critical for the latter. Therefore, the explanations and examples that follow will be *mostly* in the context of donated items. The four suggested criteria in this article are defined as follows:

1. DUPLICATION VS. DEFICIENCY. Is the item a duplicate of one you already have in your collection? Do you already have an overabundance of very similar items? Depending on your collection development policy, duplication is a criteria which can turn the decision either way. The other extreme is when an item represents a subject area where you have little or nothing or a collection deficiency. If the item fills a deficient area of your collection, you can accept it but only after considering the other criteria listed below. For example, you may be deficient in multicultural readers, but you may not necessarily accept one that is dated or heavily damaged. Related to the issue of multiple copies is class sets. If it is a class set of items (readers, textbooks, workbooks, etc.) you are considering, your deci-

sion to keep all of them, a few, or just one, depends on the space limitations and needs of your particular CMC. This should be written into your collection development policy.

2. CONDITION/FORMAT. What is the physical condition of the item? Is it torn, soiled, damaged, etc.? If it has parts (as in a kit or game), are they all present? If it is an instructional media item, such as a video or cassette, does it work properly? What is the manufactured quality—is it printed on tissue paper or newsprint with a minimal lifespan? When an item arrives in a less than ideal condition, it then requires an evaluation about the time and expense to clean/repair/preserve it. If the item is in very bad condition, it may not be worth it. But even that is negotiable; for example, if it is an extremely popular handbook, in a deficient area of your collection, then having it glued and rebound might be worth your time. (More often, though, extremely damaged items—such as a torn and yellowed paperback falling apart—are not worth the repair time.)

The physical condition also includes the question of format. Is the item a format you are accepting in your written policy? Having a policy on this is especially important, since formats change over the years. Would you accept an LP donation? A filmstrip set? How about an old cassette, or some Apple II software? It depends on your collection policy and the needs of your users. Typically, older formats are not accepted unless there is still a current demand for them or they are in a subject/area where you are very collection-deficient.

3. AUTHORITY/CONTENT. What is the authority and content of the item? Is it authoritative? Is a review available? Is the source or publisher known? Check publisher catalogs and reviews, and see if it is a state or district-adopted textbook for your area. Occasionally, members of the community may donate homemade or self-published materials (and sometimes with a particular religious or political emphasis). While generous, their content may not have gone through the scrutiny of reviews or publishers/editors. This is where having a clearly defined collection development policy is essential. Items that do not have sufficient evaluations or reviews of widespread use might be declined. The inclusion of minimum review standards, such as a review in an educational publication, in your collection development policy should be stated. Similarly, the originality of the item is an issue you must consider. Donations may come in the form of photocopied sheets, audio/video programs on unlabeled cassettes, and software on personal discs or CD-Rs. There must be clear evidence that the item is an original item, and not a copy; otherwise, you are risking accepting illegal material.

The item's content should also be evaluated. Is the information accurate? Is the content clear and usable? Does it reflect the current educational standards of your state or district curriculum? Obviously, no librarian is expected to be omniscient and know the intricacies of every subject discipline, but every librarian should have basic knowledge as well as knowledge of review sources. Basic knowledge can go a long way. For example, if a donated science book from an unknown publisher has religious explanations for all matters, it most likely will not reflect the educational content expected by the state or district curriculum. Therefore, it may be declined. However, remember that items that may have controversial or alternative ideas are not necessarily inaccurate. For example, items on whole language could still be accepted when phonics are more in vogue, and vice versa. Sometimes controversial/alternative items can be included under a classification category designated specifically for alternative curriculum or pedagogy.

Locating reviews of educational material is another way to evaluate content. Many times an item might be unfamiliar even to those who work with educational materials on a daily basis. A donated item, for example, might be praised by its donor or come with great claims by the publisher, but is it really that terrific? In actuality, it may have received negative reviews and been ignored or rejected by the educational community. There are dozens of very common sources to consult for reviews of both new and old materials, and with many of them now available in database form, the time involved for checking can be reduced. Listing all these sources is beyond the space limitations of this article; you can find an extensive list of them in the *Curriculum Materials Center Collection Development Policy* (1993).

4. RELEVANCE/CURRENCY. How relevant and current is the item to your collection? Does it fit into, or have a correlation to, your curriculum areas? Is it appropriate for PK–12 levels? Is it outdated or replaced by newer information? These are all questions to ask when considering relevance and currency. Relevance—applying to at least one of your curriculum areas and being able to be practically used—is important. The item, therefore, may not have relevance to your CMC's needs. Another example might be receiving a book on educational theory and history. While interesting, it may be an academic, university-level book for the main collection of the library, not a practical PK–12-oriented guide for teachers. Thus, it would not be relevant to the goals of your CMC to provide practical PK–12 materials. Relevance is a tricky thing, however, and can often involve strong emotions. What you may not designate as relevant, a donor may see as highly relevant. Some Education faculty members may donate old materials that they have used for decades and are near and dear to them. An example might be a professor donating a filmstrip on "Using a Slide Rule," and insisting it be added. This is where, once again, a definite written collection development policy is a must. If a policy states that "accepted materials will reflect methods currently being taught in local districts," then the material can be declined with a stated

reason. Referring to a written policy can prevent donors from taking denials personally or feeling that you are questioning their expertise.

However, determining relevance is not some autonomous prerogative or whim of the CMC staff. Consulting with others is important so decisions are not made in a vacuum. A clearly defined set of conditions for determining relevance must exist, and be followed, in your written collection development policy. (One might be the condition of being reflected in local curriculum, as with the slide rule example.) Consultation with district or state curriculum standards, or your library/institution's mission statements, or even with education faculty, can be employed. The rule of thumb is to follow your written policy. Even the example of the slide rule could change; if a university offered a course on comparative/historical methodology changes, and the donating professor wanted the filmstrip in the CMC for current evaluative use, then certainly it would be accepted.

Related to relevancy is the question of currency. For new items obtained by purchase, this is not a problem. It is when you have older, donated items that things get questionable. Some items are timeless and can be accepted regardless of age. For example, a *Tic Tac Toe* math game, published in 1975, may still be wildly popular and heavily used. A donation of such an item could be welcome, regardless of its age. Conversely, a donated history lesson plan entitled "Current US-USSR Relations: Detente," also from 1975, is clearly obsolete. Its age makes it an easy decision for rejection. The currency of items in your particular CMC will weigh against your space limitations, budget allowance, and the comparative age of your existing materials. For example, what if your CMC is a small college CMC, with an extremely limited budget, and you receive a set of elementary school science textbooks from 1989. It may be too old. But they might in fact be accepted them because: a) they would replace the 1980 copies currently in the collection; and/or b) they are only one edition older that what is currently being used in the local district; and/or c) the elementary science collection is weak or deficient. Once again, the written policy will set the guidelines. A sample CMC policy, included in Lare's work, gives one possible guideline (for textbooks in particular): "textbooks which are 10 years old shall be withdrawn annually unless their content is specialized and of current or historical value" (Lare, 207).

Examples of the Four Criteria Applied

With the criteria defined, we can now look at some examples of the criteria applied. Since new items are normally *already* evaluated through publishers' catalogs or reviews ahead of time, an example of scrutinizing a new item will not be exemplified here. The scenarios that follow, then, will focus more on donation situations. Since every CMC will have a slightly different collection development policy, and because the criteria will be adjusted to fit that policy, it is impossible to exemplify every possible outcome of a donation scenario. What one CMC might decline, another may want to accept, according to their different goals and users. What follows are a few *general* scenarios. Upon reading each one, try imagining your own CMC and its collection development policy, to see how the applied four criteria may work for you.

Scenario 1.
You have a medium-sized CMC in a local university library, with sufficient space for duplicates and you do accept various formats; your collection attempts to keep current within the last 20 years. You are given three "SRA Reading Kits" (1 teacher's book, 15 student books, 50 vocabulary flashcards, several transparencies & ditto masters) from a retiring teacher. The copyright is 1990. If we apply the four criteria to this situation, we can summarize them in the following checklist:

	Yes	No
1. DUPLICATION VS. DEFICIENCY		
• duplication: is item original to CMC? (nonduplicate)		x
• deficiency: fills/enhances a collection deficiency?		x
• (if multiple copies/class set: space available?)	x	
2. CONDITION/FORMAT		
• condition: physical condition okay?	x	
• format: acceptable?	x	
3. AUTHORITY/CONTENT		
• authority: known or reviewed author/publisher?	x	
• authenticity: original? (noncopy)	x	
• content: accurate and/or well-reviewed?	x	
4. RELEVANCE/CURRENCY		
• relevance: correlation to curriculum area(s)?	x	
• relevance: appropriate to PK–12 level?	x	
• currency: current? (or still currently/heavily used)	x	x

In evaluating the item you notice it is a duplicate; you already have one of these sets. You are strong in your reading materials so it doesn't fill a curricular void. So at first glance it seems unnecessary to add. But you consider the other criteria: as for Condition/Format, it is good and acceptable; the Authority/Content is fine since it is from an established publisher and has had many favorable reviews; on

Relevancy/Currency, it is certainly relevant, but not a current set. In fact, it is more than a decade old. Still, you check your circulation records and find that your current kit is frequently used since Education faculty mention it for sample lesson planning. So then...what is the verdict? Weighing the yeses and nos, you may not need to accept all three. But you certainly should accept at least one. The high usage is the factor weighing in heaviest here. However, if plans to purchase the newer edition are imminent, that could change your decision.

Scenario 2:

You have a small CMC in a private college. Space is limited, but you do have a variety of formats and collection areas. Your collection is a bit weak in math/science. You receive a donation of an educational game from a community member. It is a math bingo game with cards, chips, and a booklet of problems for writing on a chalkboard. The game is intact, but missing some chips and the rules sheet. You do not recognize the publisher; the copyright date is 1983.

	Yes	No
1. DUPLICATION VS. DEFICIENCY		
• duplication: is item original to CMC? (nonduplicate)	x	
• deficiency: fills/enhances a collection deficiency?	x	
• (if multiple copies/class set: space available?)		
2. CONDITION/FORMAT		
• condition: physical condition okay?	x	x
• format: acceptable?	x	
3. AUTHORITY/CONTENT		
• authority: known or reviewed author/publisher?		x
• authenticity: original? (noncopy)	x	
• content: accurate and/or well-reviewed?	x	
4. RELEVANCE/CURRENCY		
• relevance: correlation to curriculum area(s)?	x	
• relevance: appropriate to PK–12 level?	x	
• currency: current? (or still currently/heavily used)	x	

In evaluating the item, you check off your criteria. Duplication vs. Deficiency: it is not a duplicate and definitely fills a curricular deficiency. Condition/Format: although the missing chips and rules sheet are a valid concern, the game is still usable using the problems booklet. Authority/Content: here we have a slight problem. While the game is authentic and the content appears to be accurate, we know nothing about the game's educational value, appeal, or impact. We have never even heard of the publisher. After a little checking, we find that the publisher was a local company that is no longer in business, and no significant reviews were done on the product. This appears to be the primary reservation thus far. As for Relevance/Currency, the game is relevant, appropriate to PK–12, and, although made in 1983, has somewhat of a timelessness to it—various forms of Bingo are still played in schools today. Since the CMC collection is weak in math/science, this factor weighs in the heaviest, and the item should most likely be accepted. (If the reverse were true, and the math/science collection was extremely strong, with plentiful duplication, then it may not need to be accepted.)

Scenario 3:

You have a large CMC in a major state-university library. You have sufficient space, and maintain all formats, although you are trying to encourage new technology. Your collections are represented in all areas, and currently you are trying to budget in newer materials per your collection development goal to have the latest 10-years' worth. A veteran professor approaches you with a donation of some workbooks and accompanying cassettes on values for children that she has cleaned out from her office. The professor talks at length about how interesting these items were when produced, and that it's a shame the schools aren't doing more on values. The copyright of the materials is 1979, and is from a publisher that is still around, but no longer producing materials of that type.

	Yes	No
1. DUPLICATION VS. DEFICIENCY		
• duplication: is item original to CMC? (nonduplicate)	x	
• deficiency: fills/enhances a collection deficiency?		x
• (if multiple copies/class set: space available?)	x	
2. CONDITION/FORMAT		
• condition: physical condition okay?		x
• format: acceptable?		x
3. AUTHORITY/CONTENT		
• authority: known or reviewed author/publisher?	x	
• authenticity: original? (noncopy)	x	
• content: accurate and/or well-reviewed?	x	

4. RELEVANCE/CURRENCY

- relevance: correlation to curriculum area(s)?   x   x
- relevance: appropriate to PK–12 level?   x
- currency: current? (or still currently/heavily used)   x

This scenario could be difficult to call, especially since there is apparent emotion on the part of the donor. Let's examine the criteria. First, Duplication vs. Deficiency: while the item is original to your CMC, you already have a "values/morals/identity" section in your curriculum and already have many similar types of items on the same subject. The donation does not fill a deficiency at all. In regard to Condition/Format, you have a few concerns. The accompanying cassettes are already over 20 years old. While still audible, their quality is a bit muffled. Also, you are really trying to encourage new formats, such as CD and DVD. With Authority/Content, there is no real problem; they were published by a reputable publisher and received acceptable reviews at the time of publication. However, with Relevance/Currency, concerns again arise; you find the material to reflect trends from the 1970s (self-identification, Transactional Analysis, etc.). While values units are still taught in the current curriculum (state and/or local), the emphasis is a completely different approach. So the item's current relevance may not be high. Because of its age, its usage by practicing teachers or student-teachers might be nil. So, then, what decision should be made on this item? Given your emphasis on upgrading your collection to reflect newer technology and trends, the decision to decline the donation seems apparent. Your selection criteria should clearly be given to the professor when discussing the matter. Older materials may be maintained in a Historical Curriculum Collection housed either at your school or at another locations.

Applying the Four Criteria to Deselection (Weeding)

In addition to using the four criteria above for selecting or not selecting items, they may also be applied to deselection (weeding) of the entire CMC collection. In the introduction to this article, several questions were raised. First, older items that still have high demand or relevance are valuable contributions to the collection. Second, "at what point can duplicate copies be removed?" This will vary according to your space limitations, your acquisition of newer materials, and the usage/demand of the items. However, if the items have lost their relevance or currency, or their format/condition have become unusable, then they are likely candidates for weeding. Third, "should worn items automatically be withdrawn?" This is the same as the question of old items—no. Worn items should be repaired and kept if they still meet many of the criteria, and especially if they have high appeal/

demand. Of course, if budgets allow for replacements or upgrades, then certainly the worn copies can be relegated to backup copies or finally discarded. The guiding principles should be your collection development/selection policy and your four criteria.

Conclusion

Adding materials to CMCs is a continuing process. Ideally, materials will be added through new material purchases supplemented by gifts and donations. These gifts come from all types of individuals—educators, professionals, and community members—who show a genuine commitment to education. We must show genuine appreciation for this commitment but retain as paramount our commitment to our clients to have the materials that meet their needs. This commitment to our clients requires that weeding also be a continuing process as well. To develop and maintain our collections, we need effective, clearly defined criteria on the selection and deselection of CMC materials.

References:

Association of College & Research Libraries. 1993. *Curriculum Materials Center Collection Development Policy.* 2d ed. Chicago: American Library Assocation.

Buis, Ed. 1991. "Killing Us With Kindness; Or What to Do With Those Gifts." *Collection Building* 11 (2): 10–12.

Clark, A. S. 1982. *Managing Curriculum Materials in the Academic Library.* Metuchen, N.J.: Scarecrow Press.

Editor. 1993. "Weeding Media." *The School Librarian's Workshop* 14: 8–9.

Editor. 1995. "See and Weed." *The SchoolLibrarian's Workshop* 16: 10.

Farber, E. I. 1997. "Books Not For College Libraries." *Library Journal* 122: 44–45.

Gerhardt, L. N. 1990. "Ethical Back Talk, II: Librarians Must Resist All Efforts by Groups or Individuals to Censor Library Materials." *School Library Journal* 36: 4.

Guide for Written Collection Policy Statements. 1996. 2d ed. Chicago: American Library Assocation.

Huston, K. R. 1989. "How to Look a Gift Horse in the Mouth; Saying No to Donations." *The Bottom Line* 3 (1): 14–17.

Johnson, M. A. 1993. "When to Look a Gift Horse in the Mouth." *Technicalities* 13: 10–13.

Lane, A. H. 1980. *Gifts and Exchange Manual.* Westport, Conn.: Greenwood.

Lare, G. 1997. *Acquiring and Organizing Curriculum Materials.* Lanham, Md.: Scarecrow Press.

Livingston, S. 1999. "Weeding School Library Media Center Collections." *Kentucky Libraries* 63 (3): 15–19.

Magrill, R. M., and J. Corgin. 1989. *Acquisitions Management and Collection Development in Libraries.* 2d ed. Chicago: American Library Association.

Munstedt, P.A. 1995. "LP Donations: Love Them or Leave Them? A Case Study at MIT." *Music Reference Services Quarterly* 4 (2): 1–9.

Pidgeon, A. 1999. "On Writing a Deselection Policy; Or, How to Toss Books Without Public Condemnation." *Kentucky Libraries* 63 (3): 15–19.

Roy, L. 1990. "Weeding Without Tears: Objective and Subjective Criteria Used in Identifying Books to be Weeded in Public Library Collections." *Collection Management* 12 (1–2): 83–93.

Slote, S.J. 1997. *Weeding Library Collections: Library Weeding Methods.* 4th ed. Englewood, Colo.: Libraries Unlimited.

Strnad, B. 1995. "How to Look a Gift Horse in the Mouth; Or, How to Tell People You Can't Use Their Old Junk in Your Library." *Collection Building* 14 (2): 29–31.

Providing Effective and Efficient Access to Curriculum Materials

Gary Lare

Introduction

An important part of managing the CMC collection is providing effective and efficient access to the collection. This access involves both physical and intellectual perspectives. How the user finds the collection organized and how and where it is stored play a big role in any consideration of access. Another area to think about when looking at physical access is how the materials are processed to facilitate availability and efficient use by the borrower. A third area to consider relative to physical access is where the CMC is located, how it is staffed, and what its hours of availability are. Lastly, intellectual access must be considered. This involves what provisions are made for access to the collection via types of data found in the online catalog and other guides and pathfinders. In addition to the above dimensions involving access in the local CMC, providing access to curriculum materials outside of the CMC is also important. This chapter will address each of the areas of access mentioned above.

Physical Access—Organization of the Collection

CMCs vary as to how they organize or shelve the various formats of curriculum materials (textbooks, curriculum guides, teaching activities books, children's books, and AV media such as posters, kits, puppets, models, videos, CD-ROMs, games, overhead transparencies, picture sets, manipulatives, and so forth). Sometimes having different classification schemes for some of these formats of materials determines the way the collection is organized. It is more desirable, however, to base the organization of the CMC collection on meeting the needs of local users instead of the dictates of classification schemes. How is the collection used locally? What kinds of assignments are made? Are a variety of choices provided to the preservice and in-service teacher when developing curriculums and lesson plans? To have flexibility in how one organizes a curriculum materials collection, it would seem that one consistent classification scheme would be a needed common denominator. Since curriculum materials collections are used to meet the needs of school curriculums with their many concepts and topics, it would seem imperative that the classification scheme must be subject based. The CMC published literature seems to be deplete of discussions on the important subject of organization or arrangement of the CMC collection, other than perhaps some discussion on classification schemes. This writer, therefore, posted a survey on the EBSS listserv to ascertain how CMCs organize or arrange their collections. This survey was also e-mailed randomly to many of the CMCs listed in the fourth edition of the *Directory of Curriculum Materials Centers* (Anderson, 1996) that had e-mail addresses indicated. Fifty-two institutions responded to the survey.

Many of the respondents voiced their support of the Dewey Decimal System as the classification system of choice for a curriculum collection. Reasons advanced are that Dewey is very familiar to their preservice users since they used it in high school library media centers and to all users because they will probably be using Dewey in the schools in which they will teach. One respondent stated that using Dewey makes it easy for the preservice and in-service teachers to transfer what they learn in the CMC to what they will experience "on the job." Also, some feel that the Dewey system seems to lend itself better to PK–12 curriculum topics in general and to children's books particularly better than LC, for example.

The CMCs in the survey were asked how they organize their collections or, if they were not satisfied with the present arrangement, how they would ideally reorganize the collection. Specifically, they were surveyed about how they arrange or would arrange the textbooks, curriculum guides, teaching activities books, AV media, and children's books in their collections. They were asked if they intershelve all of these formats in one unit or shelve the materials separately by format or if they shelve by a combination of intershelving some formats and separately shelving others. In addition, rationales for shelving were asked for. Of the respondents, 52% shelve all formats separately; 13% percent intershelve all formats as one unit; while

Curriculum Materials Centers Collection Organization Patterns			
Institution	Intershelve	Separate	Combination
Appalachian State University	X		
Baylor University		X	
Bridgewater State College		X	
Cal Poly State University		X	
California State University-Fullerton			X
California State University-Northridge	X		
California State University-San Bernadino			X
Central Connecticut State University			X
Cleveland State University			X
Concordia College			X
Concordia University-St. Paul		X	
Chadron State College			X
East Illinois State University		X	
Framingham State College			X
Harvard University			X
Hofstra University	X		
Illinois State University		X	
Indiana University			X
James Madison University		X	
Kansas State University			X
Keene State College			X
Louisiana State University		X	
Mansfield University		X	
Minnesota State University-Mankato		X	
Mississippi College		X	
Moorhead State University		X	
McNeese University		X	
New Jersey City University		X	
Northern Michigan University	X		
The Ohio State University			X
Quincy University		X	
Radford University		X	
San Jose State University			X
Shawnee State University	X		
Southern Illinois University		X	
State University of West Georgia		X	
Texas A&M University		X	
University of Akron			X

Institution	Intershelve	Separate	Combination
University of Central Florida	X		
University of Cincinnati			X
University of Dayton		X	
University of Delaware			X
University of Illinois at Urbana-Champaign		X	
University of Iowa		X	
University of Nevada-Las Vegas		X	
University of South Dakota			X
University of West Florida	X		
University of Wisconsin-Madison	X		
University of Wisconsin-Milwaukee			X
University of Wisconsin-Oshkosh		X	
Washburn University		X	
William Patterson University		X	

35% intershelve some of the formats and separately shelve others. Some examples of the latter combination shelving are the following: 1) textbooks, activities books, and curriculum guides are combined and intershelved while children's books and AV media are separately shelved; 2) curriculum guides and activities books are intershelved while textbooks, AV media, and children's books are separately shelved. A total of nine different patterns emerged in the survey regarding what formats are combined and intershelved and which are shelved separately. It should be mentioned too that some of the arrangement patterns place teaching activities books in the general professional education book area of the library. Also, when AV media are shelved separately, they are often intershelved by media type; but some CMCs separate out some AV media to be shelved separately because of size (for example, posters or charts), or because of perceived security risks, such as CD-ROMs. Furthermore, in some CMCs broad classification numbers are used; in these situations different formats of materials in the same broad curriculum area are shelved near each other, based on a similar classification number, but then are shelved separately by format.

Those favoring a separation by format feel that this is best because students come into the CMC looking for a particular type of material, such as a textbook or piece of software, or they are assigned to compare and contrast textbooks, review software, or retrieve a curriculum guide, for example. One CMC supporter of separate formats said, "Just imagine how confusing it would be to an undergraduate student with an assignment to look at a basal math text, if he had to plow through curriculum guides, professional books, and children's books to locate a 3rd grade textbook; or how confusing it would be for a teacher involved in curriculum revision to try to locate a curriculum guide amongst all these other types of materials." Others say that if a consistent classification scheme is used and there is a desire for various materials on a given subject, their users can easily browse the collection by just going from section to section with a given class number representing the subject being sought. One respondent noted that the model of shelving by type or format of material provides an opportunity for an effective lesson on doing subject searches using the online catalog. Some say that maintaining separate areas makes it easier for student workers to shelve and maintain the order of items. Another reason advanced is that shelving by type or format allows for the most efficient use of shelf space, so that different size shelving can be utilized depending on the size of the format. Less deep shelves can be used for books, and deeper shelves can be used for media.

One can argue, however, that when materials are organized separately by format, it can become confusing to the user who must be sure to have the right location code or format in the call number when trying to locate the item. Strong attention to posting appropriate signage in the CMC and including specific location codes in the OPAC are imperative. Browsing for a variety of materials on the same subject is certainly more time consuming because of having to go to different locations.

Intershelving of the collection in various degrees is strongly advocated by other CMCs. Some of the popular intershelving combinations that appeared in the survey are: teaching activities books with curriculum guides or with textbooks, or textbooks with teaching activities books or curriculum guides. Seven of the respondents either totally intershelve or would prefer to do so. When total intershelving occurs, one will have all formats, book and nonbook, intershelved in one classification scheme run. There are certain advantages of intershelving a curriculum collection. One respondent to the survey said, "we like to keep things intershelved to assist in the serendipity part of information seeking." Some express the idea that most of the education assignments at their institution emphasize topical gathering of information more than format gathering, so an integrated CMC collection works quite well. Others stated that, when they shelved by format, their users had trouble finding materials or would not bother looking in the other collections even when it was suggested. Another respondent emphasized not only that intershelving provides definite convenience to the user but that the faculty at her institution emphasize the role of the teacher as a curriculum creator and that intershelving contributes to facilitating this activity. It is noteworthy also to mention that this individual found a substantial increase in the circulation of her CMC materials when they intershelved the collection.

With the advantages of intershelving come some challenges. It definitely takes up more space. Shelving must be adjusted higher to accommodate large items such as kits; therefore, there will be fewer shelves per section in each range of shelving. It takes more time to keep the shelves in order and maintained because smaller items can get pushed behind larger items. Books and items in pouches or envelopes next to some larger boxes and plastic tubs may fall over, and so forth. Using 14- or 15-inch-deep divider shelves will help to alleviate this problem, however. The dividers help to keep the shelves organized and materials upright and together.

Another potential problem of intershelving occurs when users need to find only textbooks or only curriculum guides or only CD-ROMs to meet the needs of a particular assignment. They have to pour through many formats to get just the ones desired. The online catalog can be an important ally in this case. It should allow one to construct searches in which topic *and* format can be combined. Then, with call numbers in hand, the user can go to the shelves and find the desired items. It is, of course, helpful if the materials' call number labels are marked with the appropriate formats, such as Textbook, Curriculum Guide, CD-ROM, Kit, and so forth. (Some CMCs even use color coding devices for this purpose.)

Having presented two different models for organizing a CMC collection which are at opposite ends of the organization scale, along with some variations or combinations, this writer prefers a hybrid of the two that seems to represent the best of both of the total intershelving and the separation by format models. This hybrid model provides for those seeking certain materials by format, the more popular being textbooks, curriculum guides, and activities books. These curriculum materials are shelved separately by format. This model also provides for those seeking a variety of materials (print and nonprint) on a specific topic by intershelving children's books with AV media (posters, kits, puppets, models, videos, CD-ROMs, games, overhead transparencies, picture sets, manipulatives, and so forth). The Dewey Decimal System is used consistently for all of the materials. This model facilitates users who often need to evaluate, compare, or contrast textbooks for a particular broad curriculum area, such as elementary science, algebra, or reading, or for a particular grade or multiple grades for a given publisher. It also provides quick access for users who need to look over a number of curriculum guides or frameworks as examples to develop a specific curriculum. For those users assigned to develop a file of teaching activities based on a theme, a good browsing collection of teaching activities books shelved in one area will make this task easier. Furthermore, having the materials shelved by subject with all of the materials of the same format together will enhance the users' ability to develop a lesson plan based on the steps usually followed in developing a lesson plan. First, the curriculum guides section could be consulted for objectives and sequencing of concepts. Then the user could move to the teaching activities books to browse for activities for the lesson plan. Usually teaching activities books are more general in nature, covering many topics. So indexes have to be browsed through to find specific activities for given lessons. Next, the textbook section could be perused to find further strategies in teacher's editions and curriculum subject matter content. Finally, the AV media/children's books intershelved would be used to find specific materials (print and nonprint) on the specific topic being taught, such as "magnetism," or "the circulation system," or "Mexico," or "Native Americans," for example. This writer feels, for the reasons advanced above, that since textbooks, curriculum guides, and activities books will usually have more general class numbers, just having them in the same relative area as the specific class numbers of the AV media and children's books, as would be the case in a totally intershelved collection, really does not contribute that much to a multiple format gathering when teaching a specific topic or concept. Therefore, more is gained by meeting the needs for those formats usually used by themselves by keeping them shelved by themselves, and the advantages gained by intershelving the AV media with children's books merits their intershelving.

It must be repeated, however, that whatever model of organization is followed, the needs of the local CMC users must be met—and the arrangement of the curriculum materials collection should reflect that. As also mentioned before, the online catalog is a crucial player in the physical access to the collection. The records should reflect the unique needs of a CMC with its needs to retrieve materials by format as well as by subject. Other important elements are adequate signage and, of course, good instruction on using the collection. Providing AV media also necessitates the provision of adequate AV media/computer equipment for using the collection, both in appropriateness for all of the types of media/computer software available in the collection and in sufficient numbers to meet the demand. Furthermore, it is important to place the equipment that goes with each type of medium as close to the AV media collection as possible. Having the equipment for utilizing the CMC AV collection in another department or another floor in the library, for example, is not providing adequate access to the CMC collection.

Physical Access—The Processing of Materials

In addition to organization and storage of the collection issues, a second area to consider in providing the CMC user with effective and efficient physical accessibility is how the materials are processed for use. Processing the materials in ways that will preserve or extend the life of the item is very important. For example, the majority of teaching activities books are published as paperbacks. They are a heavily used area of the CMC collection, getting a lot of handling as they are browsed and consulted. At the University of Cincinnati, the teaching activities books and curriculum guides are automatically bound with an economy line of binding to preserve them. The paper cover is mounted to the front of the bound cover to provide not only attractiveness but also easy recognition and accessibility by the user. Of course, if this kind of binding is out of the question because of limited budgets, then perhaps heavy, clear book tape or mylar could be applied. Either way, some kind of extra treatment to the paper cover will help to preserve the book for frequent usage right from the beginning.

It is of particular importance that AV items be appropriately packaged to preserve and provide for appropriate accessibility for users. Videos and CD-ROMs, for example, will sometimes come in slipcovers, which will not provide for protected circulation. A standard container needs to be established for different types of materials. A plastic container is recommended for videos and CD-ROMs. This might consist of an "album" type of container that not only will protect the item but will often provide an internal compartment for storage of accompanying literature. All of the material, therefore, is protected so that availability is maintained. Albums for videos and CD-ROMs come in the smaller as well as the larger size to provide for larger-sized literature. CD-ROMs sometimes come in 3-ring binders. This makes for a strong outer protection, but the CD-ROM carrier is often just in a plastic sleeve attached to the rings of the binder. In this case, the CD-ROM could be placed in a jewel case to protect it. A special plastic insert with a recessed area can be purchased to house the jewel case. This insert has three holes and can be inserted like a page in the 3-ring binder. (Regardless, CD-ROMs and audio compact discs are much better protected when placed in jewel cases.) Special plastic albums are also available for laser discs.

Overhead transparencies often provide a challenge as well. These are often produced as a set and cover a wide range of topics. If a particular topic is being taught in which an overhead transparency is desired, the user usually does not want to check out the whole set. It is better to have individual records entered in the online catalog so that each transparency can be checked out on its own. Each transparency could then be packaged in a heavy-duty envelope for circulation and shelving. Also, this separate shelving will put the specific transparencies next to other materials with the same specific classification. Kit materials sometimes have to be repackaged to provide better access for users. Kit contents may be commercially packaged in one large container. Special boxes of various sizes can be purchased from library supply companies to accommodate the repackaging of the contents. Sometimes users desire manipulatives to be packaged for individual use. Plastic boxes or tubs such as those made by Tupperware can be procured for providing for this usage pattern. Also, puppets in the collection need some special packaging too.

These could be put in boxes, but these kinds of materials are useful to be placed in containers that will allow one to view them easily on the shelf. Webbed bags or large clear plastic bags that snap closed, such as those produced by Monaco, are ideal for large or small puppets. Maps, charts, and posters need to be preserved for storage and circulation as well. Access to a large dry-mount press or laminator is very helpful for these items. Laminating these materials with heavy-duty laminating film helps to preserve and protect them for many years of usage.

Another necessary step to help ensure that the user will have everything available when needed is to be sure that all of the parts of the item are marked with the call number. Pieces of a kit or game or a teaching guide often come out and can be found in various areas of the CMC. Having the call number on the various pieces will help restore the pieces to the container quickly. Of course, one has to do this marking within reason. Marking one hundred bingo chips would be a little out of the question. In addition, marking should be avoided if the marking would detract from the instructional application of that particular piece. A preventative measure for parts and pieces falling out of containers is to keep rubber bands around those containers where pieces might slip out. In addition, a listing of the various parts of an item should be displayed on the item. This will help one to know that all of the parts are there or not when an item is being checked out. The same is true when the item is being checked in after being borrowed.

Still another area to address in trying to make sure that materials continue to be accessible to users for as long as possible is in the area of circulation carriers. We have already discussed how preservation actions can be taken for some materials such as videos, CD-ROMs, transparencies, etc., when they are initially processed for the shelf. These containers will help protect the items during circulation as well. However, some items do not need a special container for storage but do need something for protection during circulation. One such item is flat pictures. These materials typically are mounted and filed by subject and stored in vertical files. During circulation, however, they need to be protected. Nylon portfolios used in the banking industry work very well for this. These zippered portfolios can be reinforced with heavy-duty cardboard and maintained at the circulation desk for circulating these mounted pictures. A long vertical label can be placed on the outside of the portfolio on which the date due is placed. Other items that may be considered for extra preservation help during circulation might be audio compact discs. These can be stored in jewel cases on the shelf, but for circulation the jewel case can be placed in specially designed clear plastic pouches available from library supply companies. These pouches are made to house more than one CD and have a Velcro tab for securing the CDs within. A date-due label can be placed on the outside of the pouch.

All of this discussion on steps to take to preserve materials for longer life and better assurance of availability to users requires much coordination and cooperation between the CMC and the cataloging/processing department and perhaps the circulation department. This coordination, of course, will vary with complexity depending on each CMC. Some Colleges of Education administer their own CMCs and may handle all of their cataloging/circulation within their center. Other CMCs may be within the library organization and will have their cataloging and processing done by a cataloging department but will circulate their own materials from the CMC, while others will circulate from a central library circulation desk. Regardless of the administrative arrangement, to be effective, CMCs may still need to do some final preparation/processing of materials in-house.

Physical Access—Location, Staffing and Hours of the CMC

This leads us to the final areas that we will consider relative to physical access: location of the CMC, staffing, and hours of availability. Whether the CMC is administratively under the campus library or the College of Education, it would seem that the most convenient access to its materials will be provided if it is physically located within the building where most education classes are taught. Examples of this arrangement are at Brock University, Western Kentucky University, University of Southern Mississippi, University of Dayton, North Carolina State University, James Madison University, and University of Wisconsin-Madison. A second most convenient location would be if the CMC is in a building near the location of the building where education classes are taught. An example of this placement is at the University of Cincinnati. Of course, mere physical location is not the only factor in providing accessibility. Even if the CMC is located in the College of Education building, good accessibility can be limited if the CMC is not open enough hours to sufficiently meet the needs of its users. Many CMCs are located in the main library building on campus. Some examples of these CMCs are at University of Wisconsin-Stout, University of South Dakota, Moorhead State, California State University-Northridge, Midwestern State University, Louisiana State University, Kutztown University, and Central Connecticut University. It is important that the CMC have the same hours of availability as the rest of the library and be easily accessed. Longer hours of availability are usually an advantage of the CMC being located in the campus library. Also, because of the specialized materials located in the CMC with their need for particular handling, a circulation desk in the CMC provides a real plus. This arrangement of a CMC unit in the main campus library, with the CMC having its own circulation desk, can be found at Louisiana State University and Kutztown University. In addition to CMC location and hours of availability, staffing plays a big role in providing adequate access to CMC materials. Sufficient staff must be available in the CMC to provide reference help and assistance in locating materials for users. Of course, staff alone is not enough; there must be individuals available who have been trained in the curriculum materials available and how to put the user in touch with materials to meet their needs. This means that the staff (and this could be student assistants at times) should be well trained in using the online catalog as well as knowing the collection so that useful assistance can be provided to the user.

Intellectual Access

Any discussion of access must consider not only physical access but also intellectual access. This covers how the user can find out what curriculum materials are available and what kind of information is provided in the records for the user. An online catalog is the best gateway to the collection. In addition to this resource, pathfinders, guides, and class sessions can be developed to present the collection and how to access it. But the online catalog is the primary access point. Since most of the materials in the CMC collection are on the PK–12 level rather than the college level, it is useful if the online catalog can be limited to the CMC for searching. The ability to limit searching will narrow the subject search to items that the user is probably interested in finding for a particular level or type of material. Also, if the CMC is divided into sub-locations—a location for teaching activities books, a location for textbooks, etc.,—each record in the online catalog can indicate this location separate from the call number. Armed with the call number and the location from the online catalog, the user can more readily locate the item rather than only a call number with some sort of indicator in the call number alone showing the sub-location.

Although it is not the intent of this chapter to discuss the cataloging of curriculum materials, there is one area that is worth talking about. For audiovisual media, particularly, it is useful if one can search for a particular type or types of media on a particular subject and for a particular grade level. At the University of Cincinnati, a grade range and media type are entered in a local subject MARC tag (690) for PK–12 AV media materials. (This same procedure could be done for other curriculum materials, if desired.) The user then searches by subject keyword and limiting to get at this three-way match for items desired. This type of searching has greatly enhanced user access to the AV media collection.

External Access

The discussion so far in this chapter has concerned itself with access to curriculum materials in the physical collection of the CMC. We must also consider access to curriculum materials not located in the CMC. This includes items borrowed from other institutions through interlibrary loan and materials accessed on the Internet.

As more and more states and regions are forming consortia for sharing resources, a gold mine of opportunity can be made available for accessing curriculum materials. It would be impossible for one CMC to meet all the needs of all of its users in-house. By being able to borrow materials, even directly online as is done with OhioLINK in Ohio, users have access to borrow materials from the CMC collections of various institutions. In the case of Ohio, materials may be borrowed from just about all of the universities and colleges in the state. Other consortia exist throughout the United States and are growing for the purpose of resource sharing. The one area that is of concern is the packaging of AV curriculum materials for interlibrary loan. It is important that appropriate packaging be provided so that the various types of materials can be preserved and maintained in transit.

Another source of curriculum materials outside of the local CMC is the Internet, a topic that is explored in the next chapter.

Conclusion

As one can see, providing effective and efficient access to curriculum materials is a multidimensional phenomenon. Many areas must be attended to so that the curriculum materials user is given an opportunity to obtain needed materials. This chapter looked at some of the physical and intellectual issues involved in providing good access. Certainly, how the collection is organized, stored, and processed in the local CMC are important areas to address. Also, the location, hours, and staffing of the CMC play a big role in accessing materials. Furthermore, effective and pertinent cataloging records in a user-friendly OPAC, pathfinders, and guides make a difference regarding the ease with which a user can locate desired materials. In addition to the above considerations pertaining to access to curriculum materials in the local CMC, this chapter discussed access via external sources such as the Internet and interlibrary loan. Various levels of access can be afforded the CMC user. Understandably, we should always strive to provide the very best access possible.

Reference

Anderson, B. 1996. *Directory of Curriculum Materials Centers*. 4th ed. Chicago: American Library Association.

Management Tools for Maintaining a CMC Virtual Collection

Patricia O'Brien Libutti

Introduction: Curriculum Materials Choices: Breaking New Ground
CMC staff have encountered the hybrid nature of materials presently being used
in classrooms and university teaching methods classes for approximately five years.
Emerging in today's classroom materials market are materials such as those described below:

SCHOOL TECHNOLOGY BOOM INSPIRES TEXTBOOK MAKERS
Textbook makers and other content providers are moving into the growing online education market. Houghton-Mifflin, for example, is part of
the Classwell Learning Group, which is providing testing, teacher training, and curriculum over the Internet. Houghton-Mifflin's participation
marks the first time a major textbook maker has allowed online use of
its content on a large scale, says Chris Hoehn-Saric of Sylvan Ventures,
another Classwell participant. Next year Classwell plans to license standard curriculum content, with schools paying about $10,000 a year to
use the materials. Meanwhile, McGraw-Hill's Web site provides quiz-
zes, special projects, and animations that students can access by clicking

on a picture of their textbook. Harcourt General provides similar online offerings. (*Investor's Business Daily*, 9 October 2000)

Is Your CMC Ready?

This current state of Internet technology used to develop unique materials for learning presents the CMC Manager with the challenges of decisions about what to collect and how to manage a virtual collection. It is likely, as seen in a quick scan of the Fourth Edition of the *Directory of Curriculum Materials Centers* (Anderson, 1996) that almost all of the 263 CMCs described have Internet access and, in most cases, have a virtual presence themselves. What that presence is now and what will be in the future will depend on how decisions on virtual resource collections are explored.

Tool One: Use Information Auditing Strategies in the Present Situation

One of the necessary steps in examining earlier decisions as a prelude to developing a current management plan is to look at assumptions about users, institutions, and support for earlier decisions made on virtual CMC collections. It is likely that Schon's (1983) description of "decision under uncertainty" fits the CMC manager and staff in the virtual collection process:

> It has become commonplace for managers to speak of the "turbulent" environments in which problems do not lend themselves to the techniques of benefit-cost analysis or to probabilistic reasoning.... And managers have become acutely aware that they are often confronted with unique situations to which they must respond to under conditions of stress and limited time, which leave no room for extended calculation or analysis. Here they tend to speak not of technique, but of "intuition" (239).

An information audit, as described in the Special Libraries Associations Web site (http://www.sla.org/) is a tool that is customizable to the institution. An information audit of students' and faculty's actual experiences is necessary for good service planning. This should include finding the total scope of information opportunity that the students and faculty use. Knowing how resources are used should include how students are exposed to Web resources in teacher education off the campus: public schools, district technology centers, consortia resources, individual exploration, etc.

The manager and staff can develop specific information auditing strategies that may include searching for answers to questions, such as: How has the Web collection been managed during the last five years? Many sub-questions ensue from a simple beginning such as this question. If your CMC is like most, the growth of Internet resources listed on your terminal has been an organic development, replete with several overhauls. It is also likely that practice often is fast, done, and rarely reflected upon, in keeping with the pace of the learning institution.

Several recent works paint portraits to use as comparison points to the particular CMC. Libutti and Gratch (1995) collected several portraits of 1995 practice that are case studies of Internet training. Others also looked over a five-year period and provided narrative accounts of existing practice and changes observed (Libutti, 1999). It is likely that most CMC managers went through similar patterns to products on the Web. Within a five-year period, Web resources emerged from lists and handouts that were converted to Web-accessible information. When librarians first introduced Internet resources to classes and colleagues, lists of relevant links were widely available in print. These bibliographies of links evolved into Web pages on subject-specific links.

Site development on specialized topics happened rapidly in the mid-90s, with almost each university or college having specializations and Web authors coming forth in hypertext. Evaluation of and critical thinking about the importance of Web sites for instruction and information soon followed. Placement of links in online catalogs was an event for some but not all higher education institutions. Reviews and overhauls were simplified by the use of editors and technology. Now, the education market has new products that are hybrids of earlier formats of information united with Web possibility. The Web itself is now considered as a "curriculum medium" (Harris, 2000).

Tool Two: Explore Available Capital

"Capital" needs to be thought of as resources beyond financial factors. Personal skills, interests, liaisons, the positioning of the CMC for partnerships, and available Web resources are part of a comprehensive capital assessment. One way to begin is to see the CMC as part of a larger institutional picture.

Social Structure of the CMC. The organizational structure is perhaps the first factor to consider when developing managerial options for Web resource use. Factors always vary according to the social alignment of the CMC. The CMC in the university may stand alone as a source of specialized teacher preparation information, be integrated into a section of the university library, or be a part of the College of Education, as seen in the extensive survey reported in the latest *Directory of Curriculum Materials Centers* (Anderson, 1996). The Directory listed 263 discrete CMCs in 1996, and includes the data on alignment with a College of Education or library.

A CMC manager has different allies dependent on this social structure of the related units of a university for collaborative management. Each of the other components, while having similar equipment, necessarily has a unique role in the structure of the learning environment. The integrated center (part of the library) may have access to services of other subject specialists in the library, such as the education librarian, and share equipment, expertise, and expenses with the library system. It is possible that the outlay of expenses to prepare a Web product can be shared, as seen in Carr's description of the preparation of an annotated education journal list which was done using the expertise of two institutions (Carr, 1997).

The stand-alone center may be one that serves not only the College of Education but also a neighboring community of practicing teachers. This aspect brings to the assets pool the experience that teachers had with commercial Web resources, such as *Classroom Connect* (http://www.classroomconnect.com) or *Beyond Books* (http://www.beyondbooks.com). Local teachers can provide insight into the use of educational television (PBS's *Teacher Source*) as well as other portals used in a classroom setting.

Past Experience of CMC Staff. Early in the '90s, the presence of the Internet put librarians at a disadvantage. They were both learners and teachers simultaneously, usually at a rushed, frantic pace. The librarian was then forced to face educational issues that depart in significant ways from prior technology experience. Viewing Internet as a subject to be taught as well as an instructional medium to be used departed from the use of prior educational technologies.

The issues expressed by librarians in role evolution that began with each unique introduction to the Internet to diverse present implementations are described by several authors in *Librarians as Learners, Librarians as Teachers: The Diffusion of Internet Expertise in Academic Libraries* (Libutti, 1999). Many features from the anecdotes are likely similar to the learning experiences of CMC librarians with Internet. Managers often faced different pressures to learn the Internet, and often had to learn how staff built expertise and how much time that took.

Intellectual Capital. Knowing about expertise takes recognition of intellectual and social capital. Who has been writing about the impact of Internet for columns in journals? Which staff member gravitates to all things Internet? Who is the librarian who knows the latest trends in electronic gadgets? Who is working on "just one more" arrangement of a menu for the CMC Web page? Who has a small dot-com of his or her own, and devotes free time to this alternative income? Is there a staff person who was an elementary teacher and now enjoys testing out new technologies? Who volunteers as a cybrarian at a local women's center? If there is a specialist in children's literature, can this person work with tech enthusiasts to evaluate the e-books and Web-presented tales for children?

Social Capital. Which staff member is seen with faculty at institutional functions? Who shares the same interests in collection development? Who is asked by faculty to be part of a team in instruction? Which staff members complement each other's teaching style? Who follows educational market trends and can recite stock quotes on the vendors in question? Answers to these questions provide a quick assessment of social capital that can be mobilized in partnerships beneficial to the CMC.

Community Capital. What local ventures might be possible through partnership (public library–university CMC; public school system–CMC; industry or local business–CMC)? What faculty members have produced e-books or specialized Web sites and would be willing to be consultants? If educational technology courses were offered, would a faculty member give students assignments to help the CMC to have a snappy new design? A manager who looks at all the possibilities for Web development for use in the center is far ahead on the learning curve. In the complex world of higher education, the ways to produce new efforts often depend upon connections outside the university. The numbers of companies that have technology grants for higher education need assessing by the CMC manager for development. What grants are available for construction of new educational resources? Which companies are funding such production? Who on the staff would be able and challenged by the task of assessing grant possibilities? Skills seen in the staff can be integrated by able management into preparation of a virtual collection for the CMC through strategic partnerships with other interested sectors of the community, university, or school system (Bergquist, Betwee, & Meuel, 1995).

Web Capital. The array of resources that would be considered actual curriculum materials is wide. From online encyclopedias to virtual frog dissection kits, the wealth of the Internet as a curriculum materials provider is beyond estimation. The quality of resources needs to be evaluated in selected sites, so that new teachers do not have to plow their way through enormous arrays of choices. Providing allotted time for exploration of new Web materials is essential for good planning, as well as for staff morale. Good exploration is curiosity eliciting, keeps one current, and provides the basis for new ideas for in-house application. For instance, the preparation of materials by industries, businesses, and organizations is ever expanding. Government resources are rich in educational content. Beyond the work of the National Library of Education (http://www.ed.gov/NLE/) are other government sites. To examine government resources further, look into *Uncle Sam's K–12 Web* by Laurie Andriot (1999).

When thorough exploration is done by staff who have reviewed decisions, environment, and capital, selections will emerge. Since there are many pathways for exploration, considering what to include was developed for this chapter by using Elkordy's (2000) description *What to Include in a Virtual Collection* and modifying the list to display selected categories specific to a CMC Virtual Collection. Each category has from one to three examples for exploration. A deliberate effort was made to include relatively new resources, as well as those that have achieved permanence over the last five years. The categories are by no means exhaustive and should be regarded as a starting point for exploration and debate. Elkordy's list is available at http://www.thelearningsite.net/cyberlibrarian/elibraries/include.html. The appendix to this chapter contains this pathway; examples were taken from sites listed in a listing of Web sites of CMCs posted to the EBSS-List (Walker, July 2000) which is reproduced in Walker's chapter, elsewhere in this volume.

Tool Three: Prepare a Virtual Collection Plan

Collection plans that include Web resources are faced with an extremely short half-life. However, the alternative to such preparation is worse: the hidden costs of nonmanaged virtual collections eventually emerge. The user may find a display screen that is difficult to navigate or outdated links. Many of the newer resources that need evaluation and commitment in fees paid may not get much attention until the faculty use them in their coursework or the library provides access and "sells" the resource through proactive contacts. Students may well begin Web pages as part of coursework, which could become part of a collection of educational Web sites for the CMC. The existence of such factors indicates that a cycle of planning for collection needs to be rapid, with planning, actual practice, and review of practice being continuous.

There may be those who feel that the development of a plan isn't as necessary as with a physical collection plan. Perlmutter (1999) makes conscious the essential nature of the decisions involved in such planning. Ideally, managers want decisions that are made with knowledge of the right resources for the particular institution. A Virtual Collection Development Plan needs to provide for the budgeting needed for resources that are subscription based. Developing a shared understanding of scope, desirable aspects of collection, tasks that need attention and responsible allocation are all part of the planning decisions for a virtual collection. The energy (and scheduled budgetary allotments) for an excellent virtual collection will, of necessity, need to be juggled with the already existing responsibilities of staff. Decisions about what to collect, who will oversee it, and how the collection is to be used and maintained are seen with the reality of the choices already examined.

Consider the Plan as a Document in Constant Process. It is important to understand the permanence of the plan. Since the Internet is not on an easily predicted course, the plan needs to be flexible for those implementing it. Let a developed plan serve as a guiding document, rather than a collection of benchmark statements.

Purpose. These essential decisions need to be a point of consensus prior to development. Here, the CMC manager needs to exercise the role of skilled convener, since it is likely that all staff members are stakeholders in a good plan. Purposes that may be important include priority of a virtual collection, responsiveness to a college division, provision of materials in current use in teacher education programs or recognition of the role that virtual materials play in the current collection planning cycle.

Uses of a Virtual CMC Collection. Considering present and anticipated uses of a virtual collection will set some boundaries on the amount of collecting actually done. Many sites would be collected for the express purpose of use in class or in training situations.

Course Resources: On-shelf or Online? Faculty e-books and Web sites are a valuable part of a collection. Parts of courses in the education methods classes may be online, and also may be the beginning of good team teaching, seen in numerous CMC site curricula.

Students Using the Web as Curriculum Material? One of the many faculty who emphasizes the uses of the Web as a curriculum material is Judi Harris. She focuses on the process that students enjoy through collaborative learning (Harris, 2000). Her site: *In the Kitchen—Designs for Telecollaboration and Telepresence* (Access: http://lrs.ed.uiuc.edu/LRS/TE-surfing.html) provides options for learning impossible prior to the Web.

Providing Distance Education Resources? The CMC has choices to make about managing needs by offering online or on-shelf resources. Materials used in distance education for the university may include for-fee services that are restricted to those enrolled in courses offered by methods faculty. Each choice carries with it a logical task structure, which needs articulation in a plan.

Collecting For-Fee Services? A decision of that nature needs to be supplemented by other information. What is happening in the College of Education? Do courses incorporate such subscriptions? Do professors author such resources? These questions need to be answered for data on subscription expense decisions. For instance, *Columbia University's Earthscape* (http://www.earthscape.org) is an excellent resource about earth sciences, and prices access according to the number of students in an institution. Individual subscriptions are $145. Exploring the free trials available may be part of a bibliographic instruction class, with handouts providing details about individual connection.

Including Sites by and for Students? Many sites are developed that are student based and are informative to teachers in training. An archive of class projects done for Web-based instruction is foreseeable.

Including Teaching Materials? Teachers in training need examples of Internet-based lesson plans, and this category should be represented in a CMC collection, along with other approaches seen in lesson plans. Student teachers need to know how to find evaluated resources, with sites such as *Blue Web'n Learning Sites Library* (Access: http://www.kn.pacbell.com/wired/bluewebn/).

Proficiency in directory and index use online and practice with application in subject searching for specific lesson plans are topics for the bibliographic instructor in a CMC. An excellent resource for understanding the characteristics of search engines that can be used by students on their own is the University of California-Berkeley's *Internet Resources: Search Engines.* The University of California-Berkeley has led the nation in librarian-developed search engine instructions (Access: http://www.lib.berkeley.edu/TeachingLib/Guides/Internet/).

Other Bibliographic Instruction Issues. The CMC, with its emphasis on materials, is in a perfect position to provide instruction on topics relevant to future practice of teachers. The topics of intellectual property, online privacy, acceptable use policies, and plagiarism are important for the practitioner and can be developed in conjunction with curriculum material exploration (D'Amico, 1996; McKenzie, 1996; Davidson, 1999.) These topics will be integrated into the practice of teachers on the job. Collection of materials that support bibliographic instruction is not limited to articles: Web tutorials on information literacy, PowerPoint presentations on best practices in teaching, and school-produced Webs are materials that are useful for bibliographic instruction in the CMC and can be found in metasites, such as *Kathy Schrock's Guide for Educators* (http://school.discovery.com/schrockguide/).

Responsible Staff and Logistics of Planning. Considering the possible aspects of partnership, collaboration, and task sharing by others in the university is worth conscious thought. Bergquist, Betwee, & Meuel (1995) focused on the kinds of partnership seen in business environments that may well inform choices in a university environment. Since the CMC supports faculty and community through the delivery of information and collections of materials, the connections among local teachers, university faculty, and library staff needs examining. Choices that the manager needs to consider include:

• assigning one key staff person to obtain current awareness information in diverse ways.

• working with decentralized information systems: using each librarian's expertise differently (i.e., assigning different librarians the tasks of faculty liaisons, search and report, vendor relationships, according to perceived expertise and interest).

• involving faculty and local school partners to develop a plan for shared resources. Actual logistics of the Web development need to be reflected in the plan.

Web Site Design. Computer Department Staff, Librarian, or Other Producer? The designer, whether in-house or external to the CMC, will face
issues about the fit of the site to the rest of the institution, as well as aes-
thetic ones.

Web Site Content: Linkage or Original Construction? Does it serve the interests
of the CMC to develop original content? Tillman (2000), in the CMC Web site
he manages, included a *K–12 Cyberpedia*, which he designed and uses as a show-
case for curriculum and education materials. Many other sites use strategic linkage for the purpose of the collection and depend upon annotation or grouping
under chosen headings for explanation.

Organizational Schema. What classification systems are available and how do
they "fit" with the course structures of the parent institution? Consider looking at
several PK–12 guides to the Web (Polly, 2000; Junion-Metz, 1997; Berger, 2000).
It is also likely that original schema can be developed to mirror the purposes in the
plan. Polly, in developing the schema used in hierarchal tree category system, had
studied both Web classification and traditional classification before extracting
the system now in use by the author (Polly, e-mail, June 1999).

Hardware, Software, and Support Issues. What is available now, and what is
planned in a future budget cycle? Is partnership needed with the computer sciences department? What kind of support can be counted upon for mechanical
issues? What will the staff need to learn for routine maintenance? The CMC
manager needs to plan for such support needs and provide for professional development time for some of these issues.

Other CMCs' Virtual Collections

A thorough exploration of others' sites can also speed the planning with awareness
of choices of design and content. Look at others' organization and presentation of
sites for ideas. These sites are only a few of the many excellent CMC sites available
and were selected to demonstrate variation in design, choices of listing, annotation, and site selection.

K–12 Cyberpedia (Mike Tillman, California State University at Fresno). A curriculum materials center manager skilled in instructional technology developed
this method of resource presentation. Access: http://www.lib.csufresno.edu/
SubjectResources/CurriculumJuvenile/K12CyberPedia/Metasites/
SelectedMetasites.html#A-D.

Marshall University. Ed Mullen's *EdLinks* includes 36 commercial links, featuring
publishers (Scholastic, Education World, Oryx, Peterson's) and numerous con-

nections for children. Access: http://webpages.marshall.edu/~jmullens/
edlinks.html#Commercial.

Slippery Rock State University's CMC page features photos of classrooms and
pupils in much earlier times. Although this factor may take time to view, it is
visually stimulating. Webliographies on several topics, including those of local
interest (Pennsylvania Folk Tales), are available via the Web. Access: http://
www.sru.edu/depts/library/imc/index.htm.

University of Cincinnati Curriculum Materials Center. Worth exploring is Gary
Lare's *Resources to Support Pre-K–12 Curricular Instruction* (graphics, pictures, documents, maps, literary text, museums, exhibitions, primary source materials, content background materials, motion pictures, audio, etc.), as well as methods for
finding curriculum resources. This site includes an extensive set of links on review
sources, freebies, and even an archived "Rettig on Reference." Access: http://
www.libraries.uc.edu/libinfo/crc/web-resources.html.

University of Illinois, Chicago, features many Illinois sites: newspapers, organizations, schools homepages as well as curriculum guides, children's literature, and
lists. Access: http://www.uic.edu/depts/lib/documents/resources/
currinternet.shtml. These and other sites are listed in Walker's chapter, included
in this book.

Tool Four: Developing Continual Exploration for New Resources
The expansion of the number of Web sites demands an exploratory and sometimes playful attitude. Librarians are skilled searchers and are the "hunters and
gatherers" (Thomas, 1999) needed to organize the vast array of possible curriculum materials. Fortunately, even in the relatively short history of virtual collections, there are those hunters and gatherers who have done a professional job.

Hunters and Gatherers and Evaluation of Materials
The collation of evaluated Web sites by committees in the Education and Behavioral Sciences Section of Association of College and Research Libraries serves the
same function as an "Opening Day Book Collection" for the virtual collection.
Curriculum Materials are a component of this resource: CMC-PACEM
Webliography of Educational Materials (Access: http://libweb.uncc.edu/cimc/
ebsscmc/edweb.htm).

Since this resource represents the collected thinking of many librarians
from all over the United States, it is likely to serve the CMC manager well as a

benchmark against which a local collection is compared. Using evaluation tools, such as *Ed's Oasis* (Access: http://www.classroom.com/edsoasis/), not only guides the evaluation process, it becomes a learning experience to be passed onto students through bibliographic instruction. A wide range of evaluation tools can be found in *Kathy Schrock's Guide for Educators* (Access: http://school.discovery.com/schrockguide/index.html). Reviewing already evaluated resources, such as sites listed in *Blue Web'n*, saves much time.

Tool Five: Consider a Plan as Needing Regular Revisiting

Evaluation of Collection Plan. Any collection plan should have a section for weeding the older materials and maintaining good resources. Revisions are likely to be frequent, due to the ever-changing nature of the Internet. Key to successful revisions will be the awareness about the changing resources used in instruction, both in the University classroom and in the local public schools. Librarians need to be in touch with both sources here, most likely in person. Team teaching, observation, and plain talking about what is new serves many functions. New resources will appear; new work will be done by either local public school teachers, librarians, or faculty, and will need to be evaluated for placement with the existing collection.

    Evaluation Skills. Evaluation of resources calls for specific skills: matching the existing resources with newer ones, examining the online resource for stated evaluation criteria, and making solid decisions about maintenance needs to be brought into play with the specific library team. The manager needs to recognize who is likely to enjoy and be challenged with this aspect of Web resource collection. Who is always forwarding to other staff the latest Internet resource? Who is excited by novelty and the "new on the Net"? Who is likely to take the time to see if a product is what it appears to be? Who will take the necessary step of communicating the addition of the resource to faculty who will be likely to use it (Branch, Kim, & Konenecke, 1999)? Evaluation of Web sites is an active part of teaching and librarianship; examine Kathy Schrock's listing for a collation of excellent Web evaluation tools (http://school.discovery.com/schrockguide/eval.html).

    Keeping Current. Systematic awareness of Internet products is needed to maintain the collection. Reading the latest literature is a step that is totally self-directed. In addition to exploring the Web by staff, a wise CMC manager may set the task to scan specific aspects of the literature as part of the review process and divide the task among staff members.

    Expanding Internet Search Skills. The literature is at a stage where the term "cybrarian" is used and written about (Ensor, 2000). Numerous librarians have ventured into this skill subset of librarianship and have Web presence worth noting for both resources and methodologies (Berger, 2000; Polly, 2000). Scanning the online journals in ALA organizational units (AASL, ACRL, YALSA) can help as advanced organizers for the increased flow of Web resources available. The skill sets needed for this area of librarianship are those seen in the planning, evaluating, production, and development of a virtual CMC collection. These skills can be expanded to involve the CMC librarian in many subsets of Web development and information delivery to university faculty and teachers and regional schools.

The cycle of planning, reviewing, renewing, and reconstructing is likely to be ongoing and continuous, since the Internet is likely to expand. As of this writing, the number of unique Web pages has been assessed as above two billion (Microsoft, October 2000). With such extensive resources, the work of a reviewer seems endless. In the capacity of librarian, the CMC staff can be creative about delivery of services. When CMC staff see their recommendations of quality materials adopted in a school district, classroom, or another Web site, it is a moment of professional success.

References

Anderson, B., ed. 1996. *Directory of Curriculum Materials Centers*. 4th ed. Chicago: ACRL.

Andriot, L. 1999. *Uncle Sam's K–12 Web*. Medford, N.J.:Information Today.

Berger, P. 1998. *Internet for Active Learners: Curriculum-based Strategies for K–12*. Chicago: American Library Association.

Berger, P. 2000. *Infosearcher*. Accessed at http://www.infosearcher.com on December 26, 2000.

Bergquist, W., J. Betwee, and D. Meuel. 1995. *Building Strategic Relationships: How to Extend Your Organization's Reach Through Partnerships, Alliances, and Joint Ventures*. San Francisco: Jossey-Bass.

Branch, R.M., D. Kim, and L. Konenecke. 1999. "Evaluating Online Educational Materials for Use in Instruction." ERIC Digest ED 430 564; available at http://www.ed.gov/databases/ERIC_Digests/ed430564.html.

Carr, J. 1997. "EdLibWeb: A Study in Cooperative Web Site Development." Accessed at http://www.ala.org/acrl/papertxt/a12.txt on December 26, 2000.

Curriculum Materials Committee/Problems of Access and Control of Educational Materials Committee. *CMC/PACEM Webliography*. Educational and Behavioral Science Section of the Association of College and Research Libraries. Accessed at http://libweb.uncc.edu/cimc/ebsscmc/edweb.htm on December 26, 2000.

Davidson, H. 1999. "The Educators' Lean and Mean No FAT Guide to Fair Use." Accessed at http://www.techlearning.com/content/speak/articles/copyright.html on December 26, 2000.

Elkrordy, A. 1999. *What to Include in a Virtual Library*. Accessed at http://www.thelearningsite.net/cyberlibrarian/elibraries/include.html on December 26, 2000.

Ensor, P. 2000. *The Cybrarian's Manual 2*. Chicago: American Library Association.

Eskridge, S., and J. Harris. *ThinkQuest's Guiding Partner Model.* Accessed at http://www.thinkquest.org/t3/ on December 26, 2000.

Field, T. G. *Avoiding Patent, Copyright & Trademark Problems: What You Don't Know Can Hurt You.* Accessed at http://www.fplc.edu/tfield/avoid.htm#ACI on December 26, 2000.

Harris, J. 2000. *In the Kitchen-Designs for Telecollaboration and Telepresence.* Accessed at http://lrs.ed.uiuc.edu/LRS/TE-surfing.html and http://ccwf.cc.utexas.edu/~jbharris/Virtual-Architecture/ on December 26, 2000.

Junion-Metz, G. 1997. *K–12 Resources on the Internet PLUS: Instructor's Supplement.* 2nd ed. Berkeley, Calif.: Library Solutions Press.

Libutti, P. O., ed. *Librarians as Learners, Librarians as Teachers: The Diffusion of Internet Expertise in Academic Libraries.* Chicago: ACRL.

Libutti, P. O., and B. Gratch, eds. 1995. *Teaching Information Retrieval and Evaluation Skills to Education Students and Practitioners: A Casebook of Applications.* Chicago: ACRL.

McKenzie, J. 1996. *Keeping It Legal: Questions Arising out of Web Site Management.* Access at http://www.fno.org/jun96/legal.html#Concept.

Microsoft. October 2000. Software promotional letter.

Perlmutter, J. 1999. "Which Online Resources are Right for Your Collection?" *School Library Journal* 45 (5): 27–29.

Polly, J. A. 2000. *The Internet Kids and Family Yellow Pages.* 2001 ed. New York: Osborne/McGraw Hill.

Polly, J. (June 1999). E-mail.

Schon, D. A. 1983. *The Reflective Practitioner: How Professionals Think in Action.* New York: Basic Books.

"School Technology Boom Inspires Textbook Makers." *Investor's Business Daily.* October 9, 2000.

Schrock, K. 2000. *Kathy Schrock's Guide for Educators.* Accessed at http://discoveryschool.com/schrockguide/ on December 26, 2000.

Tillman, M. 2000. *K–12 Cyberpedia.* Accessed at http://www.lib.csufresno.edu/SubjectResources/CurriculumJuvenile/K12CyberPedia/ on December 26, 2000.

Thomas, C. "The ITP Program at Columbia University". In *Librarians as Learners, Librarians as Teachers: The Diffusion of Internet Expertise in Academic Libraries,* P. O. Libutti, ed., Chicago: ACRL.

Walker, J. (July 2000). E-mail posting to EBSS-L. List of Web sites of Curriculum Materials Centers.

Appendix: Virtual Curriculum Materials Center Collection: Examples of Instruction, Classroom, and Research Resources

The CMC may be the only collecting agency for a specific area, or share the responsibility with other divisions of the library or College of Education, which would affect which of the categories would be developed by a specific agency. A CMC Virtual Collection can be organized in diverse ways, as seen in the centers listed in Judy Walker's chapter, in this volume. This "example collection" is composed of three broad categories, with example(s) for each subcategory. These areas are Resource by Topic, Resource by Origin, and Resource for Information Literacy Development. The second category is included to develop the awareness of the diversity of educational materials from a wider array of sources than textbook publishers. The third category is included to promote the collection of resources related to information literacy development in the institution.

1. Resources by Topic
Education Sites

    Britannica's Internet Guide to Education Sites. Accessed at http://www.britannica.com/education/index.html on December 26, 2000.

    "Best Practices." *Teaching in the Digital Age.* George Lucas Educational Foundation: The Web site is rich in articles (downloadable in .pdf files), subject information and curriculum information, as well as a guide: Feature stories center on schools that use innovative methodologies. Other topics are examined in articles, videos, and related links. Access at http://glef.org.

Curriculum Directories

    Yahoo's Curriculum Listings: Accessed at http://dir.yahoo.com/Business and Economy/Business to Business/Education/Teaching and Learning Aids/Curriculum on December 26, 2000.

Curriculum Resources

    Curriculum Resource Center: Montclair State University: This page neatly organizes diverse resources by subject area. Accessed at http://www.montclair.edu/Pages/CRC/EdResources.html on December 27, 2000.

Subject Guides

    Children's Literature. Accessed at http://www.lib.ksu.edu/subguides/childlit/clit0001.shtml.

Lesson Plans

New York Times Learning Network is an interactive learning experience for teachers and students, based on the daily edition of the New York Times. Look at the Day in the News, the Lesson Plans (including an Archive of plans), and enjoy the integration of the New York Times with your curriculum planning! Accessed at http://nytimes.com/learning.

Illuminations Internet-Based Lesson Plans are examples of how Internet links can be used to help create effective standards-based mathematics lessons. Accessed at http://illuminations.nctm.org/lessonplans/index.html.

Teaching Methodology

Cyberteach: Look at the Lesson Plan Checklist. Accessed at http://www.econedlink.org/cyberteach/ on December 26, 2000.

Instructional Design

The Internet: Communicating, Accessing, Providing Information. Dwayne Harapnuik, University of Alberta, CA. Access at http://dte6.educ.ualberta.ca/tech_ed/. This course from the Education Division, has an overview of relevant learning theories prepared by the designer of the course, titled: Inquisitivism or the "HHHMMM???? What Does This Button Do?" Approach to Adult Education. This overview is perhaps the most concise presentation of learning theory contributions to Internet education.

Curriculum Standards

ISTE standards directly address the use of information technology in education. The standards are available as a .pdf file. Accessed at http://www.iste.org/standards/index.html on December 26, 2000.

Textbook Evaluation

Kutztown's CMC page has a textbook evaluation page: Accessed at http://www.kutztown.edu/library/curriculum/textbookeval.htm on December 26, 2000.

Curriculum Matierals by and/or for Kids

ThinkQuest is a program for integration of technology into children's learning. This site is useful for demonstration of what students are capable of producing, as well as examining their research and reporting skills. There is a searchable Library of Entries of student-produced educational Web sites. Accessed at http://www.thinkquest.org/library/.

Neuroscience for Kids. Eric Chudler. The guide to neuroscience is kid-friendly with scholarly content presented in understandable text and activities. Accessed at http://faculty.washington.edu/chudler/neurok.html on December 27, 2000.

Curriculum Materials: Software

TourMaker. This tool is used to develop systematic exploration of the Web for students and teachers. You can download a 30-day free trial copy of TourMaker by Tramline at http://www.tramline.com/ tm/download/tm_v154.exe.

Current Trends in Web based Instruction: Journals and Current Awareness Online

From Now On (http://www.fromnowon.org/) is an educational technology journal with articles of interest to educators and librarians.

Knowledge Quest on the Web: Special topics can be easily examined, such as this one on Visual literacy. Accessed at http://www.ala.org/aasl/kqweb/28 4 vandergriftlinks.html on December 26, 2000.

Information Searcher: (http://www.infosearcher.com). Pam Berger's site explores active learning with the Web, presents articles and case studies from "in the field," and reviews Web resources.

Government Agencies related to Curriculum

U. S. Dept. of Education: Examine for current awareness on legislation affecting funding of resources in schools, general education topics. Accessed at http://www.ed.gov.

Curriculum Standards, Teacher Certification, and School Issues

State: New York Department of Education: This site will provide information on curriculum standards, directories of personnel, teaching projects, and a link with the New York State Library. Accessed at http://www.nysed.gov/home.html on December 26, 2000.

Professional Resources: Collection Development of Web-based Resources Collection Development Web issues. Accessed at http://www.thelearningsite.net/cyberlibrarian/elibraries/webcoll.html on December 26, 2000.

2. Resources by Origin
University Research

Digital Dante. The Institute for Learning Technologies. The site features works in progress and a large collection of resources on the projects. Digital Dante is a good example of "growing a site." Access at http://www.ilt.columbia.edu/projects/index.htm.

The Perseus Project. A digital library on classical resources, this resources has applications in many classroom settings, with collections on topics such as Hercules and The Ancient Olympics, The English Renaissance, and California Pioneer Life. The project is located on Tufts University servers. Accessed at http://www.perseus.tufts.edu/ on December 27, 2000.

Virtual Architecture. Judi Harris. This site is an e-book that explores teleteaching and learning in depth. (Access at http://ccwf.cc.utexas.edu/%7Ejbharris/Virtual-Architecture/Foundation/index.html) One chapter is *In the Kitchen-Designs for Telecollaboration and Telepresence* (Access at http://lrs.ed.uiuc.edu/LRS/TE-surfing.html)

Resources from Organizational Sites

Xpeditions: National Geography Standards puts principles into practice. Access at http://edsitement.neh.gov/.

American Zoo and Aquarium Association (AZA). The site is designed to be highly interactive and informative for kids. The focus is preservation of wildlife and the environment. Accessed at http://www.azasweb.org on December 27, 2000.

Resources from Media

Ed's Oasis. The site, funded by AT&T is a "one-stop spot" for teachers: discussion groups, lesson plans, evaluated educational sites, conference handouts, biographies and interviews with teachers, and more. Accessed at http://www.classroom.com/edsoasis/ on December 27, 2000.

New York Kids. This character-filled site ("peopled" with The Dirtmeister, Mighty Liz, The Gameboy, and Terry the Taxi Driver) leads elementary students and teachers to subject and topical materials on the Web. Accessed at http://www.nykids.org/ on December 27, 2000.

Resources in Virtual Libraries

The Academy Virtual Library in Canandaigua, New York, began in 1996 and is maintained by Library Media Specialist Mike Nyerge. Access at http://www.canandaigua.k12.ny.us/academy/library/.

Foundations Educational Resources

George Lucas Foundation: rich in subject information and curriculum information: Access at http://glef.org.

Commercial Sites (for fee)

Earthscape. Prepared by Columbia University Press, this Earth Sciences site charges for access according to the size of the institution. An individual subscription is $145 yearly. As with other for fee-sites reviewed, there is a free trial. Accessed at http://www.earthscape.org on December 26, 2000.

Education Pages from Company Sites

Teacher's Toolkit. IBM. Access at http://www.can.ibm.com/k12/ Resource_websites.htm. Models of virtual schools are downloadable as .pdf files, as are Lesson Plans. After registering as an educator, you can download technology integrated lesson plans. The plans cover K–12, and are on diverse topics, such as: Exploring Art, Beautiful Bats, Cultures around the World, Immigration, and It's Music to My Ears.

Resources from Museums

Living Room Candidates. American Museum of the Moving Image. This resource, developed for a collection of Presidential campaign political commercials (1952–2000), includes a teacher's guide to using this Web-based resource. Accessed at http://www.ammi.org/livingroomcandidate/ on December 26, 2000.

Wet With Blood. The Investigation of Mary Todd Lincoln's Cloak. Chicago Historical Society. This Web site uses forensic evidence in an historical investigation of the clothing Mary Todd Lincoln wore when Lincoln was assassinated. Materials included are Museum publications on this subject dating to the time of the assassination. Accessed at http://www.chicagohistory.org/wetwithblood/introduction/index.htm on December 26, 2000.

Resources From Government Education Pages

New York State Teachers Union. Although not a "government site," this link provides essential material for teachers in a union-affiliated district. The electronic edition of *New York Teacher* is included on this site. Links to education associations, Teacher Centers, and Distance Education sites are also provided. Accessed at http://www.nysut.org on December 26, 2000.

New York City: *New York City Board of Education Network*: Look at the local school communities (and their Web pages), learn about education initiatives, and examine the school issues in the Big Apple. Access at http://?www.nycenet.edu/.

3. Resources for Information Literacy

"Information literacy" is a set of skills that are especially crucial for effective Web use. These skills consist of:

- Developing effective search strategies
- Locating and retrieving information sources
- Analyzing and critically evaluating information
- Using, synthesizing, and applying information

Developing effective search strategies

Web Tutorials The University of California, Berkeley, has led the nation in search engine instructions. Take the time to learn and speed your search process! Access at http://www.lib.berkeley.edu/TeachingLib/Guides/Internet.

Internet Training Program (ITP). Columbia University Libraries offers training modules to "build your own web tutorial." The handouts and resources are available. Access at http://www.columbia.edu/cu/libraries/inside/internet/.

Ask An Expert. There are questions that only an expert can answer. This site is a human-mediated Q&A service, funded by the U.S. government. Access at http://njnie.dl.stevens-tech.edu/askanexpert.html.

Locating and retrieving information sources

Web Review Sites

Blue Web'n Learning Sites Library is a database of reviewed education sites. Access at http://www.kn.pacbell.com/wired/bluewebn/.

Information Searcher. Pam Berger. (http://www.infosearcher.com). The site explores active learning with the Web, presents articles and case studies from "in the field," and reviews Web resources.

Analyzing and critically evaluating information

Intellectual Property Resources

Student plagiarism in an online world. This article demonstrates methods of detection of plagiarism. Accessed at http://www.asee.org/prism/december/html/student_plagiarism_in_an_onlin.htm on December 26, 2000.

"The Educator's No Fat Lean Guide to Copyright and Fair Use." Hall Davidson. This article, from the September 1999 issue of *Technology & Learning*, includes a 20-item test of a teacher's knowledge of copyright issues and fair use. Accessed at http://www.techlearning.com/content/speak/articles/copyright.html on December 26, 2000.

Can I Borrow a Bit of Digital? [fair use on the Web] Marie D'Amico. A legal, yet very readable, set of articles on copyright issues can be found on this site. The page includes *NetGuide*, May 1996. Access at http://lawcrawler.lp.findlaw.com/mad/.

Avoiding Patent, Copyright & Trademark Problems: What You Don't Know Can Hurt You!" Thomas G. Field, Jr. The Franklin Pierce Law Center. Access at http:/

/www.fplc.edu/tfield/ACI. One of the best parts of the page is the excellent, easy-to-follow chart: "When Works Pass Into the Public Domain." Accessed at http://www.unc.edu/~unclng/public-d.htm on December 26, 2000.

Evaluation of Web Sites: Critical Thinking about Content and Sources

Kathy Schrock has gathered many evaluation links: student, teacher skill, and Web assessment guides. Accessed at http://school.discovery.com/schrockguide/assess.html on December 26, 2000.

Using, Synthesizing and Applying Information

Construction of Web pages

Setting Up a Web Site for School. Accessed at http://bones.med.ohio-state.edu/eric/papers/primer/webdocs.html on December 26, 2000.

Collection Development for CMC Reference Materials

Peter Cupery, Lori Delaney, and Bernie Foulk

Role of the CMC Reference Department

The role of the reference department in a CMC is to support education activities and education-related research. This support occurs in a variety of ways, including providing access to ready reference sources, providing instruction in searching the library catalog as well as searching academic databases such as ERIC and Education Index/Abstracts/Full Text. Other ways that the CMC reference staff supports educational activities include assisting users in identifying and locating pertinent print and/or audiovisual resources in the physical collection, providing interlibrary loan service, and assisting in locating Internet resources in education.

With the proliferation of new technologies and especially with the complexities of existing formats, the true task is to identify and utilize the most efficient and effective way to distribute information to our clients. An hour or more may be spent instructing a new doctoral student in techniques for using the library catalog and electronic databases. However, we may spend five minutes or less with the client who needs to verify a citation for a paper that is due in an hour. The challenge for CMC reference staff is to aid in the identification of information that the user wants.

As we acclimate our clients, and ourselves, to the 21st century, the shift from print to electronic resources challenges us to balance their use. Although electronic resources often provide us with the best information in the shortest amount of time, we must also remember the power and reliability of many print resources.

Importance of a Collection Development Policy

The CMC's collection development "should be based on a sound, written policy" (ALA, 1993, 2). The policy should specifically address materials selection for the reference collection and should also include an evaluation tool. The evaluation should be done regularly and serve to identify gaps in the collection to aid in targeted collection development. But it also serves to identify items that are no longer useful to clients, such as aged editions of bibliographies or a CD-ROM that no longer works with new computer hardware and software.

In the American Library Association's publication *Curriculum Materials Center Collection Development Policy* (1993), Anderson states that "as the production of materials in all formats increases, the importance of a judicious selection to ensure a quality collection in support of the curriculum also increases. To improve the selection process, there is a need to pinpoint specific goals and find materials to meet these goals" (ALA, 1993, 2). The evaluation component of the collection development policy is the likely place where these goals are identified.

Communication with the Education Dean, Faculty and Students

The collection development policy should mirror the needs of the School of Education by clearly relating its selection of materials to the School's instructional methods and courses. This is best accomplished through communication with the Dean, faculty, other instructors, and students. Anderson states that "collaborative efforts by librarians and teacher educators are essential to identify an expanded CMC role to meet new challenges" (Anderson, 2). By participating in the School of Education's strategic planning meetings or, more specifically, its curriculum planning, the CMC can anticipate needs for new types of reference materials.

Questions to Address

The following questions should be addressed in the collection development policy and should be asked each time an item is being considered for addition to the reference collection. By doing so, the reference collection maintains its pertinence to the larger collection and supports the clients' current and evolving information needs.

- Does this item relate to the College of Education's curricula?
- Does this item relate to the College of Education's goals and policies?
- Does this item support the existing PK–12 collection?
- Does this item promote professional development in the field of education?
- Does this item fill any gaps in the reference collection?

Further considerations need to be made in terms of adding any item to the reference collection as well as to other collections in the CMC.

- Currency
- Usefulness
- Cost
- Availability at other campus libraries or online
- Inclusiveness

Challenges for the Future

CMC staff reference staff face significant challenges in the future, including:

- Technological changes and emerging formats of materials. How do we balance the need to keep current of technological advances with budget constraints? Is it necessary to retain a print copy of items that are also available on CD-ROM or online?
- Increasing costs for resources, especially electronic ones.
- Limited staffing resources to identify Internet Web sites that offer quality educational resources.

Building the Collection

CIMC staff members may find the following list of resources to serve as a basic collection to meet the needs of their clients. However, these resources and the many others that will be a part of an individual CMC's reference collection should be evaluated according to the criteria outlined above.

Curriculum Materials

The Kraus Curriculum Development Library. (2001). Lanham, Md.: Bernan.
This microfiche, soon to be a Web-based resource, contains curriculum guides from school districts throughout North America. They are reproduced on microfiche and are indexed by subject and grade level for easy access. These guides focus on objectives, programs, and teaching practices for Grades K through 12, Early Childhood Education, and Adult Basic Education.

El-Hi Textbooks and Serials in Print. (2000). 128th edition. New York: Bowker.
This core reference title is useful in locating and ordering texts, text series, workbooks, periodicals, tests, programmed learning materials, teaching aids, maps, professional books, and AV materials. The 2000 edition of El-Hi Textbooks and Serials in Print contains over 150,000 entries.

A-V Online. (2000). Boston: Silver Platter.
Compiled by the National Information Center on Education Media, this computer file includes over 430,000 titles of films, videos, audiocassettes, and software. It covers more than 100 media types in 65 languages back to the early 20th century. Citations include annotations, subject descriptions, audience level, media type, running time, language, availability status, and information about distributors and producers. A-V Online catalogs and summarizes audiovisual and multimedia materials from the Library of Congress, publishers' catalogs, and library collections.

The Educational Software Selector: TESS. (1996). Hampton Bays, N.Y.: EPIE Institute.
This CD-ROM lists approximately 20,000 software products. Included in each entry are description, grade level, target audience, and review citations. TESS is produced by Educational Products Information Exchange (EPIE) Institute, a not-for-profit independent consumer organization, and updated twice a year.

Testing Resources
Health and Psychosocial Instruments (HAPI). (1985–date). New York: Ovid Technologies.
This resource enables users to identify measurement tests used in health, psychosocial sciences, organizational behavior, and library and information. From 1985 to date (updated quarterly), HAPI is a database of evaluation and measurement tools designed to facilitate health and psychosocial studies. The measurement instruments available include questionnaires, checklists, index measures, rating scales, project techniques, tests, interview schedules, and a variety of other means of evaluation. The database currently contains more than 45,000 records.

Mental Measurements Yearbook. (2000). Lincoln, Neb.: Buros Institute of Mental Measurements of the University of Nebraska-Lincoln.
This standard resource is available in both electronic and print formats. It provides descriptive information, references, and critical reviews of commercially published English language tests. The electronic version [1989 to date (updated semiannually)] contains descriptive information and full-text reviews of commer-

cially published English-language tests. It covers more than 1,850 standardized educational, personality, vocational aptitude, psychological, and related tests. Information provided about each test includes name, classification, author, publisher, price, time requirements, existence of validity and reliability data, score descriptions, intended populations, and critical reviews.

Tests in Print. (1983). Lincoln, Neb.: Buros Institute of Mental Measurements, University of Nebraska-Lincoln: Distributed by the University of Nebraska Press
This title provides a bibliography of achievement, aptitude, intelligence, personality, and certain sensory-motor skills tests available in English-speaking countries. It also serves as a classified index and supplement to the Mental Measurements Yearbook series.

Keyser, D. J., and R. C. Sweetland. (1984–1994). *Test Critiques.* Austin, Tex.: Pro-ed.
Keyser, D. J., and R. C. Sweetland. (1997). *Test Critiques Compendium.* Kansas City, Mo.: Testing Corporation of America
These volumes provide critiques of the most frequently used psychological, educational, and business tests. Each entry includes an introduction to each test as well as a description of practical applications, uses, and technical aspects when appropriate. Entries also include supplemental psychometric information relating to reliability, validity, and normative development.

Maddox, T. (1997) *Tests: A Comprehensive Reference for Assessments in Psychology, Education and Business.* 4th edition. Austin, Tex.: Pro-ed.
The fourth edition continues the work of Keyser and Sweetland to provide consistent information for describing tests used by psychologists, educators, and human services personnel. This resource does not review or evaluate tests but provides concise descriptions for thousands of tests. Multiple indexes are provided, extending the ease of use of this resource.

Goldman, B. A., and D. F. Mitchell. (1980). *Directory of Unpublished Experimental Mental Measurements.* Dubuque, Ia.: Wm. C. Brown.
This volume, the fifth in a series edited by Bert Arthur Goldman which began in 1974, provides a listing of experimental test instruments for use in the behavioral and social sciences. It does not provide evaluations. Thirty-seven journals are examined to identify tests and other instruments that are not commercially available.

Lester, P. E., and L. K. Bishop. (2000). *Handbook of Tests and Measurements in Education and the Social Sciences.* 2nd ed. Lanham, Md.: Scarecrow Press.

This volume includes not only bibliographic information but also the actual instrument for 120 instruments in education and the social sciences. Each entry includes the instrument title, a source of the instrument and comments as well as information on scale construction, the original samples, reliability, validity, factor analysis, and scoring. References that describe the instrument or its use are also included.

ETS Test Collection Tests in Microfiche. (1975–2000). Princeton, N.J.: Educational Testing Service.
This collection includes microfiche of thousands of instruments for achievement in vocational, special populations, cognitive, intelligence, attitude, and personality tests. These tests are otherwise unpublished and therefore have not been subjected to the investigation of commercially published tests. Indexes are provided for title, subject, and author.

Children's Literature Sources
Books that provide subject access to children's literature include: *A to Zoo: Subject Access to Children's Picture Books* by Carolyn W. Lima and John A. Lima (1998. New Providence, N.J.: R.R. Bowker.); *More Books Kids Will Sit Still For* by Judy Freeman, (1995. New Providence, N.J.: R.R. Bowker); and *Children and Books* by Zena Sutherland (1997. 9th ed. New York: Longman).

CCBC Choices. (2000). *Madison, WI: Friends of the CCBC.*
This title, which is published annually, summarizes, evaluates and organizes by subject significant titles for children published in the previous year. Created by the staff of the Cooperative Children's Book Center at the University of Wisconsin-Madison, this title is based on extensive review of formal and informal discussions as well as annual awards discussions.

Something about the Author. (1971–date.) Detroit: Gale Research.
SATA is a reference series that examines the lives and works of authors and illustrators of books for children. Both authors and illustrators are included in the indexes. Information about each author includes awards, affiliations, adaptations that have been made from the author's works, photo of the author, and contact information.

Directories
QED's State by State School Guide. (2000) Denver, Colo.: Quality Education Data.
This 32-volume resource from Quality Education Data provides demographic

data, contact information and the names of administration for public, private, and religious schools across the country. While the guides are created for marketing purposes, they are perfect tools for anyone searching for employment in a specific state.

Cabell's Directory of Publishing Opportunities in Education. (1998). 5th edition. Beaumont, Tex.: Cabell Publishing Company.
A valuable resource for authors, this volume contains the names of editors and contact information for over 440 journals. *Cabell's* describes the style and format of each journal, the review process, and fees required, and classifies the journals into 27 different topic areas.

Indexes

ERIC, a product of the U. W. Department of Education, contains over a million citations and abstracts of the international journal and report literature in education and related fields. It includes all aspects of education, including child development, classroom techniques, computer education, counseling and testing, administration, higher education, library science, and vocational and adult education. Sources include more than 980 journals, educational reports, project descriptions, curriculum guides, and dissertations. It includes the complete ERIC Thesaurus and begins coverage in 1966. ERIC can be searched with products from a variety of vendors or free online. (Accessed at http://www.eric.ed.gov.)

Education Index, Education Abstracts and Education Abstracts Full-Text. (1983–). New York: H. W. Wilson.
These three products from Wilson index more than 400 English-language periodicals, yearbooks, and selected monographic series. Feature articles are indexed, as are important editorials and letters to the editor, interviews, reviews of educational films, software reviews, critiques of theses, charts and graphs without text, and book reviews. Coverage starts in 1983. Abstracts are included since 1994. Full-text articles have been added beginning with 1996.

References

Anderson, B. 1984."Curriculum Materials Center Collection Development Policy." Chicago: Association of College and Research Libraries. ERIC Document Reproduction Service ED No. 256 360.

Association of College and Research Libraries. 1993. *Curriculum Materials Center Collection Development Policy*. Chicago: American Library Association. 2nd ed. Accessed at on August 11, 2000.

Clark, A. S. 1982. *Managing Curriculum Materials in the Academic Library.* Metuchen, N.J.: Scarecrow.

Clayton, V. 1989. "Curriculum Libraries at Institutions of Higher Education: A Selective Annotated Bibliography," *Behavioral & Social Sciences Librarian* 8, (1/2): 51–66.

"Favorite Reference Books." 1999. University of Wisconsin-Madison CIMC Reference Staff.

Henderson, M. V., and B. G. Barron. 1992. "Expanding the Role of the Curriculum Materials Center: Challenges for the 21st Century." *Education* 113 (2): 254–55.

Johnson, H. R. 1973. "The Curriculum Materials Center: A Study of Policies and Practices in Selected Centers." ERIC Document Reproduction Service ED No. 081 449.

Lare, G. 1997. *Acquiring and Organizing Curriculum Materials: A Guide and Directory of Resources.* Lanham, Md.: Scarecrow.

Mace, J. 1993. "The Importance of the Curriculum Materials Centers in the Academic Library." *Library Mosaics* 4: 22–23.

Marston, C. A. 1969. "Bibliographic Organization of a Curriculum Collection." *Peabody Journal of Education* 47: 48–52.

Teclehaimanot, B. 1992. "Curriculum Materials Centers in Teacher Education: Trends for the 1990s." *Ohio Media Spectrum* 44 (1): 38–41.

Information and Instruction Services in CMCs

Adelaide Phelps and
Jeneen LaSee-Willemssen

Historical Background and Development of Information and Instruction Services in CMCs

CMCs began to develop after education libraries, library services to educators, and curriculum laboratories were already in existence. To various degrees, they have melded the services of the library and laboratory. Consequently, though all CMCs offer instructional materials and support services to teachers in training, each does so in a unique way. A brief review of the history of the education library, the curriculum laboratory, and the curriculum materials center will help to shed light on the nature of and reason behind the wide variety of information and instruction services that CMCs offer to their patrons today.

Growth of Libraries and Library Instruction for Educators

The first normal school in the United States was established in 1839 in Lexington, Massachusetts. By the post–Civil War era, normal schools had become a familiar feature of the American educational landscape (Kaestle, 1983). According to the National Education Association of the United States (NEA), normal schools of this era did not typically have libraries. It was not until 1893 that the pioneer effort toward organization of normal-school libraries (750) began and such great current collections as those at the National Library of Education and Teachers College at Columbia University had their start (NEA, 1913). "These first normal school libraries were small, unclassified, little-used collection[s] of books behind locked doors (747) and their inadequate, inaccessible collections did not encourage the introduction of instructional programs in the use of educational materials." (NEA, 1913) Early teachers neither learned nor needed the library skills considered essential today. Normal-school libraries, however, took hold quickly. By 1898, when Adams (1898) surveyed 20 of the foremost normal schools, she found that not only did they have libraries, but they also offered some sort of instruction, ranging from informal individual instruction to classroom talks by librarians and library bibliography assignments (85). According to Morrill (1981), by the following year a substantial number, though still a minority, of teachers began to be exposed to libraries and library methods in their training (65). By the time the Committee on Normal School Libraries of the NEA met at their national conference in 1913, librarians with college training in librarianship staffed many normal school libraries. Of 155 normal schools surveyed, 38 had libraries of over 10,000 volumes and 53 required lessons in the use of the library (NEA, 1913).

According to the NEA (1913), the nature of library instruction given to educators during the 1890s and the first decade of the 1900s was generally designed to prepare teachers to administer a small school library in addition to teaching (750). By 1913, however, this technical librarian training was de-emphasized in favor of practical teacher-needs training by the NEA's Committee on Normal School Libraries. Indeed, the Committee specifically recommended that normal schools, in their required library lessons, should place the emphasis on children's literature and practice lessons given by the prospective teachers and that technical library instruction be reserved for elective teacher-librarian courses (755–6). These recommendations, however, were never made into requirements, and, although most teacher education institutions now require courses in children's literature, few require library or information literacy courses.

Today, the situation has not changed much. In her article, "Up the Down Staircase: Establishing Library Instruction Programs for Teachers," O'Hanlon (1988) traces the progression of various early reports and articles that have emphasized the need for teacher education students to have bibliography, library, and research skills courses. She points out that instructional programs were shown to offer real benefits to teachers and their students, but librarians' calls for a national standard for library education of teacher trainees were and are still largely ignored and instruction in information skills in teacher training institutions is still only haphazardly provided (529).

Birth of the Curriculum Laboratory

The 1920s and '30s saw an increase in the advancement of the study of education as scientific methods were adopted and the curriculum became a focus of study. These changes helped give rise to the curriculum laboratory in the United States (Morrill, 1981) and brought about a new development in curriculum services to educators. According to Nevil (1975), many of these early curriculum laboratories were run from or for Colleges of Education. "In addition, they were dedicated to in-service workshops for the teachers they served, and the three activities [they] were most engaged in were curriculum construction and revision, the collecting and assembling of curriculum materials, and the investigation of curriculum problems." (14, 17) The curriculum materials that such laboratories collected were not normally held by academic libraries; they were geared specifically toward the practical classroom needs of teachers and included such things as curriculum guides, media, maps and globes, posters, realia, and artifacts.

Instructional services in curriculum laboratories were and are still geared toward developing, creating, and analyzing curricula and instructional materials. It is the curriculum laboratory (or the curriculum laboratory function of the modern CMC) that assists teachers in the evaluation of curricula, the creation of instructional media, the production of videos, the integration of technologies into the classroom, and the design of instructional software programs. The curriculum laboratory, rather than teaching library or information retrieval skills, deals with curriculum-related issues.

Curriculum Materials Centers

In the 1960s, many curriculum laboratories began to take on library-like qualities and lose some of their laboratory qualities, largely because Colleges of Education found they were unable to manage the organization, circulation, and storage of the laboratory materials as well as libraries could. McGiverin (1990) notes:

> By the late 1960's, institutional responsibility for many curriculum centers had moved from the colleges, schools, and departments of education to the academic library. With this shift in sponsorship, service emphases veered away from the creation and development of curricula to the issues of collection development; the functions of acquisitions, cataloging, management, and circulation; and instruction in collection use (563).

This shift of focus coincided with great growth in commercial publication of and CMC collection of ready-made curricula and children's books. This change increased the uses and appeal of the CMC, and soon preservice teachers were not the only users of the CMC; in-service teachers increased their presence, and parents and children began entering and using CMCs.

Certainly CMCs have not all given up their traditional laboratory roles, nor have they all completely taken on a library-only identity. Rather, today's CMCs have roles and responsibilities all along the laboratory-to-library spectrum. It is this diversity that makes identifying the information and instructional services offered by CMCs difficult to pinpoint. There is only one area where consistency can be noted: assisting users in selecting materials (Boudreau, 1983; Bharattari, 1972; Church, 1957; James, 1963; MacVean, 1958). It is this service that will be dealt with most extensively in this chapter.

Information and Instruction Services in CMCs
Reference Services
Similar to reference services offered in academic libraries, CMC reference services include informal instruction in information-seeking skills (using hard copy sources, nonprint media, and automated systems) and assistance in the identification, use, and selection of print and electronic reference and information sources. CMC reference services vary from the norm, however, because of the specialized nature of their materials and because of the unique needs of their user groups.

Due to their library and laboratory backgrounds, CMCs generally contain materials that vary from the very traditional (books and journals) to the unique (PK–12 textbooks, curricula, realia, media, etc.). For the same reasons, CMC users tend to need and use information in a practice-oriented way rather than the academic approach more commonly encountered in college and university libraries (James, 1985). Accordingly, providing reference services in CMCs can be a challenge unless one has a background in or knowledge of the reference materials and resources related to curriculum materials and media, and a detailed knowledge of the information needs of teachers and other CMC users. This sort of knowledge is not typically gained in one's preparation as an academic librarian. As established in the chapter by Scott Walter, CMC staff are best able to serve their clientele if they have training and/or experience in a variety of disciplines: academic and school librarianship, education, curriculum and instruction, and children's services.

To CMC staff trained as academic librarians, traditional academic information requests and the sources with which to answer those requests will be very familiar and easy to handle. Traditional information such as books and serials can generally be found easily enough with standard reference tools: encyclopedias, dictionaries, almanacs, handbooks, gazetteers, atlases, catalogs, indexes, databases, and so forth. Less academic and more practice-based requests require a more thorough reference interview and the use of multiple, specialized reference tools.

To illustrate, a CMC staff member who assists a patron in identifying a social science textbook will need to interview his or her patron in a variety of ways. Is the patron an in-service teacher, a preservice teacher, a parent, a home-schooler, or a PK–12 student? Their needs will be very different. An in-service teacher is likely to be looking for textbooks to supplement the classroom text, or may be looking for textbooks to compare with those being considered for adoption. A preservice teacher may be looking for a textbook to evaluate and critique for methods classes. A parent may be hoping to find something to supplement her child's school readings, while a home-schooler may be looking for a textbook to use to teach his child. Finally, a PK–12 student may be looking for a better textbook than the one currently assigned; may be street-smart enough to be looking for a teacher's edition of their school text; or may not be looking for a textbook at all (many children have difficulty formulating questions and CMC staff working with child patrons need to hone their interviewing skills).

Each of the above scenarios may lead the librarian to additional interview questions. Is an actual textbook needed, or just a verification that such a textbook exists? Is the teacher's edition needed, or the student edition? What about the supplementary materials? Is the textbook needed for evaluation? Will it be used as a supplement to a classroom text—for teacher or student use? What specific topical coverage might be required—history, geography, communities? What grade and/or reading levels are desired? Are a specific publisher's textbooks needed? The questions that need to be asked all relate to the CMC staff member's knowledge of the information needs of the client.

After the interview, the CMC staff member can begin looking for the information the patron really wants. At this point a thorough knowledge of the specialized resources and search strategies related to CMCs is necessary. Identifying and finding something as commonplace as a PK–12 textbook is more difficult than it seems; unfortunately, a great many CMC materials are similarly difficult to find. CMC materials are not always cataloged in the library's online catalog, and, even if they are, subject headings and notes are not always adequate to identify needed items. CMC-created bibliographies can frequently assist in identifying publishers and grade levels; and a thoughtful physical organization of the CMC can be of great assistance. Finally, CMC staff members intimately familiar with their collections are priceless.

When one is looking for textbooks beyond those held in the local collection, standard reference tools such as *Books in Print* (New York: Bowker, 1999) will not work well. Instead, *El-Hi Textbooks and Serials in Print* (New York: Bowker, 1999), textbook publisher's catalogs, and Web resources, such as the *Eisenhower National Clearinghouse's Resource Finder* (http://www.enc.org/rf/nf_index.htm) must be consulted to identify those materials that exist. Finding historical textbooks is an even greater challenge and may involve checking specialty bibliographies such as *Early American Textbooks, 1775–1900: A Catalog of the Title Held by Educational Research Library* (Washington, D.C.: U.S. Dept. of Education, 1985), and will most assuredly be helped by checking with CMC colleagues who have historical collections.

Each type of CMC patron and material presents the CMC staff member with a unique challenge, and the combinations and scenarios for reference service are endless. Let it suffice to say the primary user groups of most CMCs frequently need practice-based information: background information related to the topic(s) they are teaching, pedagogical information related to their topic(s), and/ or age-appropriate materials (including nonprint materials) for their students. These needs make reference encounters necessarily complex, and CMC staff members must be aware of and willing to work with these needs. In addition, CMC materials (audiovisual, multimedia, children's materials, and so forth) each have their own set of reference materials and access methods. To ensure adequate reference assistance, those providing CMC-related reference services must have access to a broad range of resources including in-print, virtual, academic, children's, and school library media center reference materials. Those who are looking for more information on reference sources for CMCs should consult "Collection Development for CMC Reference Materials" in this volume, which includes a thorough examination of these materials.

Information Literacy

The education of library users (bibliographic or user instruction) is closely related to reference service and encompasses a wide range of practices. The Association of College and Research Libraries' Bibliographic Instruction Section (1979) developed one definition that referred to any activities that are designed to teach learners how to locate and use information (57). According to Mellon (1987), a second generation of user instruction emerged in the 1980s and advocated a more conceptual approach that resulted in a focus on teaching principles rather than on specific methods. Bopp and Smith (1995) push this concept further by stating that the intent of teaching principles of information organization and retrieval is to provide learners with the knowledge to function in a broad range of information situations and environments (156). Recently, particular emphasis has been placed on instructing users in information literacy, defined as the ability to access, evaluate, and use information effectively while understanding the legal, ethical, and social issues involved. This type of library user education is particularly important for students in teacher education classes because teachers who lack information literacy proficiency cannot guide students in, nor model, information literacy behavior.

Unfortunately, the great attention paid to the importance of information literacy for teacher educators does not seem to be reflected in the literature about CMCs. According to research conducted by Buttlar and Tipton (1992), there is a distinct gap in formal programs related to bibliographic instruction programs in CMCs (371). On the other hand, in a recent survey almost 75% of CMCs reported providing bibliographic instruction or library user education to preservice teachers, and 50% reported providing instruction to in-service education (Teclehaimanot, 1990). It seems most CMCs offer user instruction on request or by appointment rather than through a formalized instruction program. Unfortunately, it appears that these types of classes are infrequently written up for publication. The surveys collected for this publication reveal that few CMCs have formalized instruction programs, reporting rather that *formal* library user education classes are often left to the main campus library or libraries. While this type of user education is certainly very useful, Worley (1981) states that it is important that CMCs provide more than informal user education classes because students in education need an increasingly sophisticated knowledge of library resources to access information in the discipline (209) and because the information needs of educators working with curricula are quite different from those working with research materials, which are most emphasized in academic library user education classes.

The lack of published literature describing informal and formal CMC user instruction does not mean that CMC librarians have nothing to draw upon; the literature is rich in examples related to the teacher audience. Jacobson (1988) published an article, "Teachers and Library Awareness," in which she describes a wide variety of user education models for teachers, including everything from the self-paced workbook to the faculty-centered, course-integrated class. Another exemplary piece is the book *Teaching Information Retrieval and Evaluation Skills to Education Students and Practitioners: A Casebook of Applications* (Libutti and Gratch 1995). Published by the Bibliographic Instruction for Educators' Committee of the Association of College and Research Libraries' Education and Behavioral Sciences Section (EBSS), this book, unlike the normal "how we did it right" examples of user education classes, offers candid reflections on real-life class experiences, as well as personal evaluations of what happened and what could have been changed or improved. Finally, EBSS (Worley et al., 1981) also offer CMC staff guidance in formulating learning objectives and planning formalized instruction programs. Specifically, they have outlined 13 bibliographic competencies for educators, many of which will be applicable to user education programs developed by CMCs.

Educators should be able:

1. To develop a logical approach to researching a topic
2. To identify major reference tools in education
3. To identify and describe standardized tests
4. To locate and describe print and nonprint curriculum resources and instructional aid resources
5. To locate book reviews in education and related fields
6. To utilize state and federal government publications
7. To locate statistics relevant to the school community in government publications and other sources
8. To make a general assessment of an author's competence
9. To distinguish characteristics of general, scholarly, and professional association journals
10. To understand the purpose and scope of professional associations and their major publications
11. To select and use computerized information services
12. To identify theses and dissertations
13. To identify and locate information resources available outside the local community, using general and national bibliographies (209–10).

Those looking for CMC-specific guidance and examples will find little in the literature. One exception is Clarke's *Role and Functions of Curriculum Resource Centres in Australia.* Clarke (1991) provides readers with a description of a program that many CMC staff members will recognize as a good model toward which to strive. Clarke's examples reflect what many CMCs are doing informally in their own centers: teaching a plethora of user education courses that are characterized by instruction in small groups, integrated into the faculty teaching program, scheduled as part of class times, and covering process, practical, and subject-specific instruction (238).

In our survey and in follow-up discussions, it was determined that CMC professionals provide many thoughtful and innovative user education classes. In terms of instructional design, CMC staff report creating learning experiences that allow students to take an active role in what they will learn, allowing the librarian to act as a guide. They report designing their classes to accommodate different learning styles by using a wide variety of audiovisual media and other information formats, encouraging small- group discussions, and employing hands-on and active learning techniques in their classes. Team-teaching with College of Education faculty was also commonly reported as a highly successful method to capture students' interest and to enhance learning. Some CMC staff members reported modeling pedagogical methods using curriculum materials and/or educational technology in the classroom (this type of modeling is more completely addressed and described in "Technology and the Curriculum Materials Center" in this publication). Finally, a few CMC staff members reported formally assessing and reflecting on their teaching, though many did so informally.

In terms of specific content, the most commonly reported user education classes in the CMCs surveyed included: how to identify, obtain, and evaluate curriculum guides and lesson plans; how to use ERIC; how to use Education Index/Abstracts; how to use and create bibliographies; how to identify and obtain media items; how to use equipment and software; and how to use the online catalog to find specific types of educational materials and media. More specific examples of classes currently being taught in CMCs may be readily obtained simply by asking a CMC staff member; the examples are as varied and wide ranging as CMCs themselves.

The CIMC at the University of Wisconsin-Madison offers a variety of traditional and not-so-traditional classes. In the traditional realm, there are several database-searching classes, including basic and advanced ERIC classes. These classes are taught in the CIMC and are open to the campus and community at large. Audiences are frequently made up of preservice teachers, school administrators, and in-service teachers. These database-searching classes typically begin with an introduction to the database and simple demonstration of searching techniques. Students are then encouraged to conduct some hands-on searches using the knowledge they have gained in class. Later, more advanced techniques are covered, based on the students' needs. In the nontraditional realm, the CIMC offers instructional programming for children and parents on Saturday mornings. These Saturday classes include an introduction to the Internet for both parents and children, and explanations and assistance with a variety of Web resources.

Kansas State University's CMC librarian describes a series of book-talking classes that are team-taught with education methods faculty. She and faculty members work together to explain the concept of book-talking to the students. The CMC librarian presents a series of book-talks, and the students use her presentations as a model for their own. Both the librarian and the faculty member provide discussions and critiques of the students' book-talks.

As a final example, the Educational Resources Laboratory at Oakland University in Rochester, Michigan, provides introductory database-searching classes at the beginning of each semester. A typical class centers around using the online catalog, with instruction on setting search limits, basic search strategies, and a review of finding and identifying specific types of materials, such as diversity-related materials. Students are encouraged to request individualized instruction on any of the services or resources covered during the class time. The audience is mainly composed of undergraduate students from the School of Education and Human Services, but also includes students from the Center for American English and occasionally a group from the School of Arts and Sciences.

Tours and Orientations

Tours and orientations are often part of user education related to CMCs. Tours provide current and potential users with a basic overview of the CMC's physical layout, the services offered, and the types and locations of collections. Most important, they introduce the CMC's staff as a friendly source of interested and knowledgeable assistance.

As instructional tools, tours and orientations in CMCs are offered through a variety of means: as part of a formal College of Education orientation program for new education students; as part of user education sessions; as part of course syllabi; as drop-in opportunities; and as part of one-on-one consultation sessions. According to our survey, most CMC professionals feel that tours and orientations should occur early in an education student's career so that the CMC's resources and services will begin to serve and enhance learning experiences from the start.

One example of a tour and orientation program that is tied to the curricula of the College of Education is the program at the University of Dayton, Ohio. There, the education students are required to attend an orientation of the CMC as part of their introductory teaching courses. During their visit, they become familiar with the building and the services and then complete activities in eight areas of the center to familiarize themselves with the CMC collection and borrowing procedures.

Workshops and In-services

For our purposes, workshops and in-services provide training related to the laboratory aspects of CMCs, specifically those functions that are related to curriculum development and those that are not traditionally dealt with in a library setting. Many CMCs may not offer these types of classes at all because other agencies are taking care of these types of services. CMCs in our survey that do maintain instructional services related to curriculum laboratory functions report offering workshops and inservices related to the use of audiovisual equipment, computers and computer software, presentation techniques, materials production and production equipment, and curriculum development.

The CMC at Moorhead State University in Moorhead, Minnesota, offers a workshop that features instruction on the use of CD-ROM workstations. Oakland University in Rochester, Michigan, presents workshops in a variety of technologies, including scanner use, connecting laptops to projection equipment, presentation techniques, and the creation of overlays and underlays using overhead transparencies. The CIMC at the University of Wisconsin-Madison offers workshops in video editing and production. The CMC librarian at the University of North Carolina Charlotte has offered a class on Page Maker and basic book production. Louisiana State University's CMC offers computer clinics, and, finally, the CMC at Brock University in St. Catherine's, Ontario, Canada, features introductory hands-on workshops in computer applications using e-mail, Internet resources, and multimedia.

Bibliographies

CMCs frequently own a wide variety of commercially published bibliographies to meet the needs of the educators they serve. These bibliographies may be available in reference or in the circulating collection. CMC-created bibliographies are also very common and are normally available in handout form or on the Web. Bibliographies commonly found in CMCs include everything from a listing of the works by a certain children's author or on a certain subject, like Thanksgiving, to a listing of PK–12 textbooks available for purchase from publishers.

CMC-created bibliographies are particularly useful in enhancing the informational and instructional services that CMCs offer to their educators. CMC-created bibliographies can be highly focused and specific to the interests and curricula of the educators they serve and are therefore a very highly used service and in great demand. An example of just such a bibliography is *The Never Ending Never Done Bibliography of Multicultural Literature for Younger and Older Children* (Toni Walters, Paula Webster, and Amy Cramer [Rochester, MI; Oakland University, 1998]). It contains more than 1,400 titles with an emphasis on authentic and realistic voices related to multicultural issues.

In addition to traditional bibliographies, CMCs also create bibliographies that specifically address three unique information needs of educators: materials for student use, background materials for teachers, and pedagogical materials to assist teachers in choosing a method to convey content to their students. An example of such a CMC-created bibliography is *Children's and Young Adult Books About Disabilities* (Jeneen LaSee-Willemssen and Jennifer Bergen [Manhattan, KS: Kansas State University, 2000]) at http://www.lib.ksu.edu/depts/cmcjuvlit/disabilities/. This bibliography offers a traditional bibliography of children's books about disabilities or with characters with disabilities. It also provides listings of commercially published bibliographies on disabilities, curriculum and lesson planning resources on disabilities for teachers and background resources about disabilities for both teachers and parents.

Pathfinders

Bopp and Smith (1995) provide a fine definition of pathfinders: guides with suggested search strategies that include standard reference tools and their appropriate subject headings (276). Pathfinders such as these are fairly common in CMCs, though they are called by many different names. These types of guides, which provide self-help for searching, are particularly effective when used for recurring and popular topics and are typically found in the form of handouts, signs, or as Web sites.

In CMCs, pathfinders often focus on the needs of education students. One of the most typical questions CMC staff encounter is the identification and location of lesson plans; thus, the pathfinder Finding Lesson Plans is one of the most common. Examples of this type of pathfinder include:

> *Finding Lesson Plans, Activity Guides, and Curricula*
> Kansas State University's CMC
> http://www.lib.ksu.edu/depts/cmcjuvlit/activities.html

> *Finding Lesson Plans, Curriculum Guides, and Standards*
> University of Wisconsin Madison's CIMC
> http://cimc.education.wisc.edu/userguides/lessplans.html

> *Instructional Activities: Lesson Plans and Instructional Units*
> University of North Carolina Charlotte's CIMC
> http://libweb.uncc.edu/cimc/activities.htm

In addition to the pathfinders focused on lesson plans, CMCs offer guides on many other topics, such as: specific educational subject areas, multimedia materials, tests and scales, research, full-text electronic journal articles, and subject-specific children's materials. Pathfinders can be found on many CMC Web sites; an exemplary site is the Pathfinders site at: http://www.lib.ua.edu/mclure/pathfind.htm, produced by the McLure Education Library at the University of Alabama.

Future of CMC Information and Instruction Services

Today's changing information environment makes it important that CMCs adjust all of their services in relation to the times, and, more specifically, that CMCs adjust their information and instruction methods to meet the needs of today's educators. The advent of rapid technological innovations such as e-mail, the Internet, educational Web sites, interactive television, and distance learning have caused information and instruction services to change dramatically. Suddenly, information can be easily published and disseminated without the aid and filtering of traditional editorial gatekeepers, and reference questions and answers can be transmitted instantly and on demand. According to Bopp and Smith (1995), the ability to change rapidly provides both opportunities and challenges to librarians (28). These challenges and opportunities face CMC professionals as well.

The Coalition for Networked Information (CNI) New Learning Communities (NLC) provides a model for the collaborative teamwork that will be necessary for high functioning CMCs of the future. According to Tompkins, Perry, and Lippincott (1998), the future of CMC information and instructional services revolves around the combination of three trends: the increased availability of computer networks in higher education, specifically the Internet; the need for students to develop information literacy skills as part of curriculum; and the increasing importance of collaboration in both teaching and learning and technological society (100). These trends offer opportunities for CMC professionals of the future to focus their attention on providing guidance in the development of information literacy skills as they apply to education students.

Roberta Matthews, the keynote speaker at the New Learning Communities (NLC) Conference in 1996, offers this challenge for future librarians, one that is particularly important to CMCs. Librarians must be in the forefront of helping students and faculty locate, evaluate, and incorporate the new sources of knowledge at their fingertips. You might also be in the forefront of creating new models of learning communities that depend, from the very beginning, on the incorporation of information technology into the very fabric of the teaching/learning experience. She suggests that there is a natural convergence between collaborative learning and technology. Contrary to an earlier belief that technology would isolate the learner, it actually offers greater opportunities for collaboration through e-lists and specialized chat rooms. For example: Course Content Web and Blackboard provide templates for uploading information on individual classes. Within each program, chatrooms and discussion boards can be tailored to each class and secured with a password for security.

The instructional role of the CMC of the future will need to expand to provide workshops that develop the thinking and learning skills necessary to participate in university courses that are already utilizing mid- to high-end technology. If students are to become proficient in using distance learning, print and nonprint search strategies, and the Internet, it will be even more important for

CMC professionals of the future to be prepared to teach information literacy that bridges electronic formats and print resources. Teaching students to integrate information resources and services into their classrooms will be a top priority.

Like the Coalition for Networked Information (CNI) New Learning Communities (NLC), the National Council for Accreditation of Teacher Education (NCATE) emphasizes school district collaboration. CMCs may take NCATE's *Major Themes of the NCATE Standards* (available at: http://www.ncate.org/accred/initial/themes.htm) and use them to initiate and help develop user education programs of the future:

- Collaboration with PK–12 schools
- Provisions for adequate access to computers and other technologies
- Training for faculty and students on the use of computers and other technologies
- Resources that support the divergent backgrounds of students of the 21st century
- Collaboration with Colleges of Arts and Sciences that encourages a strong foundation in the liberal arts for future teachers

In addition to the above recommendations, NCATE has also published *Future Teachers* (available at: http://www.ncate.org/future/m_future.htm). The advice that is offered in this work is invaluable to CMC instructional staff.

> Teaching is about conveying a love of learning and discovery, and giving children the tools they can use throughout their lives to make their own discoveries. Teachers must be prepared to work as part of a team, combining their efforts with colleagues, supervisors, and parents to create the best possible learning environment for their students. In addition, teachers must continually educate themselves learning about new advances in education, new technologies, and new ways to inspire students to reach their full potential.

Finally, NCATE's *Future Teachers* also offers advice on selecting a College of Education. Answering yes to the following questions is essential:

1. Does the institution have the resources necessary to support each of the programs that it offers?

2. Does the institution prepare candidates to work with the growing diversity of America's school population?

3. Does the institution prepare candidates to work with the merging technologies that will certainly change teaching and learning in our schools?

CMC instructional staff might use these same questions as a guide to developing instructional programs that will help ensure that these teachers will be successful.

Since education students come to their certification programs with different levels of experience, it can never be assumed that they are information literate or technology savvy. CMCs of the future will have the responsibility of supporting the development of the skills that will bridge the gaps in information literacy and technology. According to Tompkins, Perry, and Lippincott (1998): "The need for information literacy has taken on a new urgency in the Information Age because use of new information technologies will play a role in many individual's [sic] ability to complete higher education and find gainful employment" (104). They further state that "schools and universities can play an important role in keeping the society from fragmenting into a population of information haves and have nots by incorporating information literacy into the curriculum and making available hardware, software, network connections, and networked information resources to all students" (104). This is particularly true for education students. It is also the connecting point for CMCs.

CMCs will have the responsibility of identifying new and innovative electronic media using similar evaluation skills that are essential to literature selection. The ability of CMCs to provide learners with space, resources, instructional services, and support that foster the transfer of skills is crucial to the future of education. Another important aspect of this evaluation process will be accountability regarding how the hardware will be used to enhance learning.

Learning to incorporate educational technologies into instruction is closely linked to curriculum standards and technology innovations for education students. For example, in Michigan, the Consortium for Outstanding Achievement in Teaching with Technology (COATT), which includes some 11 institutions, has the following as its goal (http://www.coatt.org/about.html)

Meeting the challenges of the 21st century through the recognition of Michigan educators who have achieved excellence in teaching with technology. COATT will begin awarding a certificate to preservice teachers who demonstrate excellence in the use of technology to enhance student learning. This certificate will exist independently of both degree programs and the state certification process. It will allow educators to demonstrate their proficiency in this area and will help school administrators who make hiring decisions identify teachers who can be technology leaders in their schools. The certificate will also allow institutions of higher education to benchmark their achievements in teacher training in technology against an independent standard of excellence.

Due to COATT, future user education programs in Michigan's CMCs will be based on meeting the criteria set up for achieving COATT certification. CMC professionals will be responsible for designing instructional programs that allow student teachers to experiment with various technologies and practice teaching while using technologies.

As electronic media continues to evolve, copyright issues will continue to be a hot topic for CMCs. As CMC instructional professionals continue to assist education students with everything from portfolio building to creating lesson plans that utilize Web-based information and scanned materials, it will be imperative that copyrights be addressed. Education students of the future will depend on information professionals in their CMCs to provide them instruction and information about how to stay legal and avoid accidental copyright infringement. Up-to-date copyright information will need to be provided in CMC workshops, as well as instruction on how to access this information.

Copyright issues will evolve right alongside electronic resources to which the plethora of current articles can attest. Blumenstyck (1999), in his article "Putting Class Notes on the Web: Are Companies Stealing Lectures," discusses the pros and cons of notes that are taken in class by students and posted to a public Web site. Judi Repman and Elizabeth Downs (1999) discuss the effect of technology on school media center policy in their article "Policy Issues for the 21st Century Library Media Center." They pay special attention to the emerging technologies and how copyright issues impact them. Finally, in the article "Distance Education and Intellectual Property," the American Association of University Professors' Special Committee on Distance Education and Intellectual Property (1999) joins the highly volatile discussion on the rights and responsibilities of faculty, teachers, institutions, and third parties as they apply to distance education. CMC instruction professionals will need to include information from all of these sources, and more, in their teachings to better prepare future teachers for their real-world experiences in the classrooms of tomorrow.

According to Rapple (1997), CMC information professionals of the future will be responsible for developing online information spaces that support the curriculum and provide guidance to students and faculty on their way to access, use, and evaluate information resources (50–51). In addition, Rader (1995) states that research and demonstration projects have already begun to assess the effect of information management skills on academic performance. Further, her writings support the idea that the emerging role of the CMC is to function as an information center and CMC professionals are to function as teachers of information skills for education students (277).

Future CMC user education will not begin and end with technology. The American Library Association Presidential Committee on Information Literacy (1998) emphasizes the need to communicate that quality education requires investments not only in technology, but also in programs that empower people to find, evaluate, and use all information effectively. CMCs will need to provide instructional programs in ways that are education-specific. For example: using print and electronic resources to evaluate children's literature for cultural diversity, integrating that knowledge with methods courses and providing a selection of the materials for education students to peruse. The American Library Association's American Association of School Librarians *Information Power* initiative (http://www.ala.org/aasl/ip_toc.html) includes a set of information literacy standards that will also come into play in determining how to teach information literacy and evaluation skills.

In her 1995 article, "Information Literacy and the Undergraduate Curriculum," Rader shares her insights regarding the future role of academic librarians, which also apply to CMC professionals. Specifically, they must:

• understand the curriculum and have effective liaison relationships in collection building with faculty;

• foster support from administrators and faculty leaders;

• be well prepared for teaching, understand different learning styles, and engage students actively in the teaching process;

• be flexible to accommodate the range of the curriculum and disciplines, as well as a diversity of faculty and students;

• use effective marketing techniques to demonstrate the importance of information and technology literacy and their crucial role in it; and

• stay somewhat ahead of the technology developments so they can be the first to teach new information formats and networks (273).

Conclusion

The future of CMC instructional services will depend on how well they can ride the winds of change. CMCs will be responsible for acquiring and teaching the effective use of electronic media before it hits the classroom. They will need to design programs that support the learning of the new technologies. They will be responsible for instructing teachers about the relationship between electronic media and print materials and how they apply to information literacy. They will need to assist future teachers in creating electronic portfolios that will be presented to prospective employers. They will be key players in developing instructional collaborations with PK–12 schools, academic faculty, and the public to ensure future teachers are exposed to and experience a broad knowledge base for curriculum development purposes. They will be responsible for providing and training teachers in the use of resources that will serve the diverse academic and PK–12 communities. In CMCs of the future, teaching students how to learn will be as important as teaching content and methods. The ever-changing landscape of electronic media and its increasing scope of information will merge with teacher education as it creates new paths to the future.

References

Adams, E. L. 1898. "Instruction in the Use of Reference Books and Libraries." *Library Journal* 23: 84–86.

American Association of University Professors' Special Committee on Distance Education and Intellectual Property. 1999. "Distance Education and Intellectual Property." *Academe.* 85 (3): 41–45.

American Association of School Librarians. (1999). *Information Power: Building Partnerships for Learning.* Accessed at http://www.ala.org/aasl/ip_toc.html.

American Library Association's Presidential Committee on Information Literacy. 1998. *A Progress Report on Information Literacy: An Update on the American Library Association Presidential Committee on Information Literacy: Final Report, March 1998.* Accessed at http://www.ala.org/acrl/nili/nili.html.

Association of College and Research Libraries, Bibliographic Instruction Section, Policy and Planning Committee. 1979. *Bibliographic Instruction Handbook.* Chicago: American Library Association.

Bhattarai, M. D. 1972. Plan for the Development of a Curriculum Laboratory in Nepal. Ed.D. thesis, George Peabody College for Teachers.

Blumenstyck, G. 1999. "Putting Class Notes on the Web; Are Companies Stealing Lectures?" *Chronicle of Higher Education* 46 (6): A31–A32.

Bopp, R. E., and L. C. Smith. 1995. *Reference and Information Services, an Introduction.* Englewood, Colo.: Libraries Unlimited, Inc.

Boudreau, B. 1983. "Curriculum materials centres in teacher education institutions." *CLJ* December: 379–82.

Buttlar, L., and M. Tipton. 1992. "Library Use and Staff Training in Curriculum Materials Centers. *Journal of Academic Librarianship* 17 (6): 370–74.

Church, J. G. 1957. The Development of Criteria for Evaluating Curriculum Laboratories in Teacher Education Institutions. Ph.D. dissertation, University of Utah.

Clark, A. 1982. *Managing Curriculum materials in the Academic Library.* Metuchen, N.J.: Scarecrow.

Clarke, N. 1991. "The Roles and Functions of Curriculum Resource Centres in Australia." *Australian Library Journal* 40: 232–41.

Consortium for Outstanding Achievement in Teaching with Technology. 1999. *About the Organization.* Accessed at http://www.coatt.org/about.html.

Cullinan, B. E., and L. Galda. 1998. *Literature and the Child.* 4th ed. Philadelphia: Harcourt Brace College Publishers.

Jacobson, F. 1988. "Teachers and Library Awareness: Using Bibliographic Instruction in Teacher Preparation Programs." *Reference Services Review* 16 (4): 51–55.

James, M. L. 1963. The Curriculum Laboratory in Teacher Education Institutions: Its Essential Characteristics. Ph.D. dissertation, University of Connecticut.

James, R. 1985. "Teacher Education Students—Different Needs, Different Solutions." In *Reader Services in Polytechnic Libraries*, ed. J. Fletcher, 140–58. Brookfield, Vt.: Gower.

Kaestle, C. E. 1983. *Pillars of the Republic: Common Schools and American Society, 1780–1860.* New York: Hill and Wang.

Libutti, P., and B. Gratch, eds. 1995. *Teaching Information and Retrieval Skills to Education Students and Practitioners: A Casebook of Applications.* Chicago, Ill.: ACRL.

Matthews, R. S. 1996. *Technology, Collaboration, and Democratic Practice.* Presentation at Librarian Leaders in New Learning Communities, ACRL/CNI Preconference, American Library Association Annual Meeting, New York City. Accessed at http://www.cni.org/projects/nlc/nlc96.keynote.html.

MacVean, D. S. 1958. A Study of Curriculum Laboratories in Midwestern Teacher-Training Institutions. Ed.D. dissertation, University of Michigan.

McGiverin, R. 1990. "Curriculum Materials in Online Catalogs." *College & Research Libraries News* 51 (6): 562–65.

Mellon, C., ed. 1987. *Bibliographic Instruction: The Second Generation.* Englewood, Colo.: Libraries Unlimited.

Morrill, R. 1981. "Library Service in Teacher Training Institutions." *Education Libraries* 6 3: 64–78.

NCATE. 2000. *Future Teachers.* Available at: http://www.ncate.org/future/m_future.htm.

NCATE. 2000. *Major Themes of the NCATE Standards.* Available at: http://www.ncate.org/accred/initial/themes.htm.

NEA. 1913. "Report of the Committee on Normal School Libraries." *Journal of Proceedings and Addresses of the National Education Association of the United States of America.* 51st Annual Meeting. NEA.

Nevil, L. 1975. *A Survey of Curriculum Laboratories in Selected Colleges in Pennsylvania.* ERIC Document Reproduction Service: ED No. 112 909.

O'Hanlon, N. 1988. "Up the Down Staircase: Establishing Library Instruction Programs for Teachers." *RASD* 27 (4): 528–34.

Rader, H. B. 1995. "Information Literacy and the Undergraduate Curriculum." *Library Trends* 44 (2): 270–79.

Rapple, B. 1997. "The Electronic Library: New roles for Librarians." *CAUSE/EFFECT* 20 (1): 50–51.

Repman, J., and E. Downs. 1999. "Policy Issues for the 21st Century Library Media Center." *Book Report* 17 (5): 8–11.

Teclehaimanot, B. 1990. The Nature, Function and Value of the Curriculum Materials Center in Colleges of Education. Ph.D. dissertation, University of Toledo.

Tompkins, P., S. Perry, and J. K. Lippincott. 1998. "New Learning Communities: Collaboration, Networking, and Information Literacy." *Information Technology and Libraries* 17 (2):100–6.

Worley, J. et al. 1981. "Bibliographic Competencies for Education Students." *College & Research Libraries News* 42 (7): 209–10.

Collaborative Activities with Faculty: Grant Writing, Action Research, and Scholarly Activities

Martha Henderson

Introduction

Collaboration: defined as a cooperative endeavor in which professionals identify common goals, coordinate efforts to achieve objectives, and share responsibilities for achieving outcomes, is not a new concept for librarians. CMC staff regularly participates in collaborative activities that relate to the information needs of faculty and students and address information literacy skills, library instruction, and collection development. However, changes in the field of information science provide opportunities to advance the librarian's role as a "partner with faculty," acting as an analyst, a consultant, and a participant in the cycle of scholarly endeavor and communication (Veaner, 1985).

This is a modification of the perception held by academic faculty, as well as many librarians, who view the role of the CMC librarian only in the context of service. Both groups fail to recognize and utilize the CMC librarian's multidisciplinary strengths and research knowledge and skills. The librarian, to become a partner, must take an active part in establishing that role by identifying and initiating collaborative activities.

Fortunately, significant opportunities exist for enhancing collaboration between the CMC librarian and faculty members. Major changes in curriculum and information resources, in the design and delivery of courses, and in technological applications provide a variety of avenues for collaboration. Librarians are usually at the forefront in recognizing trends, identifying and reviewing literature related to innovations, and responding to those factors that positively impact the field of education. They can be significant partners in planning for and implementing change.

Three areas that afford opportunities for faculty-librarian collaboration are grant writing, action research, and scholarship. Not only do these areas address resource and information needs common to most institutions, but they are components of merit, evaluation, and faculty tenure and promotion policies.

Initiating Collaboration

The effective librarian knows the faculty, is aware of the curriculum, and initiates communication in relation to faculty interests and activities. Collaboration usually develops as a result of similar interests or needs, knowledge about colleagues and the curriculum, and establishment of contacts with faculty. Johnson and Hedrich (1994) describe a database project to track faculty research specialties, grant funding, and faculty publications. A survey by Schloman, Lilly, and Hu (1989) was used to gather information about faculty. Both of these activities can be utilized to develop a profile of the individual faculty member. This information can then be used to initiate dialogue, provide services, and develop partnering projects.

Additional ways to develop knowledge about faculty and curriculum and to identify collaborative activities include:

1. Identify faculty who are actively involved in scholarly pursuits and initiate discussions, ask questions, provide information, and express your interest in participating in similar activities.

2. Identify new inexperienced faculty who are just becoming involved in issues related to higher education and have merit, tenure, and promotion concerns and suggest collaborative activities.

3. Identify experienced faculty who are effective mentors. These faculty members, who enjoy working with other people, usually have experience in a variety of activities, and willingly participate in collaborative endeavors.

4. Develop cooperative and collegial relations with lab school and professional development school librarians and collaborate to address common interests and needs.

5. Identify faculty needs. If the new mathematics methods teacher wants manipulatives or kits that are not available in the CMC, suggest that you cooperatively write a grant proposal.

6. Review faculty syllabi to identify resource needs, research interests, and topics for action research projects or publications.

7. Attend meetings of curriculum committees or review their minutes to stay informed about changes in courses and programs. Identify topics for research studies or publications.

8. Maintain a "grants information center." Notify faculty about relevant materials and funding opportunities and suggest collaborative activities.

9. Circulate pertinent information—RFPs, research data, new curriculum guides, ERIC abstracts—to interested faculty and indicate your willingness to participate in activities.

10. Establish a working relationship with the regional educational or professional development center to ensure knowledge about current issues and resources. Share information with faculty or work with center staff members to design grants, research, and publications.

The time element involved in scholarly production is often a handicap to librarians. It is certainly easier if one works with colleagues. However, Jackson (1997) emphasized that librarians need to know their own personal working styles. Deciding on a collaborative strategy needs to be a personal and conscious decision.

Grant Writing

Grant seeking is a complex and detailed process requiring organization and dedication. However, decreasing budgets and increased competition for grant monies make it even more important to develop skills related to grant writing. The components involved in grant activities are identifying appropriate and relevant funding sources, preparing a competitive grant proposal, and conducting the project if funding is received.

Large amounts of grant monies are available from national and state agencies for varied projects, including curriculum revision, resource acquisition, studies about teaching and learning processes, and technology acquisitions and upgrades. Ideas for grant proposals range from acquiring and implementing reading programs to purchasing vast amounts of equipment for implementing new technologies to implementing simple proposals that enhance or improve on an existing idea. Winning proposals must indicate knowledge and expertise, including in the academic emphasis, about use of technology in classrooms and how that technology affects effective instruction and academic achievement. (Schnitzer, 1995).

Writing the Proposal

Some private agencies that provide funding for educational activities accept a brief description of the project summary. However, most funding agencies in the announcement of a competition or in the request for a proposal (RFP) will have a detailed format to follow. In each case, the evaluation procedures will be described. Often these criteria provide the best overview for preparing the proposal. Many agencies provide samples of funded proposals. In addition, the U.S. Department of Education and the National Endowment of the Humanities will provide sample proposals on request.

Reif-Lehrer (1995) identified the proposal idea as the most important part of a grant application: "The research plan should be innovative, have a clear rationale, and have obvious significance; it should be focused, well thought out, and timely." Any proposal should address a specific problem that can be solved by a logical process. The description should be clear and concise with appropriate details. Each goal should be performance based and one that can be assessed.

Resources

Many valuable print resources are available to assist in developing skills, providing information, and identifying funding sources. Sample titles include:

Bauer, D. 1998. *The Teacher's Guide to Winning Grants.* San Francisco: Jossey-Bass. Step-by step primer for selecting funding sources, organizing proposal ideas, writing the proposal, and implementing the project.

Directory of Grants in the Humanities. 1999. Phoenix: Oryx Press. A listing of sources with a guide to proposal planning and writing.

Reif-Lehrer, L. 1995. *Grant Application Writer's Handbook.* Boston: Jones Bartlett. Comprehensive work includes: detailed overview, procedures, and checklists.

An annotated bibliography of print resources is available at: http://www.library.wisc.edu/Memorial/grants.

Most higher education institutions have an office that is responsible for assisting with grant and research activities. Personnel in these areas assist faculty with developing skills in writing grants, identifying sources of funds, editing a proposal, and providing access to print and Web-based resources.

Academic libraries usually have a center or section in their collection devoted to grant writing. This area houses current print resources and webliographies, which provide information about available Internet resources. The library's homepage may also have information about grant activities and provide pointers to Web-based resources.

Some links to these resources include:

Webliography, Grants: Northwestern State University. Available at http://www.nsula.edu/watson_library/index.html.

Grants Information Center at University of Wisconsin-Madison. Available at http://www.library.wisc.edu.libraries/Memorial/grants/proposal/.

Grant Getting Page: University of Illinois at Chicago. Available at http://www.uic.edu/depts.ovcr/.

Faculty and Research: Writing a Grant Proposal at Columbia University. Available at http://cpmcnet.columbia.edu/research/writing/htm.

Tips for Writing Grants at North. Available at http://www.ncsa.uiuc.edu/people/bievenue/gw.html.

Reference: Tools for Writing Grants at Kansas University Medical Center. Available at http://library.kumc.edu.

The U.S. Department of Education and other federal agencies provide an abundance of resources and information. These documents are available in government documents collections in academic libraries or on the Web:

http://www.ed.gov.legislation/FedRegister/announce

http://www.access.gpo.gov/su_docs/aces/aces140.htm

http://www.web.fie.com/

http://gcs.ed.gov/

http://www.ed.gov/pubs.KnowAbtGrants/

Other valuable sources of information include the Cisco Educational Archives (CEARCH), a meta-library of K–12 links—http://sunsite.unc.edu/cisco/ ; the Foundation Center which fosters understanding of the foundation field and provides access to "A Proposal Writing Short Course"—http://fdncenter.org/ and professional organization web sites such as the Association for Supervision and Curriculum Development—http://www.ascd.org/services/grantingo/tips9.html.

Successful Activities

North Carolina State University reported collaborative grant activities in the EBSS Survey on the Management of Curriculum Materials Centers. These grants were written with specific units within the college and benefited the CMC by providing additional materials. College of Education faculty and librarians at Northwestern State University of Louisiana collaboratively wrote several grants to the Louisiana Board of Regents:

"Technological Enhancement of Teacher Education with Government Documents"—$52,000 for purchase of computers and printers to access Web-based educational resources.

"Preventive Law Initiative for Educators"—$42,000 for purchase of an NT server and computers and printers, and development of a curriculum guide and database guide to Lexis-Nexis Academic Universe.

"N.S.U.: A Site for Systemic Initiatives in Math/Science for Middle School Educators"—$16,000 for materials and part-time staff.

Action Research

Action research is designed to improve knowledge about effective teaching/learning practices and to promote collaboration among preservice and in-service educators and between PK–12 schools and higher education personnel (Henderson, Hunt, Wester, 1999). Sparapani (1996) describes action research as an effective strategy to help school-based professionals connect classroom theory and classroom practice. A model described by Marquardt (1998) consisted of five steps: (1) decide on a strategy or program to study; (2) implement the strategy in a classroom; (3) collect data; (4) evaluate the effectiveness; and (5) make decisions about future instruction.

Emphases on reorganizing and restructuring schools fueled the number of action research projects and provided sources for funding such activities. Collaborative activities among various educational entities developed and expanded, including those between colleges of education and PK–12 schools; among colleges of education, other colleges within the university, PK–12 schools, and school agencies; and between academic and PK–12 school librarians.

Data from a survey of institutions with membership in the American Association of Colleges of Teacher Education (Henderson, Hunt, Wester, 1999) indicated that the topic of action research is included in the curriculum of 85% of the institutions. Over 75% designed or implemented action research projects in cooperation with local school districts. Topics for the projects ranged from reading instruction to teaching strategies in mathematics to technology implementation. A large number of the projects resulted in program or curricular changes.

Resources

Educational Action Research, published by the Collaborative Action Research Network, is a full-refereed international journal that reports on action research and related studies. Free online access to this journal and other educational titles is available at http://www.triangle.co.uk. "An Introduction to Action Research," a presentation at the National Association for Research in Science Teaching, is available at http://www.phy.nau.edu/.

Mid-continent Research for Education and Learning (http://www.mcrel.org/), the Ohio Literacy Resource Center, (http://archon.educ.kent.edu/OASIS/Pubs/), and Southern Cross University, (http://www.scu.edu.au/schools/sawd/ari/ar.html) maintain lists of Web-based resources pertaining to action research. In addition, an article describing action research is available on the Center's homepage.

Additional resources, including articles, descriptions of successful projects, and URLs, can be located at a variety of sites, including:

http://www.parnet.org (Cornell)
http://www.imlab.uiuc.edu (University of Illinois at Urbana-Champaign)
http://info.csd.org/WWW/resources/
http://www.accesseric.org/

Successful Activities

The education librarian and director of field experiences at Northwestern State University collaborated to conduct research relative to the information needs of students in field placements. These students were located at PK–12 institutions distant from the main campus. Students were in these locations for 16 weeks and had limited physical access to library resources. An initial survey sought information about topics of student information needs and the student's access to resources available through the Internet, either from the site, from a personally owned computer, from a convenient public library, or from another source. Information about accessing library resources and electronically communicating with personnel related to information needs was then sent to each student. Student evaluations of the project were very positive.

A similar project, "Profiling information needs to design library services for distance learners," was a collaborative effort between the education librarian and faculty who were teaching courses at distant sites (Henderson, Jarred, 1996). Data from this study indicated that students need additional information about technological access to library resources and services.

Scholarly Activities

Scholarly activities include endeavors such as publications, presentations, and curriculum development. Curriculum innovation, grant-funded projects, and action research activities often provide data and information that can be used to develop an article or make a presentation.

Curriculum changes are occurring today, gradually in some cases and dramatically in others. Donham (1998) identified six trends that have particular impact: emergence of the cognitive theory of constructivism, emphasis on higher-order thinking skills, integrated disciplines, development of graduation standards, acknowledgement of social learning, and recognition of a variety of learning styles.

As Colleges of Education redesign curriculum to prepare teachers to address performance-based standards and assessment issues, the CMC librarian can play a key role. The availability of professional standards, current textbooks, teaching aids, and professional journals enables the librarian to identify new trends and issues.

Many CMCs serve as textbook depositories. Publishers deliver new texts that are under consideration for adoption. Member of textbook-selection committees and in-service teachers visit the CRC to evaluate the textbooks. These new materials provide a resource for the librarian in staying current with curriculum design.

References

Aspen Publishers. 1999. Grantseeking 101. Available at http://www.grantscape.com/omaha/grants/.

Austin, A., and R. Baldwin. 1992. Faculty Collaboration: Enhancing the Quality of Scholarship and Teaching. ERIC Document Reproduction Service ED No. 347 958.

Bluh, P. 1997. "Tips for the aspiring authors" *Library Administration and Management* 11 (1): 9–25.

Boyer, P., and L. Cockriel. 1998. "Factors Influencing Grant Writing: Perceptions of Tenured and Nontenured Faculty." *SRA Journal* 29 (3–4): 61–68.

Clark, C. et al. 1996. "Collaboration as Dialogue: Teaches Ad Researchers Engaged in Conversation and Professional Development." *American Educational Research Journal* 33 (1): 193–231.

Couch, T., and R. Knack. 1996. "Get that Grant: How to Write a Winning Proposal." *Planning,* 62 (12): 17–20.

Donham, J. 1998. *Enhancing Teaching and Learning.* New York: Neal Schuman.

Grover, R., and M. Hale. 1988. "The Role of the Librarian in Faculty Research." *College and Research Libraries* (Jan.): 9–15.

Grants to Teachers. Available at: http://www.ofe.org/lef/grants.html.

Haycock, K. 1995. "Research Imperatives for Information Professionals: Developing Foundations for Effectiveness." *School Library Media Annual* 13, 113–26.

Henderson, M., S. Hunt, and C. Wester. 1999. "Action Research: A Survey of AACTE-Member Institutions." *Education* 119 (4): 663–67.

Johnson, J., J. Johnson, and A. Hedrich. 1995. "The University Library as Information Provider and Communication Facilitator: A Faculty Research Database." *Proceedings of the ACRL 7th National Conference,* 309–16.

King, J. A., and M. P. Lonnquist. 1992. "A Review of Writing on Action Research." Madison, Wisc.: Center on ORganization and Restructuring of Schools. ERIC Document Reproduction Service ED No. 355 664.

Lanning, J. A. 1988. "The Library-Faculty Partnership in Curriculum Development." *College and Research Libraries News* (Jan.) 7: 10.

Marquardt, F. M. 1998. "Implications of Teacher Action Research for In-service Teachers' Professional Development." Accessed at http://www.unf.edu/dept/juep.

Schloman, B., R. Lilly, and W. Hu. 1989. "Targeting Liaison Activities: Use of a Faculty Survey in an Academic Research Library." *RQ* (summer): 496–505.

Schnitzer, D. 1995. "How to Fund Technology Projects." *Educational Leadership* 53 (3), 71–74.

Sparapani, E. F. 1996. "Action Research: A Strategy for Bridging the Gap between Theory and Practice." ERIC Document Reproduction Service ED No. 398 194.

Outreach and Public Relations in CMCs

Harriet Hagenbruch

Introduction

CMCs may vary in size, title, administrative structure, and physical location on campus (main library, College of Education building or another location entirely), but they share at least one thing in common—a unique collection of instructional materials designed to support the needs of school professionals, particularly those of teachers and teachers-in-training. Over the years, the value of these collections has been increasingly recognized. In 1960 the National Council for Accreditation of Teacher Education (NCATE) indicated that a "materials laboratory or center should be maintained either as part of the library or as a separate unit" and that "it should be directed by a faculty member well informed in the various instructional media and materials at different grade levels." (Buttlar, 371) The 1990 revised NCATE standards, as part of their criteria for compliance, also call for "an iden-tifiable and relevant media and materials collection accessible to education stu-dents and faculty." (59) Recently, the NCATE 2000 Unit Standards stated in conjunction with Standard 6 "Unit Governance and Resources" that as a target:

> The unit aggressively and successfully secures resources to support high quality and exemplary programs and projects to ensure that candidates meet standards .... The unit serves as an information technology edu-

cation resource in education beyond the teacher preparation programs—
to the institution, the community and other institutions. Faculty and
candidates have access to exemplary, library, curricular, and/or electronic information resources that serve not only the unit but also a
broader constituency." (25)

Many educators and/or librarians have stressed the need for teachers to be
knowledgeable about the practical materials needed for unit and lesson planning.
Edwards (1996) goes as far as to refer to CMCs as a "vital link in the educational
process." Directors of CMCs have become especially adept at promoting the
importance of their collections, often assuming a proactive role as they utilize
every resource within their power to develop partnerships on campus and in the
community beyond.

The following chapter is based on the experience of the Curriculum Materials Center/Education Librarian at Hofstra University, the experience of members of the Education/Curriculum Materials Centers Librarians Group (an
interest group of ACRL/NY), recent discussion that appeared on the EBSS
electronic discussion list, and an EBSS survey of CMCs throughout the country.
According to the EBSS survey, collaboration is defined as forming partnerships
with a variety of constituencies on campus such as College of Education faculty,
academic librarians, the Center for Computing, etc., while outreach is defined as
reaching out to the community beyond. However, sometimes the lines between
collaboration and outreach may blur; and, very often, outreach may be necessary
as a first step to form collaborative relationships with colleagues on campus. In
addition, according to the survey, the majority of directors of CMCs seem to be
academic librarians, some of whose main discipline is education. For purposes of
this chapter, "librarian" will be the primary term used in this discussion.

Outreach to the College of Education Faculty

While CMCs are usually open to anyone on campus, and while they may invariably interact with a number of departments and/or units, they primarily serve the
needs of students and faculty within the College of Education. It is therefore
essential that the person in charge of the CMC reach out and collaborate fully
with the various people who are part of the College of Education. Regardless of
where the CMC is located, the fact remains that it is necessary to maintain a high
degree of visibility as well as to form strong working partnerships with College of
Education faculty. This can be accomplished in a number of ways, including writing letters of introduction to new faculty in which the CMC librarian describes
his/her background as well as what the CMC has to offer. To personalize the

letter, it pays to learn a little about the new faculty member's areas of research and exactly what type of courses this person will be teaching. Usually, this type of information can be acquired by access to the new faculty member's curriculum vitae. Lists of new faculty can often be obtained directly from the College of Education itself—or, perhaps, from the Provost's office—and should be updated at the start of each semester. Of course, it is wise to re-inforce existing relationships with the College of Education faculty as well. This can be accomplished by correspondence (e-mail or traditional letter writing) and simply, from time to time, picking up the telephone. Beyond that, meeting in person with faculty in either a formal sense or in a social situation is an excellent way to remind them that the CMC is there to serve their needs.

Attending the College of Education's faculty meetings is also important in terms of maintaining a high profile. These meetings may consist of general faculty meetings, or they may be departmental meetings where some CMC librarians feel more central issues are actually discussed. The protocol of most institutions requires that individuals who are not members of the department obtain permission to attend. It is useful to receive advance notification of these meetings including the agenda, location, and time so that the CMC librarian is prepared for any issues that may arise. Attendance at these meetings provides a wonderful opportunity to learn exactly what concerns are particularly important to the College of Education faculty and staff, as well as what courses and programs are being developed. It also provides the opportunity to talk, on an individual basis, to the College of Education people about the CMC and what it has to offer. It is helpful to the College of Education faculty, particularly at the beginning of the academic year, for the librarian to attend departmental meetings to formally describe the new materials and services at the CMC as well as in the library. Beyond attendance at meetings, serving on College of Education committees may also be extremely beneficial. The CMC librarian may serve on committees continuously or may participate when a committee is focused on specific activities such as preparing for accreditation. For example, when the College of Education is NCATE accredited, the CMC librarian may be actively involved in the accreditation process—submitting reports, serving in an advisory capacity to some of the NCATE-related committees, and possibly being interviewed by the members of the accreditation team. In certain instances, planning for additional technology or, perhaps, even a new CMC may lead to membership on a committee. For example, the CMC librarian at Hofstra University served on a committee, along with faculty from the College of Education as well as another librarian, that was charged with developing a "Proposal for an Integrated, Comprehensive Technology in Education Center" that would combine traditional print and nonprint resources with a host of new technologies in an attractive, up-to-date setting. The development of this very ambitious proposal turned out to be a cooperative effort that established a basis for future endeavors. In a similar vein, the director of the CMC at the University of Dayton cochaired their School of Education and Allied Profession's (SOEAP) Technology Visioning Committee and, in addition, served on a SOEAP support staff committee and a faculty subcommittee to develop plans to fulfill the "Vision." In several instances, CMC librarians serve as library liaisons to their respective Colleges of Education as well as serving on a number of committees. One CMC librarian at Kansas State University reports she works closely with the College of Education's Professional Development Coordinator to make sure that library-related topics are part of the College of Education's Professional Development Workshops and include sessions on such topics as the Kraus Curriculum Development Library, how to locate lesson plans in the ERIC database, and what's new in the CMC. At the Educational Resource Center (ERC), Boston College, the School of Education has set up a faculty advisory board consisting of four faculty members and the Dean's administrative assistant to advise the ERC librarian. A librarian at Ohio State University was involved in a seminar devoted to technology that was sponsored by the College of Education and serves as a member of the College's Administrative and Professional Staff Advisory Committee.

Attending conferences and workshops sponsored by College of Education faculty can be a valuable learning experience as well as a means of collaboration in terms of sharing ideas. Since the College of Education often sponsors many conferences during the course of the academic year, it is probably a good idea to obtain a list of upcoming events from the Dean's office or from the person who is responsible for scheduling. However, the CMC librarian also has the opportunity to sponsor or cosponsor events and workshops for education faculty as well as the community at large. The librarian at the University of South Dakota mentions presenting frequently at reading conferences with the reading faculty. The Curriculum Lab at the Central Connecticut State University reports hosting two teas for education faculty as well as local teachers; at these teas they set up subject-related displays of various curriculum materials. Two librarians at Teacher's College, Columbia University, have conducted a series of teleconferences within the library that consist of monthly U.S. Department of Education town meetings as well as other special events. These are brought into the library by means of satellite and are targeted for education faculty and students, people in the community, and other special guests. Some of the topics included "Smart from the Start: Strengthening Early Learning, from Infants to Preschoolers," "Powerful Middle Schools: Influencing Teaching and Learning for Young Adolescents," and

"Multiplying Excellence: Ensuring Quality Mathematics & Science Teaching," among many others.

While the CMC librarian is a subject expert who is primarily responsible for the development of the CMC collection, collection management is another area where opportunities for collaboration abound. Almost all of the librarians who participated in the survey reported working with College of Education faculty in terms of acquiring materials. Frequently, College of Education faculty will donate materials that are extremely expensive if purchased otherwise. A perfect example of this is textbooks. At one time, publisher's representatives were only too willing to donate sample copies or even whole series of current textbooks. That is no longer true, yet it behooves CMCs to have samples of the latest textbook series. Purchasing these texts can readily eat up what usually amounts to a limited CMC budget. Often, education faculty members are in a better position to acquire sample textbooks and, on occasion, donate whole series of textbooks to the CMC. In turn, College of Education faculty will rely on the CMC as a place where students can come to examine textbooks. Furthermore, while the CMC librarian may be an expert in many areas of education, it is literally impossible for one person to be an expert in every area. Therefore, it is invaluable to rely on the subject expertise of fellow education faculty in terms of the collection. This is true in terms of acquisition and, at times, deselection.

Outreach to College of Education Students

While it is important to reach out to College of Education faculty to form meaningful partnerships as well as promote the Curriculum Materials Center, it is perhaps even more important to reach out to education students since they constitute the primary users of the CMC. In interacting with students, the CMC's size and specialized nature (referred to in the opening paragraph) may actually serve as an advantage. Very often, the CMC librarian and/or staff have an opportunity to work more closely with students on a one-on-one basis and can establish a close and positive relationship that may last even after graduation. This is in keeping with Claudia J. Morner's advice to let education students know they "have a friend in the Library"—a comment which appears in her contribution to *Teaching Information Retrieval and Evaluation Skills to Education Students and Practitioners* (Libutti, 66). While she is referring specifically to doctoral students, this can apply to education students at either the undergraduate or graduate level. Furthermore, as Jo Ann Carr states in her article "Information Literacy and Teacher Education," "if teachers are to use information so that others can learn from them, then teachers must be information literate" (Carr, 2). However, for this to happen, education students need to feel comfortable using a library. This is more likely to occur if they have a positive library experience—the type of experience they usually have within the CMC. Additionally, the more students come to regard the CMC as their Center—a place where they can receive assistance in meeting their educational needs as well as meet and collaborate with colleagues on various projects - the more they are likely to "spread the word" to their classmates or fellow teachers.

Of course, it is important that students learn about the CMC as early in their educational career as possible. Here the cooperation of the College of Education may be vital. Orientations that are held at the CMC for incoming education students or even students considering an education major can convey to them that they will receive the support they need as aspiring teachers. For example, the University of Wisconsin-Madison has orientations for potential education students held with their CIMC, allowing them to view the wonderful resource at their disposal. Also, classes conducted within the CMC on behalf of the College of Education faculty can serve as an important introduction to the types of services offered as well as materials available. In fact, while "Information and Instruction Services in CMCs" forms the basis of another chapter in this volume, there is no escaping the fact that instruction is a powerful tool in terms of outreach to students as well as collaboration with faculty. It is also worth noting that colleagues in the academic library may play a key role in promoting the CMC to incoming freshmen, transfer students, and beginning education majors. Very often, librarians conduct tours of the library for new students and may, in addition, participate in freshmen seminars and other events that are designed to acquaint students or potential students with what the college or university has to offer. Including the CMC as part of these tours or mentioning the CMC to possible education majors can certainly help students be aware of the CMC's existence. It is also important for librarians (reference and otherwise) who conduct classes in the use of the library to mention all public service areas including the CMC.

Many strategies that were designated previously as working with faculty are useful with students as well. These can include workshops on topics of interest held at the CMC that can, in many instances, be specifically targeted for students. Maintaining bulletin boards as well as signs describing the CMC in College of Education buildings can also serve to arouse interest. Displays at the CMC can also draw students as well as other library patrons into the center. As mentioned earlier, a subject-centered display of curriculum materials is promoted by the Central Connecticut State University Curriculum Lab. The CMC librarian at Hofstra tries to coordinate displays of children's literature with other events taking place on campus such as Black History Month or Women's History Month.

At other times, she will create displays built around a theme or a genre of literature such as poetry or mystery stories. The librarian at the University of Wisconsin-Stout mentioned a display of children's books in conjunction with Children's Book Week, and, in developing the display, she indicated that she collaborates with reading classes or with such campus organizations as the National Art Education Association. Often, CMCs mount displays of education students working in the CMC, thereby effectively modeling the use of curriculum materials. All of these different types of displays serve to make the CMC a visually more attractive place, but, to serve as a form of outreach, they must be promoted through fliers or newsletters. Bibliographies are also an invaluable means of promoting the collection as well as another means of assisting students who use the CMC. Bookmarks that include CMC hours and the names of staff as well as other handouts help to publicize the collection, as well as providing useful information. Also, maintaining a strong presence on the Web in the form of a CMC homepage may be a powerful form of outreach to students as well as faculty. This may be particularly true if, once again, the homepage includes basic information about the CMC (hours, staff, policies) as well as the electronic version of a CMC newsletter that highlights events as well as different parts of the collection. In addition, incorporating the E-mail address of the CMC librarian and/or members of the CMC staff as part of the homepage may further illustrate that the CMC staff is truly responsive to student needs. Finally, reaching out to students may involve going outside the CMC. While classes are traditionally taught in a classroom located at the CMC, at times CMC librarians also teach in classrooms in other areas on campus, laptop in hand, to promote their collections and services. If education students have organizations on campus, it is important for the CMC librarian to find out about them and, if possible, speak at and/or attend meetings. For example, at one point Hofstra University had an undergraduate education society. Notices of meetings of this organization were posted outside the Curriculum Materials Center, and the CMC librarian attended a number of their meetings. All of these activities and strategies combine to make students aware that the CMC staff is readily available to offer assistance.

Outreach to Other Units on Campus

Frequently, the CMC does interact with other units on Campus and building collaborative partnerships with them may be important as well. At Hofstra, the CMC librarian has worked closely with the Child Care Institute (a facility designed to provide day care for Hofstra employees as well as people in the community), reading aloud to youngsters in the Institute, providing input about computer software, and conducting a session pertaining to children's literature for teachers in the Institute as well. In addition, some of the programs in the Hofstra Summer Camp have used the CMC facilities as well as parts of the collection as part of their activities. Moreover, if there is a separate area on campus devoted to educational technology, many CMCs establish a close working relationship with these centers as well. For example, the University of Delaware indicates that their Education Resource Center and the Instructional Technology Center have co-sponsored joint technology workshops to education faculty as well as in-service teachers. In addition, they have joined forces to apply for a grant to a state agency to establish a county center for the previewing of educational software as well as professional development.

Partnerships with Other Academic Librarians on Campus

The role of other academic librarians within the library in promoting the CMC has already been mentioned. Beyond this, there is not a function of the CMC that is not enhanced by the CMC librarian working collaboratively with other academic librarians—librarians who invariably represent almost every library department. In many CMCs, the materials in the collection are cataloged by a separate cataloging department; it is essential that the CMC librarian establish a close working relationship with the librarian who catalogs his/her materials so that access to these materials is handled in the most efficient manner. Working with other academic librarians in terms of collection development is another form of collaboration for many CMCs. Usually, the CMC contains the more practical materials needed for lesson and/or unit planning while the more theoretical materials are housed in the general collection. However, when it comes to education, the theoretical and practical can frequently overlap. Therefore, it is essential that the CMC librarian work with the librarian responsible for collection development to avoid unnecessary duplication. Moreover, if a collaborative relationship is established, both librarians may be in a position to recommend materials to each other.

Instruction is another area where collaborative partnerships can be forged between the CMC librarian and other academic librarians. This is especially true since technology has, to a great extent, broken down barriers between library departments. Certainly, there was a time when the presentation of materials at the CMC was very distinct from instruction in the use of reference tools including the use of the ERIC database. Now, with almost every computer in a library connected to the LAN and, as a result, providing access to both CD-ROMs and the Internet, this is no longer true. As a result, CMC staff frequently provide individual and group instruction in ERIC and other education-related databases. Working cooperatively with other academic librarians in developing classes for education students addresses "the big picture" in terms of the discipline and ultimately serves to promote the CMC collection as a necessary component in the instruction of teachers and teachers-in-training.

Partnerships with Other Librarians in the Community

It is also important for CMC librarians to work cooperatively with other types of librarians as well as attended conferences sponsored by school library media specialists and public librarians. This is particularly true since CMC librarians share many concerns and interests with their professional colleagues. For example, since many CMCs house collections of children's literature, this is a subject area of interest to many CMC librarians. Very often, public librarians in the area of children's services sponsor conferences and workshops pertaining to children's books that feature famous authors and illustrators as keynote speakers or the discussion of selected titles. Attendance at these conferences can only help to expand knowledge and, ultimately, enhance the collection as well as those classes taught by the CMC librarian that are related to children's literature. Also, CMC librarians have much in common with school library media specialists both in terms of collections and client groups. CMC librarians and school media specialists can cosponsor workshops and events as well as addressing areas of mutual concern. In fact, many CMC librarians belong to local School Library Media organizations or are involved on the national level as part of the American Association of School Librarians. Furthermore, CMC librarians are in a unique position to promote the importance of the school library media center to the various teachers and teachers-in-training with whom they interact. It is especially important for CMC librarians to reach out to other CMC librarians within their local area. As a group, CMC librarians find themselves somewhat isolated because of the unique position they occupy as either part of the main library or, for that matter, within the College of Education. Several years ago, the CMC librarian at Hofstra started a new Interest Group as part of ACRL/NY consisting of education and Curriculum Materials Center librarians who meet at least twice a year and communicate frequently. Their meetings have addressed all kinds of issues including the impact of technology and have included such guest speakers as textbook representatives and school library media specialists. Also, another way for CMC librarians to share with each other is through electronic discussion lists such as the one provided by EBSS.

Outreach to School Districts

However, it is in the area of working with local school districts that the CMC librarian really has the opportunity to play a major role. Once again, such outreach can build on the CMC librarian's knowledge of such specialized areas as technology and children's literature. For example, as a result of an endowment received by the University of Wisconsin-Stout, a center was established with the purpose of providing local educators with access to, as well as instruction in, the latest technology. The Education Materials Center librarian not only served on the Center's Outreach Committee but also played a major role in setting up and participating in a weeklong, summer, technology-related workshop for PK–12 educators. The CIMC at the University of Wisconsin-Madison is involved (through grant money) in offering technology training to teams of five teachers and five instructors in the various methods classes with the goal of integrating technology into the curriculum. They have applied for funding for the following year and plan to add teacher education students to their teams. Furthermore, many other CMC librarians are presently involved in technology-related workshops for their neighborhood schools or are planning workshops of this type in the near future. These workshops may take place at the CMC or in the schools themselves. The Educational Resource Center in Boston, working with the Foundation for Children's Books, has hosted a "Conversations with . . ." series which explores the exciting world of children's and young adult literature and, in the process, has invited many famous authors as guest speakers. The CMC librarian at Moorhead State University, through grant money, selected books for a traveling exhibit, "Windows on Our World: An Exhibit of International Picture Books." In addition, she wrote annotations for each book, coauthored a 90-page guidebook which accompanied the exhibit, and saw to it that audiocassettes were produced that contained readings of the books in their original language as well as in English. This CMC librarian is also a team leader for "Children's Choices" and, in this capacity, sends out multiple copies of recently received new children's books for evaluation by children and young adults in two local school districts. The librarians in the resource center of Milbank Memorial Library, Teacher's College, have developed an exciting series of read-aloud sessions of children's books for youngsters in local schools. The program has proved quite successful and has drawn upon the talents of Columbia University administrators and faculty as well as educators from the community. Not only do these people all take part in these sessions, but the series is also promoted by the resource room librarians who utilize a variety of strategies including a video that describes the program. Also, many of the events that CMC librarians promote within their centers that are directed toward education faculty and students can include teachers and administrators from local schools as well. Finally, CMCs act as a resource to the community by encouraging local teachers and administrators to examine the various curriculum materials that are part of their collections. In many instances, local teachers are able to obtain borrowing privileges.

It is worth noting that while local PK–12 educators can learn about current materials and technologies from CMC librarians, the relationship is a mutually beneficial one. Close ties with the local school districts allow CMC librarians to gain a full understanding on what is going on in the schools around them in terms of both educational trends and materials utilized in the classroom.

Conclusion

CMCs play an important role in the education and training of classroom teachers. Furthermore, they are a valuable resource in the community beyond. However, all of this is meaningless if the people who stand the most to benefit from using the CMC are unaware of either its existence or what it has to offer. Alice Clark considers outreach so essential that in her classic, *Managing Curriculum Materials in the Academic Library* (1982), she includes a section on "A Public Relations Program" that suggests many of the same strategies cited in this chapter (162). Certainly, it would seem that promotion in the form of both outreach and ultimate collaboration is the key to the success of the Curriculum Materials Center. Most CMC librarians do well in this area, but by sharing ideas and strategies they can continue to expand their role as teacher educators well into the future.

References

Buttlar, L. and M. Tipton. 1992. "Library Use and Staff Training in Curriculum Materials Centers." *Journal of Academic Librarianship* 17 (January): 370–76.

Carr, J. A. 1999. *Information Literacy and Teacher Education*. Washington, DC: ERIC Clearinghouse on Teaching and Teacher Education. Digest 97-4. Available at http://www.ericsp.org.digests.

Clark, A. S. 1982. *Managing Curriculum Materials in the Academic Library*. Metuchen, N.J.: Scarecrow.

Edwards, R. G. 1996. "Curriculum Materials Centers: The Vital Link to Teacher Education Programs." *Ohio Media Spectrum* 48 (spring): 13–15.

Morner, C. J. 1995. "One-on-One Instruction for Doctoral Students or Faculty." In *Teaching Information Retrieval and Evaluation Skills to Education Students and Practitioners: A Casebook of Applications*, P. O. Libutti and B. Gratch, eds. 65–71. Chicago: American Library Association.

National Council for the Accreditation of Teacher Education. 1990. *Standards, Procedures and Policies for the Accreditation of Professional Education Units*. Washington, D.C.: NCATE.

National Council for the Accreditation of Teacher Education. 2000. *NCATE Unit Standards*. Accessed at http://www.NCATE.org.

Technology and the CMC

Judith Walker

Introduction: Availability vs. Utilization

Education in the 20th century saw myriad changes: shifts in demographics, a progression of new pedagogies, changes in curriculum paradigms, and, central to this discussion, new instructional technologies. Pedagogies and paradigms have shifted and been debated for centuries. But the introduction of so many new technologies into the classroom is unique to the 20th century. Although none of these technologies—film, filmstrips, slides, overheads, television, video, records, cassettes, compact discs, or computers—were designed specifically for use in the classroom, they have found their way there. Some have been superseded by newer technologies but most were hailed as revolutionary for teaching and learning. Whether or not they have revolutionized education is not within the scope of this discussion, but the fact that educational technologies are an integral part of today's classroom has significant ramifications for CMCs.

A 1995 report by the Office of Technology Assessment indicated 90% of American classrooms have access to a VCR and 78% have television access (U.S. Congress, 1995). Older technologies such as overhead projectors and audiocassettes are so ubiquitous they didn't even bother to record their presence. Another report from the Center for Research on Information Technology and Organizations (CRITO) indicates that in 1998 there were 8.6 million computers in schools across America, an increase of 150% from 1992. This is an average of six students per computer nationwide (Anderson and Ronnkvist, 1999). Yet another report from CRITO indicates 90% of all schools have some type of Internet access somewhere in the school, with over a third of the teachers having direct access in their classroom. The report also reveals that 59% of teachers have access to the Internet from home and only 27% have no access at either school or home (Becker, 1999). Although these statistics were collected in 1998 and probably have already increased dramatically, it would appear they are proof that educators are committed to the use of technology in the classroom.

But does the presence of technology in the classroom assure their incorporation in the learning process? According to Marshall-Bradley and Bradley (1998), simply placing technology in front of preservice educators and administrators will not ensure that they use this medium of information acquisition to effectively instruct students or improve the quality of their work. Statistics from the same report that indicate the near-saturation of technology in classrooms support this point. Even the older technologies with which teachers should be very comfortable, of those 90% who have access to a VCR only 64% actually use it. The same is true for the television: 78% have access but only 52% use it. The gap between access and integration into the curriculum is even greater. Although a majority of teachers (68%) use the Internet for finding information resources such as lesson plans, very few teachers have had their students involved in Internet-based activities such as communicating to other individuals, to collaborate with classes in other schools in joint projects, or to become experts on a topic and publish their findings on the World Wide Web (Becker, 1999). The overwhelming conclusion from the literature is that, even though the technologies are available to teachers, they are not being integrated into the classroom curriculum.

Seeing this disparity, the National Council for Accreditation of Teacher Education in their 1997 report, *Technology and the New Professional Teacher*, stated, "The nation's teacher education institutions must close the teaching and learning technology gap between where we are and where we need to be. Teacher education institutions must prepare their students to teach in tomorrow's classrooms" (National Council for Accreditation of Teacher Education, 1997). This call-to-arms by the nation's leading teacher accreditation organization has set into motion a wave of activity which has major implications for CMCs. Since the primary function of a CMC is to support the education curriculum of its parent institution, any changes to that curriculum will impact the CMC. In the past CMCs could fulfill their function by providing a specialized collection of materials which consisted of both print and nonprint materials. But now, according to Bently, as we have moved into the computer age and, more recently, telecommunications and other higher technology capabilities for education, the CMC may no longer be the focal point for these technologies that have become a vital part of teaching and learning (1994).

Bently's prediction does not have to become a reality. CMCs can and should continue to be a vital part of the education curriculum for preservice and in-service teachers. To do so, they will have to take a serious look at the role their collections and instructional services provide students and faculty in their respective departments/colleges of education.

Technology and Teacher Education

Even before the 1997 NCATE report, professionals were already aware of the disparity between access and use. Handler in 1993 concluded, "Today, educators basically agree that preparing preservice teachers to use media and technology in the classroom should be one of the goals of teacher education programs in the Information Age" (1993). This realization led to a rush to create standards, which would guide teacher preparation institutions and school districts in developing curriculum and/or professional development programs which would better prepare teachers for teaching with technology.

According to Kent and McNergney (1999), at least 32 states have established technology requirements as part of their teacher certification process. The proliferation of these requirements has led to an intensified use of technology in the preservice courses, assignments requiring students to develop materials that demonstrate their competence with the use of computers, and additional attention to the computer-related practices they observe in the classrooms in which they are doing their preservice training (Love and McVey, 2000). For example, the University of North Carolina at Charlotte, in response to a state mandate, has developed a Technology Passport which students use to develop a professional portfolio. As they progress through the education curriculum, students must have professors, supervisors, cooperating teachers, and/or the Curriculum Materials Librarian sign off on the passport indicating they have met various benchmarks. Then physical representation must be included in their portfolio along with the passport.

In 1997, NCATE joined forces with the International Society for Technology in Education (ISTE) by adopting ISTE's recommended *National Standards for Technology in Teacher Preparation* (ISTE Accreditation and Standards Committee, 1997) as its guidelines for evaluating teacher education programs. These standards are at the core of state requirements as well. According to ISTE, students seeking initial certification or endorsements in teacher preparation programs should have opportunities to meet the educational technology foundation standards. The standards address three basic areas:

• Basic Computer/Technology Operations and Concepts: Focuses on how to operate the computer; understanding terminology; basic troubleshooting; using peripherals such as scanners; and knowledge of how technology is used in business, industry, and society.

• Personal and Professional Use of Technology: Focuses on learning how to use technology to enhance their own professional growth and productivity. This includes learning how to use word processing, spreadsheets, databases, grading programs, etc.; creating multimedia presentations; using computers to support problem solving, data collection, information management, communications, presentations, and decision making; and identifying technology resources for facilitating lifelong learning. Knowledge of equity, ethical, legal, and human (i.e., adaptive assistive devices) issues concerning the use of technology is also addressed.

• Application of Technology to Instruction: Focuses on how to apply technologies to support instruction in their classroom. To demonstrate mastery of this goal, educators need to plan and deliver instructional units that integrate a variety of technologies and reflect effective grouping and assessment strategies for a diverse population. Ethical, equitable, and legal issues are also addressed (ISTE Accreditation and Standards Committee, 1997).

As standards were being created, it became apparent that emphasis should move away from the mechanics of using technologies to actually integrating the learning capabilities of the technologies into the curriculum. As pointed out by Cradler, Executive Director of the Far West Lab, despite available technologies in schools a substantial number of teachers report they do not use computers and other technologies regularly for instruction. A majority of teachers report feeling inadequately trained to use technology resources, particularly computer-based technologies. Training focuses on the mechanics, not on integrating technology in the curriculum (Cradler 1995). The President's Committee of Advisors on Science and Technology concurred with Cradler, stating that what teachers actually need is in-depth, sustained assistance as they work to integrate computer use into the curriculum and confront the tension between traditional methods of instruction and pedagogic methods that make extensive use of technology (President's Committee of Advisors on Science and Technology, 1997, 49). This is not a new concept; Bitter and Yohe in 1989 felt the integration of media and technology into teacher preparation curriculum is the single most pervading issue relating to technology today in colleges of education. The literature reverberates with this concept: Teachers lack an understanding of curricular uses of technology and lack models of technology for their professional use (Cradler 1995). Researchers concluded that teachers are being inadequately prepared to use instructional technology and consequently, are unable to integrate technology effectively into classroom teaching practices (Northrup 1995).

It is not sufficient to confer technical ability on a particular topic or device. Such training is of little value unless preservice students also learn how to incorporate this technology into their future classrooms in a sound and meaningful manner. The ability to integrate new technology successfully into one's everyday teaching style is crucial to its success (Halpin and Kossegi, 1996). Faculty must include current technologies in their curricula, thereby empowering graduates with the knowledge and understanding of appropriate and productive use of technology (Marshall-Bradley and Bradley, 1998). Integration, integration, integration is the new mantra for educational technology. It is also emphasized in the ISTE standards.

Technology and the CMC Instructional Role

How do these two developments in the education curriculum, technology competencies and integration of technology, affect the instructional role of the CMC? Since the CMC's function is to support the education curriculum, any type of instruction the CMC undertakes with educators—whether it be face-to-face or via the Internet—should incorporate instructional experiences that will help students meet technology competencies. Strategies should be developed to provide students opportunities to meet the educational technology foundation standards as laid out by ISTE/NCATE. There are a number of activities described in the ISTE standards which can be easily integrated into instruction provided by a CMC, particularly in the areas of personal and professional use of technology and application of technology in instruction.

Although most CMCs are not in the business of training students in the mechanics of particular programs, it is the CMC's business to train students and faculty in how to search for information resources. It does not matter whether the student or faculty member needs research articles or bulletin board ideas. The CMC staff must instruct them in the basic principles of how to locate resources in a wide variety of electronic databases, including the World Wide Web. These skills are necessary for educators to become lifelong learners that will enhance their own professional growth. This instruction can be accomplished individually, in small or large groups, and/or asynchronously via the Internet. Each delivery method has its own unique set of challenges, but CMCs need to provide instruction in as diverse a manner as possible to better meet the wide variety of student and faculty needs.

Another way the CMC can effectively support the ISTE standards is through modeling. To a large extent, a teacher's ability to integrate technology into the classroom depends on the modeling and classroom experiences he or she had as a preservice teacher (Luke, Moore, and Sawyer, 1998). The simplest way CMC staff can implement modeling is by using PowerPoint presentations and/or Web sites to instruct students in how to locate education resources. By doing this, CMC staff provides an instructional model for students which: 1) demonstrates that producing instructional technologies such as a PowerPoint presentation or a Web site is not beyond their capabilities; 2) illustrates good instructional design principles; and 3) provides examples of good integration skills. Providing students with e-mail addresses for contacting CMC staff and making handouts and bibliographies available via the World Wide Web takes them a step further by encouraging them to actually use the technology.

All CMCs should be providing the minimum instructional services mentioned above. Depending on the size and resources of a CMC, several other instructional activities may be provided to help promote the ISTE standards. Most of these activities involve collaboration with faculty and/or students. One is providing demonstrations of specific equipment and/or software to students during a methods or instructional design course. At the University of North Carolina Charlotte, the Curriculum Materials Librarian works with education faculty to identify what software and equipment are most appropriate for their subject area. The professor chooses one or two of the programs to incorporate into his or her teaching. Others are demonstrated in the CMC during a session designed to expose students to a wide variety of resources in a particular subject field. For example, during the secondary science methods class the Curriculum Materials Librarian discusses and demonstrates the characteristics, advantages and disadvantages of laser discs, the visual presenter, and student production with HyperStudio as related to the middle and secondary science curriculum.

Another instructional service that can occur in the CMC is instructional consultation. As mentioned earlier, students are being asked to demonstrate their competence with educational technology by integrating it into their instructional units. Students should be able to set up an instructional consultation with CMC staff during which the CMC staff can help the student choose appropriate instructional technologies for their particular unit. This time could also be spent demonstrating to a student how a particular program works or discussing how it might be used in the classroom. Of course, this instructional consultation does not have to be limited to students. Faculty members frequently need this type of assistance as well because they do not always have time to keep up with new technologies and/or software.

Probably the most involved instructional support the CMC can offer faculty in the area of technology is to actually team-teach a complicated project such as assisting students in developing a HyperStudio stack or creating an instructional Web site. A good example of this type of collaboration occurs at the University of North Carolina Charlotte. An elementary language arts professor decided she wanted her students to publish a book using the writing cycle they discuss in class. She also wanted them to publish it electronically, so the Curriculum Materials Center became involved. When she first made the assignment there were no education computing labs, but the Center had several computers that the students could use.

On the surface this appears to be a simple assignment. Students could in theory use any number of programs available at the elementary level such as BankStreet Writer and the Children's Publishing Center software. The professor, however, wanted the students to assemble the book the same way real publishers do it by sewing down the middle of folded sheets. With this caveat the project became a problem-solving experience as well. How do you get the pages in the right place?

When she first assigned the project, the only program available to create the book using her directions was the desktop publishing program PageMaker. Although this is not a simple program to master, it would not be difficult to learn the basic skills needed to complete this project. The problem at first, however, was not the program but rather that most of the students were basically computer illiterate. They were still having difficulties with word processing. Most did not have computers at home and had to use campus labs to key in their stories.

With basic training provided by the Curriculum Materials Center staff, students were able to complete the project. They liked scanning and taking their pictures digitally. Since a color ink-jet printer was available at the time, the books were printed in color. The students were very proud of their work. During their discussion evaluating the project, the professor reminded them that their students will experience the same feelings of accomplishment and self-worth, if they provided their students with the same experience.

As semesters pass, students' computer skills have improved greatly, and most now have computers at home. The project is still part of the language arts curriculum, but students are now using Microsoft Word instead of PageMaker. Using a program that is already familiar to the students lessens the anxiety, but it also illustrates that they are probably not using this very common program to its fullest potential. Although they are more familiar with the technologies of scanning and digital imaging, they still are incredibly proud of their product because it looks so professional.

This is only one example of how CMC staff, if available, can collaborate with education faculty to help students master technology skills. Other centers are involved in assisting students in learning how to use camcorders and create HyperStudio programs. This type of collaboration is limited only by the imagination of the education faculty and CMC staff.

Technology and the CMC Collection

Traditionally, the CMC has provided specialized collections of print materials such as textbooks and children's books. Larger CMCs with more substantial budgets also included nonprint materials such as transparencies and filmstrips. CMCs have been a little more reluctant to purchase newer technologies for several reasons: the rate of platform/format changes (i.e., from disks to CD-ROMs to the Web in less than a decade); lack of equipment; cataloging difficulties; shelving considerations and circulation issues. However, if students are being required to demonstrate competencies in integrating technology into their instructional units, they must have access to a wide variety of instructional technologies.

Why are these resources important? Because using a variety of technologies and teaching methods in the classroom helps accommodate different student learning styles (Newby, 2000). Also the newer technologies (computers and the Internet) are more compatible with current teaching methods such as cooperative learning, guided discovery, and an integrated curriculum (Serim & Koch, 1996). In addition, almost one-half of all teachers in a 1998 national survey indicated that resources such as the Internet were essential for their teaching, and nearly 90% reported that they would consider these resources either valuable or essential (Becker, 1999). To effectively and efficiently purchase resources it is helpful to know how the materials are going to be used. According to Bently (1994), utilization of educational software in CMCs by students and teachers fell into three categories: 1) familiarizing themselves with a wide variety of programs; 2) evaluating the content of instructional programs; and 3) using word processing. Becoming familiar with what is available and evaluating its contents are basic to integrating technology into the curriculum.

Knowing what is available in the schools is also important if a CMC wants to reflect current school usage. In his national survey of computer and Internet use, Becker (1999) discovered the most common software programs were word processing (95%), spreadsheets (83%), databases (81%), and drawing/paint (80%) programs. Next came reference or research CD-ROMs (51%) and finally came subject area–specific software in math (50%); language arts (45%); social studies (36%); and science (31%) .

These figures provide an interesting snapshot of how computers are used in schools. The most common programs, as can be expected, are utility or productivity programs. These programs have become essential tools for both students and teachers. They enable students and teachers to do their work. They have no inherent teaching characteristics, although in the hands of an expert teacher they can be used as problem-solving tools.

Reference tools may also be a questionable purchase for CMCs, especially those at the secondary level. Many of them will be available from the institution's library. However, specialized reference tools for the elementary level might be helpful, since the language arts and social studies curricula include a number of research skills. The subject-specific software figures reflect availability of quality software and types of software used in a specific discipline. Elementary math uses a lot of drill and practice software, which is readily available. On the other hand the science curriculum requires more hands-on, simulation types of software that are not as prevalent. If a CMC collection of software reflected approximately the same distribution listed above, it would be a fairly accurate representation of what is found in the schools.

Of course, having a quality collection is worthless if students don't have access to the materials. No matter where the CMC is located or how it is structurally administered, it is first and foremost a library—a collection of materials—regardless of format. Because the CMC is a library, it can benefit greatly from advances in information technology that allow patrons to find resources quickly and easily. Finding things in a CMC can be daunting. Even with a well-designed classification system, it can be difficult to determine if a CMC actually owns a specific item. For this reason alone, all CMCs should have some type of electronic access for their collection. Larger institutions should have records of their holdings in an online catalog (either the library's or their own) which is accessible via the World Wide Web. For smaller institutions a simple searchable database like Microsoft Access or FileMaker Pro would allow educators to search for specific items. If at all possible, it should be put on the Web. If not, it should be available in the Center itself.

Once resources are identified and located, students should be able to either preview the materials in the Center or check the materials out for preview in another lab or at home. For most formats circulation is not a problem, but, unfortunately, computer software can present circulation problems. Licensing agreements can restrict usage so they should be read carefully to avoid any legal problems. In some circumstances, software may have to be returned because of the licensing restrictions. If the materials are not going to circulate, are there enough computers for previewing? There is also the problem of older programs not running on new machines and vice versa. If the software is going to circulate, students should be instructed on how to determine if the program will run on their machine. And they need to know there is no guarantee that it will work on their machine. Policies concerning the use of all software should be carefully developed and clearly written so everyone understands them.

The Internet and the Curriculum Materials Center

According to Becker's 1998 national survey of teachers and students, searching the World Wide Web has become the third most common use of computers by students at school, after word processing and the use of CD-ROMs for research. In addition, a majority of teachers (68%) use the Internet in their efforts to find information resources for use in their lessons, and more than one-quarter of all teachers report doing this on a weekly basis or more often (Becker, 1999). Most of the CD-ROM research tools used in 1998 are now available via the Internet, thus increasing the use of the World Wide Web as a research tool for students. Since more teachers are connected and there are more resources for them on the World Wide Web, they are spending more time searching it. The fact that students have become so dependent on the Internet can present a problem for CMCs. If a CMC does not have a Web page and their collection is not accessible via the Internet, connecting with many students will be extremely difficult. Internet savvy students will find other places on the World Wide Web to locate the materials they need or do without. For all but the smallest CMCs, the question is not whether to have a Web page but what information will be provided on it. Careful thought and planning should go into the design of a Web page. Who is going to use it? What are their information needs? When will it be used? Where will it be used: in a classroom, computer lab, or somebody's bedroom? Will it be used in research or instruction? Whatever the answers are to these questions, one thing all CMC Web pages should do is provide access to their collection by linking to either a library catalog or a database—one that has been created specifically for the CMC. Instructions for using the catalog or database should be just a click away.

Many CMCs are using the Web as a teaching tool as well. First information that has been distributed as handouts should be included on their Web page. If a large part of that information probably refers to Web-based information sources, they can link directly to the resources. Second, CMC staff are using their Web pages as presentation tools. Students see exactly how to use the Web page to their advantage; this is modeling of research skills at its best.

Probably the most significant effect the Internet has on CMCs is its ability to extend the resources of a CMC. There are hundreds of thousands of Web sites that can be used by teachers. Lesson plans abound. Teaching ideas for teachers are available from a wide variety of sites: museums, the government, and commercial sites. There are sites where students and teachers can talk to other professionals or experts in a particular field. But the major drawback of the World Wide Web is that these wonderful resources are not organized in any logical way. Web search engines are becoming more sophisticated and doing a better job of narrowing the number of hits. There are also more sites like LightSpan [http://lightspan.com/], Classroom Connect [http://www.connectedteacher.com/home.asp] and GEM: Gateway to Educational Materials [http://thegateway.org/] that provide organized access to educational resources on the Internet. But if CMCs are to take advantage of the resources on the Web and help their students locate information, CMCs will either have to impose some type of organization on these resources or teach students how to use web search engines effectively—or both.

Listed below are 25 Curriculum Materials Center Web sites, which represent the wide variety of design formats and information. Some are very extensive. Others are simple and to the point. This is neither an exhaustive or evaluative list. Remember, though, that Web addresses do change. These Web sites were current and viable when this chapter was written.

Boston College, Educational Resource Center
   http://www.bc.edu/bc_org/avp/ulib/ERC/ERChome.html
California State University Fresno, Curriculum/Juvenile Library
   http://duchess.lib.csufresno.edu/SubjectResources/
   CurriculumJuvenile/
California State University Fullerton, Audiovisual and Curriculum Center
   http://www.library.fullerton.edu/audiovis.htm
Gonzaga University (Washington), Curriculum Center
   http://www.foley.gonzaga.edu/pubserv/curric.html
Kansas State University, Curriculum Materials and Juvenile Literature
   Center
   http://www.lib.ksu.edu/depts/cmcjuvlit/index.shtml
Kutztown University (Pennsylvania), Curriculum Materials Center
   http://www.kutztown.edu/library/curriculum/homepg.html
Louisiana State University, Education Resources
   http://www.lib.lsu.edu/edu/er/index.html
Midwestern State University (Texas), Moffett Library Curriculum
   Materials
   http://www.mwsu.edu/~library/departments.html

Montclair State University (New Jersey), Curriculum Resources Center
http://www.montclair.edu/Pages/CRC/CRC.html
Slippery Rock University (Pennsylvania), Instructional Materials Center
http://www.sru.edu/depts/library/imc/index.htm
Texas A&M University-Kingsville, Education Materials Center
[Click on "EMC" in the frame on the left.]
http://oasis.tamuk.edu/
University of Lethbridge (Alberta, Canada), Curriculum Laboratory
http://www.edu.uleth.ca/currlab/
University of Central Florida, Curriculum Materials Center
http://library.ucf.edu/CMC/default.htm
University of Cincinnati, Curriculum Resources Center
http://www.libraries.uc.edu/libinfo/crc/index.html
University of Delaware, Education Resource Center
http://www.udel.edu/educ/erc
University of Illinois Chicago, Curriculum Library
http://www.uic.edu/depts/lib/collections/govdocs/curr.html
University of Maine, Learning Materials Center
http://libraries.maine.edu/orolmc/default.htm
University of Nebraska Kearney, Curriculum/Non-Book Department
http://www.unk.edu/acad/library/curric/curric.htm
University of North Carolina Charlotte, Curriculum and Instructional
Materials Center
http://libweb.uncc.edu/cimc
University of Southern Mississippi, Gunn Educational Materials Center
http://www.lib.usm.edu/~gunn/
University of Vermont, Curriculum Materials Center
http://bailey.uvm.edu/cmc/
University of Wisconsin-Madison, Center for Instructional Materials
and Computing
http://cimc.education.wisc.edu/
University of Wisconsin Oshkosh, Educational Materials Center
http://www.uwosh.edu/library/emc
Washburn University (Kansas), Curriculum Resource Center
http://www.washburn.edu/mabee/crc.html
Western Carolina University (North Carolina), Curriculum Materials
Center
http://www.wcu.edu/library/about/curriculum/index.htm

Computers in the Curriculum Materials Center

To use new technologies well, teachers need more than just access to these resources; they also need opportunities to discover what the technologies can do, to learn how to operate them, and to experiment with ways to best apply them in their classrooms (Congress of the U. S., 1995). It is obvious that one of a CMC's primary purposes is to provide access to resources. They can and should also assist students in finding the best ways to apply them in the classroom. However, providing opportunities to learn how to operate and experiment with them introduces the question of whether CMC should include a computer lab. To some extent the answer to this question will depend on the size and administrative structure of both the CMC and the larger institution.

Every CMC should provide equipment for educators to preview all formats of materials in its collection. This mini-lab should include at least a videocassette player and a computer. An audiocassette or CD player would also be useful. The computer should be able to serve the dual purposes of previewing materials and accessing resources on the Internet. The availability of additional computers in the CMC will provide access to resources and allow for previewing materials, one-on-one instruction and assistance, and limited production of materials by students.

A number of CMCs such as those at Montclair State University (http://www.montclair.edu/Pages/CRC/CRC.html) in New Jersey and the University of Cincinnati (http://www.libraries.uc.edu/libinfo/crc/crclabs.html) have larger and more complex instructional technology labs. Montclair State University's lab has been developed to be a model classroom with laser disc players, computers, multiple CD-ROM drives, scanners, digital cameras, audio-video equipment, and projectors. It is used for microteaching, small and large group instruction—and it has distance education connectivity. The University of Cincinnati (UC) has several labs. The computer lab accommodates both College of Education instructional technology courses and library instruction classes. When it is not being used for classes, students use it to preview and experiment with software programs and work on their assignments. In addition to its computer lab, UC has a video lab where students and faculty can be videotaped doing lessons and/or lectures. Finally, UC has a media production lab where students and faculty can produce a wide variety of instructional materials such as transparencies and bulletin boards.

Whether the CMC has a large or small number of computers, Northrup (1997) suggests the following benchmarks for a state-of-the-art laboratory: 1) multiple platforms; 2) adherence to current industry standards; 3) connectivity to the Internet; 4) current software titles for productivity tools, integrated software, desktop publishing, and graphics; 5) one or more multimedia development stations with memory and hard disk capability to capture and play back video and sound; 6) Point-to-point and multipoint desktop video conferencing; and 7) authoring tools (Northrup, 1997). These are broad benchmarks, which need to be tailored to individual circumstances. However, adherence to current industry standards, Internet connectivity, and current software are essential for any instructional technology lab.

If it is beyond the scope and/or capability of a particular CMC to provide such state-of-the-art services, the CMC staff should work closely with those entities on campus that can and do provide these services. At many institutions, the "make-and-take" production of transparencies and bulletin boards is available in a student media center or, more recently, an on-campus copy center (similar to a Kinko's). The computing services department of an institution is frequently responsible for the computer labs across campus. A campus computing services department may have more responsibility for supporting faculty than for services to students. If a CMC cannot provide extensive computer services to education students, then the CMC staff should work closely with their computing services department to develop programs and services that will meet the needs of the education students. The CMC does not have to be all things to all educators, but it can act as a liaison to other services on campus that can meet the needs of their students and faculty.

Conclusion

The literature will and should continue to debate the efficacy of instructional technology in the educational curriculum, but one thing is certain: technology in one form or another is here to stay. It is vitally important that Curriculum Materials Centers keep abreast with these changes to support the teacher preparation and educational research curriculum at their institutions. NCATE standards dictate that CMCs need to be selecting a variety of instructional software that will enable educators to integrate technology into the classroom. They need to be using technologies such as electronic databases and the Internet to provide access and instruct students and faculty in how to locate resources. In doing so they are modeling for both students and faculty how to incorporate technology into teaching. Finally, they should be working closely with education faculty and other institutional departments to ensure that services are available which provide opportunities for education students to become competent in the operation and use of all instructional technology, especially computers. These services may or may not be available within the confines of the CMC; but, regardless of their location, the CMC staff should be able to promote them to students and faculty.

References

Anderson, R. E., and A. Ronnkvist. 1999. *Presence of Computers in American Schools: Teaching, Learning, and Computing: 1998 National Survey Report #2. Center for Research on Information Technology and Organizations.* Online. University of California, Irvine and University of Minnesota, Center for Research on Information Technology and Organizations. Accessed at http://www.crito.uci.edu/TLC/findings/Internet-Use/startpage.htm on July 14, 2000.

Becker, H. J. 1999. *Internet Use by Teachers: Conditions of Professional Use and Teacher-Directed Student Use: Teaching, Learning, and Computing: 1998 National Survey: Report #1. Irvine, CA: Center for Research on Information Technology and Organizations.* University of California, Irvine and University of Minnesota, February 1999. Center for Research on Information Technology and Organizations. Accessed at http://www.crito.uci.edu/TLC/findings/Internet-Use/startpage.htm on July 14, 2000.

Bently, C. L. 1994. "Are Preservice Teachers Acquiring Skills in Educational Technology, How and Where? Results of a National Survey." Paper presented at the Annual Meeting of the Mid-Western Educational Research Association, Chicago, Ill., October 13–15, 1994. ERIC Document Reproduction Service ED No. 381 585.

Bitter, G., and R. L. Yohe. 1989. "Preparing Teachers for the Information Age." *Educational Technology,* 23 (3): 22–25.

Halpin, P., and J. D. Kossegi. 1996. "The WWW, Preservice Teachers and Their Mathematics Courses." In: *Association of Small Computer Users in Education (ASCUE) Summer Conference Proceedings 29th, North Myrtle Beach, S.C., June 9–13, 1996.* ERIC Document Reproduction Service ED No. 405 819.

Handler, M. G. 1993. "Preparing New Teachers to Use Computer Technology: Perceptions and Suggestions for Teacher Educators." *Computers and Education* 20 (2): 147–56.

ISTE Accreditation and Standards Committee. 1997. *National Standards for Technology in Teacher Preparation.* Online. Eugene, Ore.: International Society for Technology in Education. Accessed at http://www.iste.org/Standards/NCATE/found.html on July 14, 2000.

Kent, T. W., and R. F. McNergney. 1999. *Will Technology Really Change Education? From Blackboard to Web.* Thousand Oaks, Calif.: Corwin Press.

Love, R., and M. Mc Vey. 2000. "Teachers' Use of the Internet." *Teachers College Record* 6/21/00. Online. New York: Teachers College, Columbia University. Accessed at http://www.tcrecord.org/PrintIdKwParam.asp?@IdNumber=10538 on July 14, 2000.

Luke, N., J. L. Moore, and S. B. Sawyer. 1998. "Authentic Approaches to Encourage Technology-using teachers." In: *SITE 98: Society for Information Technology & Teacher Education International Conference 9th, Washington, D.C., March 10–14, 1998. Proceedings.* ERIC Document Reproduction Service ED No. 421 083.

Marshall-Bradley, T., and G. C. Bradley. 1998. "Starting from Ground Zero: Integrating technology in Education Programs." In: *SITE 98: Society for Information Technology & Teacher Education International Conference 9th, Washington, D.C., March 10–14, 1998. Proceedings.* ERIC Document Reproduction Service ED No. 421 082.

National Council for Accreditation of Teacher Education. 1997. *Technology and the New Professional Teacher: Preparing for the 21st Century.* Washington, D.C.: NCATE.

Newby, T. J., et al. 2000. *Instructional Technology for Teaching and Learning.* 2d ed. Saddle River, N.J.: Merrill/Prentice Hall.

Northrup, P. T. 1997. "Instructional Technology Benchmarks for Teacher Preparation Programs and K–12 School Districts." In: *Proceedings of Selected Research and Development Presentations at the 1997 National Convention of the Association for Educational Communications and Technology 19th, Albuquerque, N.M., February 14–18, 1997.* ERIC Document Reproduction Service ED No. 409 858.

President's Committee of Advisors on Science and Technology (U.S.) Panel on Educational Technology. 1997. *Report to the President on the Use of Technology to Strengthen K–12 Education in the United States.* Washington, D.C.: President's Committee of Advisors on Science and Technology (U.S.) Panel on Educational Technology.

Serim, F., and M. Koch. 1996. *Netlearning: Why Teachers Use the Internet.* Sebastopol, Calif.: Songline Studios.

U.S. Congress, Office of Technology Assessment. 1995. *Teachers and Technology: Making the Connection: OTA Report Summary.* Washington, D.C. ERIC Document Reproduction Service ED No. 386 154.

Willis, E. 1998. "An Interdisciplinary, Problem-centered Methods Module for Preservice Elementary Teacher Education." In: *SITE 98: Society for Information Technology & Teacher Education International Conference (9th, Washington, D.C., March 10–14, 1998). Proceedings.* ERIC Document Reproduction Service ED No. 421084.

A Selective Annotated Bibliography

Ann E. Brownson

Curriculum materials centers have been a part of teacher education programs since the 1920s, either as part of the college of education or as part of the academic library. One would expect that there would be a wide range of library and education literature describing their place in the preparation of teachers. There are a few important works about CMCs; however, many of the articles and books chosen for inclusion in this bibliography are only tangentially related to curriculum materials centers.

The items chosen for this bibliography do address many of the issues facing CMCs in the 21st century. These issues include the professional education of CMC personnel; budgeting and financial planning; collection development, including physical and bibliographic access to the collection; instruction in the use of the CMC and its collections by students and education faculty; the need to collaborate with faculty and to reach out to other constituencies; and issues related to technology.

History and General Works

Baughman, S. S. 1984. "Education Libraries in the United States." *Education Libraries* 9: 45–48.

A general overview of education libraries in the U.S. is given, with note of special types of libraries including curriculum materials libraries. Small, but strongly service oriented, most curriculum materials libraries were established between 1955 and 1975 and typically house current textbooks, curriculum guides, audiovisual materials, and microcomputer software collections.

Boudreau, B. 1983. "Curriculum Materials Centres in Teacher Education Institutions." *CLJ (Canadian Library Journal)*, 40: 379–82.
This article surveyed curriculum libraries at schools of education in Canada. They are described in this study according to name, role, administrative status, collection, and services offered. In addition, education faculty members were surveyed and found to be unfamiliar with their CMCs. This was thought to be a result of a lack of communication and coordination between all of the services in the Schools of Education related to curriculum materials.

Carr, J. A., and K. Zeichner. 1988. "Academic Libraries and Teacher Education Reform: The Education of the Professional Teacher." In *Libraries and the Search for Academic Excellence*, ed., P. S. Breivik and R. Wedgeworth, 83–92. Metuchen, N.J.: Scarecrow.
This article describes common threads in recommendations made by five reporting bodies during the mid-1980s about the nation's teacher preparation programs. Of particular interest to curriculum materials centers was the call for strengthening of academic and field experience components of teacher education, including instruction in the use and evaluation of curriculum materials.

Clark, A. S. 1982. *Managing Curriculum Materials in the Academic Library*. Metuchen, N.J.: Scarecrow.
This book was the first major attempt to provide practical information needed by academic librarians charged with managing a curriculum materials center. Clark sifted through the literature about curriculum laboratories, much of it unpublished doctoral dissertations, and included information on the history, administration, collection development, acquisition and organization of materials, and management of the CMC. Though now somewhat dated, the book still provides useful information to CMC librarians.

Clarke, N. 1991. "The Roles and Functions of Curriculum Resources Centres in Australia." *Australian Library Journal* 40: 232–41.
Clarke describes the development of CRCs in Australia, beginning in the 1970s. Ideals have been agreed upon to which the CRCs should aspire: support all courses provided by their education faculty; stock a wide range of resources in print and

nonprint including equipment and a current collection with a quantity of innovative material; provide an appropriate information retrieval system and user education programs; and develop close cooperation between the centre staff and academic staff to ensure that new directions in teacher education are reflected in both the collection and services.

Edwards, R. G. 1996. "Curriculum Materials Centers: The Vital Link to Teacher Education Programs." *Ohio Media Spectrum* 48: 13–15.
Edwards gives an overview of the historical development, services, collection and scope, and future of curriculum materials centers. Because of increased demand for services and often a lack of resources to meet that demand, CMCs must develop plans to effectively eliminate impediments to their growth.

Henderson, M. V., and B. G. Barron. 1992. "Expanding the Role of the Curriculum Materials Center: Challenges for the 21st Century." *Education*, 113: 254–55.
According to this article, the traditional CMC has not changed significantly since its inception in 1922. Henderson and Barron call for expansion of the CMC's role by identifying trends in teacher education, goals for the CMC, and activities to achieve these goals. A collaborative effort between librarians and teacher educators is called for to identify this role.

James, M. L. 1963. "The Curriculum Laboratory in Teacher Education Institutions: Its Essential Characteristics." Ph.D. diss., University of Connecticut.
An attempt was made to discern the essential characteristics of CMCs through a survey sent to 210 institutions listed in NCATE's Eighth Annual List. 138 institutions returned questionnaires and data were analyzed. A large variance of opinion regarding essential characteristics was discovered, with different opinions about administrative organization, relationship with other agencies, functions of the CMC, services and clientele, the collection, personnel, physical facilities, and financial support.

Johnson, H. R. 1973. "The Curriculum Materials Center: A Study of Policies and Practices in Selected Centers." Ph.D. diss., Northern Arizona University. ERIC Document Reproduction Service ED No. 081 449.
Before establishing a curriculum library at Northern Arizona University, Johnson visited five curriculum materials centers and surveyed the practices and policies of 66 libraries in 39 states. Using the results of his study, he describes the curriculum library established at his university and provides suggestions for establishing a curriculum library.

Kerr, L. F. 1979. "Materials Centers: A Dream of their Future." Park Forest South, Ill.: Governors State University. ERIC Document Reproduction Service ED No. 188 635.
An overview of the rational of CMCs in academic libraries from their formation to current status is presented. Two types of CMCs are discussed: one which provides a collection of teaching materials of all kinds to be available for use and study by students, faculty, and teachers; and the other to be a workshop or laboratory for developing and constructing curriculum and supplementary teaching materials.

Mace, J. M. 1993. "The Importance of the Curriculum Materials Centers in the Academic Library." *Library Mosaics* 4: 22–23.
The need for CMCs to evolve to meet student and faculty needs is addressed. This evolution is especially needed in the types of materials provided in the CMC. There is a discussion of the move of curriculum centers from Schools of Education to libraries primarily because of the library's expertise in technical processes of information organization.

MacVean, D. S. 1958. "A Study of Curriculum Laboratories in Midwestern Teacher Training Institutions." Ph.D. diss., University of Michigan, Ann Arbor.
The author examined 15 Midwestern curriculum laboratories and attempted to identify those characteristics that make them successful or outstanding. He determined that the two distinguishing characteristics necessary for an outstanding curriculum library were adequacy of personnel in numbers and training and adequate financial support. MacVean's suggestions for further study included determining the best organization for curriculum materials, whether printed and nonprint materials should be integrated in the CMC, criteria for selection, evaluation, and weeding of materials, and criteria for general evaluation of curriculum laboratories.

McGiverin, R. 1988. "Curriculum Material Centers: A Descriptive Study." *Behavioral & Social Sciences Librarian* 6: 119–28.
A lack of a common set of standards for CMCs makes them difficult to compare to one another. Statistics are reported differently, and there is a lack of a standardized description of the scope and boundaries of the collection. A need for a method of evaluation of centers is also discussed.

Morrill, R. L. 1981. "Library Service in Teacher Training Institutions." *Education Libraries* 6: 64–66+.

The history of library service in teacher training institutions from its inception in the mid-1800s through World War II is described. Of special note is a statement from the 26th yearbook of the American Association of Teachers Colleges 1947. that it is not desirable to set definite standards for library service to those institutions.

Povsic, F., and G. Junion. 1983. "Organization of and Access to Curriculum Resource Center Materials: A Response to Standards." *Ohio Media Spectrum* 35: 3–7.
Povsic and Junion look at the organization of curriculum collections and access to those materials in light of standards set forth by the National Council for Accreditation of Teacher Education (NCATE) and Ohio Department of Education Standards for Colleges or Universities Preparing Teachers. They determined that the physical arrangement and proper organization of all types of instructional media supports the ultimate aim of the curriculum center: the training and enabling of new teachers to effectively use instructional materials in the classroom.

Teclehaimanot, B., and A. Patterson. 1992. "The Nature, Function and Value of the Curriculum Materials Center on Colleges of Education." Paper presented at the Convention of the Association for Educational Communications and Technology. ERIC Document Reproduction Service ED No.348 030.
One hundred three institutions in 19 states were surveyed to provide information to administrators for planning and managing CMCs, to obtain data of CMC staff, services, facilities, and collections, to determine strategies for developing instructional media support, to examine the effect of National Council for Accreditation of Teacher Education (NCATE) standards on CMCs, and to develop a model to improve planning and integration of CMCs in teacher education programs.

Toifel, R. C. 1992. "A Survey of Curriculum Materials Centers in Teacher Education Institutions." University of West Florida. ERIC Document Reproduction Service ED No. 343 904.
A two-part questionnaire was sent to teacher training institutions accredited by NCATE. The first part sought descriptive information about curriculum materials centers; the second part consisted of an attitudinal survey with questions about policies/administration; funding; staffing; services; resources; and physical facilities. Twenty-nine percent of CMCs were administered by Schools of Education; 63% were administered by libraries. Respondents expressed concerns about lack of financial support and about a need for clear mission and collection development statements.

Professional Education of Curriculum Materials Center Personnel

Althage, J., and D. Stine. 1992. "Curriculum Centers as Support to Education Programs in Illinois Academic Programs. *Illinois Libraries* 74: 516–23.

Thirty Illinois academic institutions were surveyed related to services and materials offered to education faculty, staff, and students. It was determined that a wide range of services and materials were offered, and that most of the centers surveyed had librarians as directors, with half of them also having a teaching background. Most librarians handled bibliographic instruction, conducted tours, and provided lectures to students in education methods classes.

Haskell, J. D. 1984. "Subject Bibliographers in Academic Libraries: An Historical and Descriptive Review." *Advances in Library Administration and Organization* 3: 73–84.

The role of subject bibliographers to provide specialized knowledge and skill at developing the library collection in assigned subject areas is discussed. Education for these subject specialists is expected to be a minimum of a master's degree in a subject area as well as a master's degree in librarianship. Bibliographers are also expected to be able to provide reference and bibliographic instruction and work closely with teaching faculty on a regular basis.

Herubel, J. V. M. 1991. "To Degree or Not to Degree." *Indiana Libraries* 10: 90–94.

In this general work on academic credentials for academic librarians, Herubel argues that to enhance a subject librarian's credibility, a second master's degree in addition to the library master's degree is highly desired.

Ho, M. L. 1985. "Competencies of Curriculum Materials Center Directors in Teacher-Education Institutions." Paper presented at the annual convention of the Association for Educational Communications and Technology, Anaheim, California, 1985. ERIC Document Reproduction Service ED No. 256 319.

A survey of 183 CMC directors and 100 educators in the fields of educational media and technology was conducted. Two different questionnaires were developed that investigated tasks performed by directors and characteristics of the directors and libraries. Thirty-eight competencies that should be held by directors were identified, but a similar list of characteristics for libraries could not be identified. Neither the identified competencies of directors nor the questionnaires themselves are available in the report for review.

Skinner, A. 1980. "The Academic Departmental Library—Is It Special?" In *Special Librarianship: A New Reader*, ed. Eugene B. Jackson. 290–97. Metuchen, N.J.: Scarecrow.

Skinner describes the role of the librarian in an academic departmental library as that of an "outsider" until proven to be a competent provider of information and solver of problems to the satisfaction of faculty and students. Knowledge of the curriculum and research activities of the department contributes to the success of the librarian.

Administration of CMCs

Carrigan, D. 1992. "Improving Return on Investment: A Proposal for Allocating the Book Budget." *Journal of Academic Librarianship* 18: 292–97.
The author proposes that the book budget be allocated consistent with proportional use of the collection. For a period under review, total book circulation is allocated among the various subject areas on a percentage basis. Similarly, total holdings are allocated among the same subject areas on a percentage basis. A given subject's proportional use statistic is calculated by dividing that subject's percentage of circulation by its percentage of holdings. A proportional use statistic greater than 1 indicates that circulation is relatively greater than holdings, and a statistic less than 1 indicates the reverse.

————. 1996. "Data-guided Collection Development: A Promise Unfulfilled." *College and Research Libraries* 57: 429–37.
In this article, Carrigan proposes that data which can be provided by automated systems be used to guide collection development and allocation of materials budgets. A survey determined that data is not used because of limitations of the automated systems, as well as limitations in the number of years the data has been collected. The survey also found that the data is not used because needed programs are unavailable, and administration is not convinced of the value of the data.

Devlin, B. 1988. "Basic Budget Primer: Choosing the Best Budget for Your Library." *The Bottom Line* 2: 20–24.
Devlin provides information about four main budgeting techniques and evaluates its usefulness to libraries. He concludes that all four approaches to budgeting are needed to meet the requirements of successfully presenting the library's case for support.

Houlihan, B. 1978. "The University Curriculum Library: Evaluate, Update, Renovate." *Curriculum Review* 17: 361–63.
Houlihan notes a need for standards for curriculum libraries that would address the function of the library, the nature of the collection, the budget, audiovisual

facilities, and personnel issues, including education and training of the director and other staff.

McLaren, M. B. 1994. "The Miracle of Money! Managing LRC Budgets, Funds and Fundraising." *Tech Trends* 39: 12–16.
Practical ways to approach utilization of budget funds are discussed in this article, with special attention paid to the importance of accurate record keeping, management of grant funds, and capital outlay. A variety of strategies to stretch budget dollars is also listed, including gifts and donations, contingency set-asides, and discount purchases. In addition, ten tips for effective fundraising are outlined.

Prentice, A. E. 1996. *Financial Planning for Libraries*, 2nd ed. Lanham, Md.: Scarecrow. This book discusses the impact of the economic environment on libraries, the interrelations of financial and service planning, thorough attention to budgeting, the impact of new technology and information infrastructure, and a realistic appraisal of the prospects for the support of libraries. Prentice also spends considerable energy evaluating some of the newer budgeting techniques—performance, program, and zero-based—that stress the importance of planning.

Scherdin, M. J. 1984. "A Marriage That Works: An Approach to Administrative Structure in Curriculum Centers." *College and Research Libraries* 45: 140–47.
A brief historical review is given regarding the lack of uniformity in the administrative structure of curriculum centers and a lack of established core standards to be followed by administrators in planning curriculum centers. The remainder of Scherdin's article focuses on the development and implementation of a successful administrative structure at the University of Wisconsin-Whitewater.

Collection Management

Beck, S. R. 1982. "Bibliographic Access to Curriculum Guides." *Behavioral & Social Sciences Librarian* 2: 41–50.
A commercially available collection of curriculum guides, now known as the Kraus Curriculum Development Library (KCDL), is described, and its usefulness to both educators and librarians is discussed. The collection attempts to minimize the output of a librarian's time and money in selecting, acquiring, and processing hundreds of guides.

Education and Behavioral Sciences Section, Association of College and Research Libraries. 1993. *Curriculum Materials Center Collection Development Policy* 2nd ed. Chicago: American Library Association. Accessed at http://www.lib.msu.edu/

corby/ebss/cmcpolicy.htm/ on July 22, 2000.

This monograph, developed by an ad hoc committee consisting of members of the Curriculum Materials Committee and the Problems of Access and Control of Education Materials Committee of EBSS, provides a model collection development policy for a curriculum materials center and includes sample policies from SUNY-Binghamton and the University of North Carolina-Charlotte. Collection development areas include objectives of the collection, clientele, scope and boundary of the collection, review sources and selection criteria, staffing, gifts, deselection, and interlibrary loan.

Ellis, E. V. 1969. "The Role of the Curriculum Laboratory in the Preparation of Quality Teachers." Ph.D. diss., Florida A&M University. ERIC Document Reproduction Service ED No. 031 457.

Three hundred thirty-one institutions responded to a survey instrument designed to identify organizational and administrative patterns in CMCs and to identify the influences that innovations in teacher education have on the curriculum library. In addition to providing general information about lines of authority, names given to the curriculum laboratory, staff and personnel, and service hours, a manual of procedures for processing of book and nonbook materials in curriculum centers is provided. Though dated and geared toward print resources, this manual does contain information about processing and cataloging nonbook materials.

Gerhardt, L. N. 1990. "Ethical Back Talk, II: 2) Librarians Must Resist All Efforts by Groups or Individuals to Censor Library Materials." *School Library Journal* 36: 4.

Point #2 of the American Library Association's *Code of Ethics* is discussed, particularly as it relates to gift materials given by individuals or groups with their own agendas. The *Code of Ethics* speaks only to the resistance of censorship, not to those putting pressure on governing boards to accept their gifts. Gerhardt calls on the American Library Association to add a statement on the duty of librarians to ensure that their libraries' users are not bartered for free equipment or materials.

The Interactive Multimedia Guidelines Review Task Force. 1994. *Guidelines for Bibliographic Description of Interactive Multimedia*. Chicago: American Library Association.

Objectives of this guide are to facilitate and clarify the descriptive cataloging of interactive multimedia resources; to balance the cataloging description by giving the cataloger the latitude necessary to highlight specific media; to remain in compliance with AACR2R; to develop new cataloging instructions which address the complication of media integration; and to provide fully cataloged examples.

Kranz, J. 1987. "Cataloging of Curriculum Materials on OCLC: A Perspective." *Cataloging & Classification Quarterly* 8: 15–28.
The availability of online bibliographic records for curriculum collections is described. A major concern is that a large proportion of CMCs are not yet automated and do not have their collections cataloged and available online. Among automated CMCs, a wide variety of cataloging systems are in use.

Lare, G. A. 1997. *Acquiring and Organizing Curriculum Materials: A Guide and Directory of Resources*. Lanham, Md.: Scarecrow.
This book describes types of materials traditionally collected in CMCs including curriculum guides, courses, of study, unit and lesson plans, curriculum bulletins or reports, textbooks, teaching activities, audiovisual media, sources on the Internet, and professional education resources to support the CMC and discusses means to acquire and organize such materials. In addition, extensive resource helps are provided, including textbook publishers, media/instructional materials producer and distributor sources; and Web sources. Of special interest is an appendix that provides guidelines for curriculum materials centers adopted by CMC directors in Ohio.

Livingston, S. 1999. "Weeding School Library Media Center Collections." *Kentucky Libraries* 63: 15–19.
Although geared for school library media centers, this article provides guidance for the removal of materials from CMCs. Criteria for weeding include record of use; currency of content; technical quality; physical condition; and dispensability. Of particular use is a timeframe for weeding of textbooks and various other materials often collected by CMCs.

Magrill, R. M., and J. Corbin. 1989. *Acquisitions Management and Collection Development in Libraries*, 2nd ed. Chicago: American Library Association.
Of special interest in this general book on collection management in libraries are chapters on acquisition of special types of book materials and nonbook materials. These materials may include government publications, state and local documents, technical reports, CD-ROMs, video and sound recordings, maps, music, pamphlets, and pictures. A chapter on evaluation of the collection is also useful.

Morse, H. 1988. "Withdrawal Criteria in a Teaching Practice Collection." *Audiovisual Librarian* 14: 31–35.
As part of any CMC's collection development policy, policies and procedures for weeding the collection need to be included. Because a teaching collection is in-

tended to show preservice teachers the kinds of things they may use in the class-room, it is of major importance that the collection reflect what is indeed being used, and materials damaged, out of date, racist/sexist, or in obsolete formats be discarded.

Pidgeon, A. 1995. "On Writing a Deselection Policy; or, How to Toss Books Without Public Condemnation." *Against the Grain* 7: 68–69+.
This article provides information on development of a weeding policy, including, in addition to specific weeding criteria, information about who will weed the collection and when it will be done.

Slote, S. J. 1997. *Weeding Library Collections: Library Weeding Methods.* 4th ed. Englewood, Colo.: Libraries Unlimited, Inc.
Besides providing extensive information on weeding a library collection, Slote describes core collections for school library media centers and for special libraries. He describes goals and objectives for weeding a collection and gives examples of criteria and processes to be used in deselection.

Smith, H. F., and C. A. Gardner. 1956. "Curriculum Materials in the Teachers College Library." *College and Research Libraries* 17: 311–15.
Curriculum materials are defined in this article as "aids or devices to help the teacher in the development of a curriculum, or to help him improve an existing curriculum, or materials that will aid the teacher in instruction." Examples given of types of materials to be collected include textbooks, courses of study (curriculum guides), units of work, and a test collection.

Stine, D. 1991. "Suggested Standards for Cataloging Textbooks." *Cataloging & Classification Quarterly* 13: 67-86.
As a result of a study done comparing cataloging records for textbooks using OCLC, Stine found many duplicate records and a lack of uniformity in cataloging practices. This paper suggests standards to be considered to alleviate the duplication and to make textbook cataloging easier.

Smith, J. 1991. "But, How Do You Barcode a Puppet? (Nonbook Collection at the Learning Resource Center at Northern Kentucky University)." *Ohio Media Spectrum* 43: 23–25.
Practical concerns about automation, classification, and access to some of the more unusual materials found in a curriculum materials collection are discussed.

Subcommittee to revise the *Guide for Written Collection Policy Statements*. 1996. *Guide for Written Collection Policy Statements*, 2nd ed. Chicago: ALA Editions.
This guide provides a step-by-step outline for creating a practical and flexible collection development policy statement.

Wilson, C. F., M. M. Finley, and A. S. Clark. 1986. "Cataloging Practices and Resource Sharing of Curriculum Collections in Academic Libraries." *Journal of Library Administration* 6: 81–88.
Curriculum centers were surveyed regarding cataloging, classification, and resource sharing of materials. A variety of practices and limited input of records into OCLC were discovered. Therefore, standardization and usage of curriculum materials was limited. It is suggested that curriculum collections be treated as important, special collections with the goal of inclusion in bibliographic utilities and in campus OPACs.

Instruction

Buttlar, L., and M. Tipton. 1992. "Library Use and Staff Training in Curriculum Materials Centers." *Journal of Academic Librarianship* 17: 370–74.
A study was conducted to provide information about bibliographic instruction in CMCs, particularly in relation to the use of the online catalog. A conclusion of the study was that curriculum centers were not initiating bibliographic instruction with their users despite literature that commented on the importance of such training for teachers.

James, R. 1985. "Teacher Education Students—Different Needs, Different Solutions." In *Reader Services in Polytechnic Libraries*, John Fletcher. Aldershot, England: Gower Publishing Company, Ltd. 140–58.
In the past 20 years library service to teacher education students has moved from a very low position to a leading place in the development of new services to users. Teacher education libraries developed a range of reader services that have become an accepted part of general library services, including the publication of research guides and instruction in computer use.

Libutti, P.O., and B. Gratch, eds. 1995. *Teaching Information Retrieval and Evaluation Skills to Education Students and Practitioners: A Casebook of Applications*. Chicago: ACRL.
This book provides a variety of examples of teaching information literacy skills to many groups of students, from high school to faculty and practitioners. These information literacy concepts were based on the document "Information Re-

trieval and Evaluation Skills for Education Students" published in *College and Research Library News*, October 1992 and in *ERIC ED* 351038.

Mellon, C. A., ed. 1987. *Bibliographic Instruction: The Second Generation.* Littleton, Colo.: Libraries Unlimited, Inc.
This book provides a historic overview of the development of bibliographic instruction in academic libraries; characteristics of bibliographic instruction (BI) as it has developed in the past 15 years; and reflects on the future of user education. Of special interest to CMC librarians are chapters on the place of BI in the university curriculum and bibliographic instruction in science education.

National Education Association on the United States. 1913. "Report of the Committee on Normal-School Libraries." In *Journal of Proceedings and Addresses of the Fifty -first Annual Meeting.* 747–56.
This report reflects the status of libraries at normal schools in the early part of the 20th century. Information is included about training of librarians and administration of the library. Library instruction in 53 normal schools is discussed, with the number of lessons on use of the library varying from 1 to 60 hours, and the number of lessons in children's literature varying from 1 to 20. One recommendation to come from this report was "that normal colleges and state universities should give library instruction to the end that the leaders of the educational world may recognize the value of the school library" (755).

O'Hanlon, N. 1988. "Up the Down Staircase: Establishing Library Instruction Programs for Teachers." *RQ* 27: 528-34.
Librarians have attempted to convince educators of the value of bibliographic instruction to preservice teachers for a very long time with little success. This article calls for combined efforts of ALA, the American Association of School Librarians, and NCATE to move library literacy programs for teacher trainees to "the top of the staircase." In her article, O'Hanlon describes four library skills instruction programs being taught to education students.

Walter, V. A. 1994. "The Information Needs of Children." *Advances in Librarianship* 18: 111–29.
A model of the information needs of children in southern California was presented. According to Walter, it is distressing that the people who are responsible for providing services to children see that they are lacking in information that they need to thrive. She sees an important role of the children's librarian in providing and disseminating information about basic survival skills, cultural diversity, and

ethics and values to children and also in designing delivery systems that get informa-tion to children rather than waiting for children to come to the information.

Worley, J., et al. 1981. "Bibliographic Competencies for Education Students." *College and Research Libraries News* 42: 209–10.
The Bibliographic Instruction for Educators' Committee of ACRL's Education and Behavior Science Section developed a list of 13 competencies that identify minimal skills in the use of educational materials that should be demonstrated by students at both undergraduate and graduate levels. Among the competencies listed are "1) to develop a logical approach to researching a topic... 4) to locate and describe print and nonprint curriculum materials, instructional aid resources... 11) to select and use computerized information services." Although many of the specific sources cited as important for education student competence are now available in electronic format, the types of information with which those students should be familiar is still important.

Collaboration and Outreach

Austin, A. E., and R. B. Baldwin. 1992. "Faculty Collaboration: Enhancing the Quality of Scholarship and Teaching." *ERIC Digest*. ERIC Document Reproduc-tion Service ED No. 347 958.
This summary report reviews how college faculty are increasingly collaborating to do much of their work. Ways in which administrators can assist this collaboration are given, including resource allocation; developing supportive policies rewarding collaborative efforts; and removal of certain organizational barriers.

Boyer, P., and I. Cockriel. 1997. "Factors Influencing Grant Writing: Perceptions of Tenured and Nontenured Faculty." *SRA Journal* 29: 61–68.
The focus of this study is the differing perceptions of tenured and nontenured College of Education faculty in the United States. It is recommended that admin-istrators and tenured education faculty use the results of this study to plan faculty development programs that assist junior faculty in developing greater knowledge of external funding sources and proposal development.

Couch, T. 1996. "Get That Grant." *Planning* 62: 17–19.
Couch gives a brief overview of the grant-writing process. Steps included are: roughing out a project concept and documenting it as an abstract or discussion paper; researching the type of funding available for your kind of project; main-taining a personal resource file with newspaper and magazine clippings, ap-plication kits, instruction manuals, requests for qualifications (RFQs) and

requests for proposals (RFPs); making contact with the program officer; and following through.

Donham, J. 1998. *Enhancing Teaching and Learning: A Leadership Guide for School Library Media Specialists.* New York: Neal-Schuman.
This book is a guide for effecting change in a library media program by integrating it into the school's instructional program. By integrating the agenda for developing information literacy, advocating for reading, and facilitating effective uses of information technologies into the curriculum, the impact on students is increased. This speaks to the CMC librarian by encouraging collaboration between education faculty and the staff of the CMC to increase information skills in preservice teachers.

Henderson, M. V., S. N. Hunt, and C. Wester. 1999. "Action Research: A Survey of AACTE-member Institutions." *Education* 119: 663–67+.
Action research is defined as "a systematic method of inquiry in a collaborative effort between P–12 schools and SCDE (schools, colleges, or departments of education) personnel for the purpose of reflecting upon and improving classroom teaching and outcomes." An 18-item questionnaire was distributed to AACTE member institutions to answer questions about various aspects of action research. Although less than 50% of institutions responded to the questionnaire, it was determined that many institutions are participating in action research and most are taking advantage of grant monies presently available to encourage it. Many of the projects are planned by one entity, usually higher education, and conducted in collaboration with another.

King, J. A., and M. P. Lonnquist. 1992. "A Review of Writing on Action Research (1944–present)." ERIC Document Reproduction Service ED No. 355 664.
Because teachers work with students on a daily basis, their experiences are a potent source for improving education. King and Lonnquist define action research as trying out ideas in practice to increase knowledge about curriculum, teaching, and learning. Action research is frequently localized and therefore has limited applicability, with results not being published or distributed widely. This paper includes five sections: a history of action research, the action research concept, a theoretical rationale, practical issues of implementation, and types and categories of action research.

Lanning, J. A. 1988. "The Library-faculty Partnership in Curriculum Development." *College and Research Libraries News* 49: 7–10.

This paper, by a chemistry faculty member, presents the importance of library-faculty participation in core curriculum development. Lanning makes the following observations: at least one faculty member in each department should recognize the importance of information literacy skills; librarians should be familiar with requirements of accrediting agencies to facilitate better relationships with departments; librarians should be willing to serve on curriculum development committees and be vocal advocates for their points of view; current campus discussions of education assessment provide an excellent opportunity to integrate library and faculty skills in curriculum development; and librarians and faculty should seek opportunities to team-teach a course on information literacy.

Miller, M. L. 1989. "New Partnerships for School Library Media Education: ALA/AASL and NCATE." *Illinois Libraries* 71: 259–63.
This article describes the new relationship between the American Library Association and its division the American Association of School Librarians and the National Council for Accreditation of Teacher Education. This partnership enables AASL to develop professional competencies that entry-level school library media specialists should have when completing a preparation program in school library media education. An important benefit cited to both ALA and AASL is opportunities for communication and liaison with other NCATE organizations whose members know little about the educational contributions librarians make. As other educational groups struggle with new curricula to produce information-literate students, the opportunities for ALA representatives to interpret the role of libraries will be timely and valuable.

Schnitzer, D. K. 1995. "How to Fund Technology Projects." *Educational Leadership* 53: 71–72.
As local education budgets become tighter, it becomes more important to meet the challenge of obtaining money through the competitive grants process. This article provides a brief overview of the grant proposal process.

Sparapani, E. F., F. J. Abel, S. E. Easton, P. Edwards, and D. L. Herbster. 1996. "Action Research: A Strategy for Bridging the Gap between Theory and Practice." Paper presented at the Association of Teacher Educators' 76th Annual Meeting, St. Louis, Missouri. ERIC Document Reproduction Service ED No. 398 194.
According to Sparapani et al., teaching is often an isolated profession, with most interaction with other professionals about mostly everyday issues. Action research provides school-based professionals with opportunities for interaction with

colleagues and other professionals in an intellectually stimulating environment in a forum for sharing opinions. It provides opportunities for in-service and pre-service teachers to become effective practitioners and knowledgeable profession-als. Four examples of action research occurring through universities involved in teacher education are discussed.

Technology Issues

Anderson, R. E., and A. Ronnkvist. 1999. *Presence of Computers in American Schools: Teaching, Learning, and Computing: 1998 National Survey Report #2. Center for Research on Information Technology and Organizations.* Online. University of California, Irvine and University of Minnesota, June 1999. Center for Research on Information Technology and Organizations. Acessed at http://www.crito.uci.edu/TLC/find-ings/Internet-Use/startpage.htm on July 14, 2000.
This paper discusses the challenges facing American schools in planning and imple-menting new policies and procedures that integrate computing technology into instruction. Concerns addressed include cost; access to current technology; and whether technology actually enhances learning. Results are presented from a 1998 national survey of teachers and students.

Becker, H. J. 1999. *Internet Use by Teachers: Conditions of Professional Use and Teacher-Directed Student Use: Teaching, Learning, and Computing: 1998 National Survey: Report #1.* Online. University of California, Irvine and University of Minnesota, February 1999. Center for Research on Information Technology and Organizations. Ac-cessed at http://www.crito.uci.edu/TLC/findings/Internet-Use/startpage.htm on July 14, 2000.
This online paper presents findings from a 1998 national survey of teachers and students on Internet use (See also Anderson, above). Included in the findings are frequency of use; perceived value of the Internet in the classroom; access; and effects of Internet use on all predicting factors (e.g., technology expertise; staff development; school professional climate; and teacher's pedagogical approach).

Bentley, C. L. 1994. "Are Preservice Teachers Acquiring Skills in Educational Technology, How and Where? Results of a National Survey." Paper presented at the Annual Meeting of the Mid-Western Educational Research Association, Chi-cago, Ill., October 13–15, 1994. ERIC Document Reproduction Service ED No. 381 585.
Directors of 32 curriculum centers completed a survey designed to acquire infor-mation about the preservice training of teachers in technology. Results of the survey showed that this training is inconsistent and not focused, and that while

telecommunications technology exists at nearly all schools, training in the use of telecommunications is at a minimum level at most institutions.

Bitter, G., and R. L. Yohe. 1989. "Preparing Teachers for the Information Age." *Educational Technology* 23 (3): 22–25.
In this early article on technology and teacher education, Bitter and Yohe suggest that the integration of technology into the teacher preparation curriculum is the single most important issue in Colleges of Education. Of particular interest in technology training is the development of the teacher's competence in using exist-ing methods and also in adapting to future developments. In addition, there must be focus on both knowledge about technology beyond the application of products (hands-on experiences) and on the understanding of the processes (theoretical investigations).

Evans, A. D., and M. H. Tipton. 1999. "The Shift from the Older Media to the 'State-of-the-Art' Technology in Teacher Education Media Centers." *Ohio Media Spectrum* 41: 7–10.
The authors suggest that teacher education programs must teach the process of how instructional equipment works as well as how it should be integrated into the teaching/learning process. Because technology is changing so rapidly, learning about technology must be conceptual rather than procedural so that adaptation to new equipment can quickly occur.

Halpin, P., and J. D. Kossegi. 1996. "The WWW, Preservice Teachers and their Mathematics Courses." In *Association of Small Computer Users in Education (ASCUE) Summer Conference Proceedings 29th, North Myrtle Beach, S.C., June 9–13, 1996.* ERIC Document Reproduction Service ED No. 405 819.
This paper describes a course in problem solving required for all secondary math-ematics majors at SUNY-Oswego. One project during the term was to find a mathematics problem suitable for secondary students on the Web and to make a presentation based on this problem to the class. By finding Web sites with infor-mation beneficial to the mathematics community, the students determined that the use of modern technology as a teaching tool will have a positive impact on their teaching careers.

Handler, M. G. 1993. "Preparing New Teachers to Use Computer Technology: Perceptions and Suggestions for Teacher Educators." *Computers and Education* 20 (2): 147–56.
This study asked whether new teachers were prepared to use technology during

their preservice education and identified factors that impact on new teachers' sense of preparedness regarding the use of technology in the classroom. Some of those factors included specific courses on the uses of computers in education, uses of technology in methods courses, and technology experiences in student teaching. In addition, ways for teacher educators to implement technology into their own instruction are provided.

ISTE Accreditation and Standards Committee. 1997. *National Standards for Technology in Teacher Preparation.* Eugene, Ore.: International Society for Technology in Education. Online. Accessesd at http://www.iste.org/standards/ncate/found.html on July 14, 2000.
ISTE has developed recommending guidelines for accreditation to NCATE for both programs in educational computing and technology teacher preparation and recommended foundations in technology for all teachers. Among the recommended foundations in technology for all teachers are standards related to basic computer/technology operations and concepts; personal and professional use of technology; and application of technology in instruction.

Kent, T. W., and R. F. McNergney. 1999. *Will Technology Really Change Education? From Blackboard to Web.* Thousand Oaks, Calif.: Corwin Press.
This short work addresses questions about the use of technology; historical patterns of technology adoption by schools; how technology might be adapted to instructional models; and what the future might hold for teachers and teacher education.

Kerr, S.T., ed. 1996. *Technology and the Future of Schooling.* National Society for the Study of Education Yearbook. Chicago: NSSE. Distributed by the University of Chicago Press.
Significant questions about the field of educational technology are asked and discussed in this book. These questions include asking what technology in schools is good for; issues concerning funding for technology; concerns about technology driving education rather than the other way around; and, finally, how teachers can be encouraged to feature a thoughtful, reflective use of technology in their classrooms.

King, T., ed. 1997. *Technology in the Classroom: A Collection of Articles.* Arlington Heights, Ill.: IRI/SkyLight Training and Pub.
This book contains a collection of articles divided into the themes "The Difference Technology Makes," on the appropriate use of technology; "Transforming

Teaching with Technology," about using technology in new ways; and "Making Technology Work," which provides case studies of schools that have successfully implemented technology in their classrooms.

Love, R., and M. McVey. 2000. "Teachers' Use of the Internet." *Teachers College Record*, 6/21/00. NewYork: Teachers College, Columbia University. Accessed at http://www.tcrecord.org/Content.asp?ContentID=10538 on July 14, 2000. This commentary on the Center for Research on Information Technology & Organizations' national survey of teachers and students (See also Anderson and Ronnkvist, 1999 and Becker, 1999. proposes three reasons that relatively few teachers with Internet access are making full use of that resource, including lack of technological skills; teachers' views about children and technology; and additional demands on time and focus associated with current standardized testing practices.

Luke, N., J. L. Moore, and S. B. Sawyer. 1998. "Authentic Approaches to Encourage Technology-using Teachers." In *SITE 98: Society for Information Technology & Teacher Education International Conference 9th, Washington, D.C., March 10–14, 1998. Proceedings*. ERIC Document Reproduction Service ED No. 421 083. For students to be better prepared to learn with technology, teachers need to be better prepared to teach with technology. In this paper, Luke, Moore, and Sawyer suggest using preservice teacher education, and in-service teacher training, and providing additional field experiences involving the use of technology for preservice teachers in actual classrooms.

Marshall-Bradley, T., and G. C. Bradley. 1998. "Starting from Ground Zero: Integrating Technology in Education Programs." In *SITE 98: Society for Information Technology & Teacher Education International Conference 9th, Washington, D.C., March 10–14, 1998. Proceedings*. ERIC Document Reproduction Service ED No. 421 082. According to Marshall-Bradley and Bradley, the idea of using technology in the classroom has been articulated by some Colleges of Education, but assumptions have been made that, when students take a basic course in technology, they are prepared to use the concepts as a part of their training in education. By encouraging education faculty to design and develop Web-based applications, faculty will model the use of technology in teaching.

National Council for Accreditation of Teacher Education. 1997. *Technology and the New Professional Teacher: Preparing for the 21st Century*. Washington, D.C.: NCATE.

Accessed at www.ncate.org/accred/projects/tech/tech-21.htm on July 14, 2000. This report is the culmination of a year of deliberations by NCATE's Task Force on Technology and Teacher Education that was commissioned to help guide the development and implementation of technology expectations for teacher candidates and for accredited schools of education, and to guide the organization's use of technology in the accreditation process.

Newby, T. J. et al. 2000. *Instructional Technology for Teaching and Learning.* 2nd ed. Saddle River, N.J.: Merrill/Prentice Hall.
This integrated textbook provides basic information about both the instructional material planning process (based on the PIE Model—Planning, Implementation, and Evaluation) and about the computer as a tool to develop and execute the plan. Of special interest in the book are the companion Web site <http://www.prenhall.com/newby>; toolboxes throughout the text that present relevant tips, tools, and techniques; and appendices that provide a quick guide to computer systems, sample forms for the review of instructional materials, and ISTE "Recommended Foundations in Technology for All Teachers" and "Standards for Basic Endorsement in Educational Computing and Technology Literacy."

Northrup, P. T. 1997. "Instructional Technology Benchmarks for Teacher Preparation Programs and K–12 School Districts." In *Proceedings of Selected Research and Development Presentations at the 1997 National Convention of the Association for Educational Communications and Technology 19th, Albuquerque, N.M., February 14–18, 1997.* ERIC Document Reproduction Service ED No. 409 858.
This study provides clearly defined systematic benchmarks in preservice teacher preparation and in K–12 education that can be used as a guide to teacher preparation programs and K–12 school districts wishing to facilitate this change in the use of instructional technology.

Peterson, S. L. 1999. *Teachers and Technology: Understanding the Teacher's Perspective of Technology.* San Francisco: International Scholars Publications.
In addition to pointing out problems with lack of funding, low priorities manifested in lack of time and training for teachers, and technophobia among the nation's teachers, this book also attempts to provide solutions to those problems. Of particular interest are prompts, checklists, and other handout templates to guide teachers and administrators in their thinking about technology.

President's Committee of Advisors on Science and Technology (U.S.) Panel on Educational Technology. 1997. *Report to the President on the Use of Technology to*

Strengthen K–12 Education in the United States. Washington, D.C.: President's Committee of Advisors on Science and Technology (U.S.) Panel on Educational Technology. ERIC Document Reproduction Service ED No. 410 950.
Through a literature review and written submissions and briefings from a number of individuals, agencies, and organizations involved with the application of technology education, the Panel on Educational Technology offers several recommendations related to the use of technology in K–12 education. Among those recommendations are: 1) focus on learning *with* technology, not *about* technology; 2) emphasize content and pedagogy, and not just hardware; 3) give special attention to professional development; 4) engage in realistic budgeting; 5) ensure equitable, universal access; and 6) initiate a major program of experimental research.

Serim, F., and M. Koch. 1996. *Netlearning: Why Teachers Use the Internet.* Sebastopol, Calif.: Songline Studios.
This book addresses the value of the Internet to educators in addition to answering technical questions about getting connected. While a linear reading of the book is recommended for "newbies," experienced Internet users may find the chapters "Teachers Creating Online Collaborations," "The Innovative School," and "The Connected Community" of special interest.

U.S. Congress, Office of Technology Assessment. 1995. *Teachers and Technology: Making the Connection: OTA Report Summary.* Washington, D.C. ERIC Document Reproduction Service ED No. 386 154.
This report summary discusses the need for teachers to be adequately trained and for new teachers to be adequately prepared for the role of technology in education. The report states that often, when teachers' needs are addressed at all, it is in terms of the "one-shot" short-term training to familiarize the teacher with a specific application or piece of hardware rather than on the relationship between technology and the teacher's role. Seldom has the connection been made between teachers and the vision of technology that includes all parts of their job: classroom instruction, administrative tasks, communication with parents, and continuing professional development. The role of Congress in providing access to technology for teachers and schools is also discussed.

Williams, C. 2000. *Internet Access in U.S. Public Schools and Classrooms: 1994–1999.* (NCES Publication No. 99017). Online. Washington, D.C.: U.S. Department of Education, Office of Educational Research and Improvement, 2000. National Center for Education Statistics. Accessed at http://nces.ed.gov/pubs2000/qrtlyspring/4elem/q4-8.html on July 14, 2000.

Statistical evidence related to various aspects of computer and Internet access in public schools is presented here. These aspects include progress in connecting to the Internet; connecting individual classrooms; ratio of students per computer; how schools are connecting to the Internet; and how they are funding advanced telecommunications.

Willis, E. 1998. "An Interdisciplinary, Problem-centered Methods Model for Preservice Elementary Teacher Education." In *SITE 98: Society for Information Technology & Teacher Education International Conference 9th, Washington, D.C., March 10–14, 1998. Proceedings.* ERIC Document Reproduction Service ED No. 421 084. This paper discusses a class at Northern Arizona University that teaches the integration of technology into the elementary classroom through the use of a constructivist model. The preservice teachers in the class became active learners who were confident in their ability to integrate technology into an interdisciplinary curriculum when presented with that model in a learning environment that made them responsible for their own learning.

Contributing Authors

Ann Brownson is a reference librarian and coordinator of the Florence Coles Ballenger Teacher's Center at Eastern Illinois University in Charleston. She holds a B.A. from Grinnell College and Master's degrees in Postsecondary Student Development, and Library and Information Science from the University of Iowa. She presently cochairs an Education and Behavioral Sciences Section ad hoc committee charged with developing guidelines for curriculum materials centers.

Jo Ann Carr, Editor, is the director of the Center for Instructional Materials and Computing for the School of Education at the University of Wisconsin-Madison. She holds a B.A. and an M.L.S. from Indiana University-Bloomington. She has published in the areas of information literacy and electronic publishing. She has an extensive record of service to education and library associations, including being a member of the National Education Network Executive Board and the Science and Mathematics Advisory Board for the Eisenhower National Clearinghouse. She was named the 1999 Distinguished Education and Behavioral Sciences Librarian.

Peter Cupery is the information services librarian at the Center for Instructional Materials and Computing for the School of Education at the University of Wisconsin-Madison. He holds a B.S. in Zoology and an M.L.S. from the University of Wisconsin-Madison and a B.A. in Industrial Education from the University of Wisconsin-Stout. His ten years as a public school teacher and more than a dozen years as a university library reference coordinator were put to use in constructing the chapter "Collection Development for CMC Reference Materials".

Lori Delaney received a B.A. from the University of Minnesota-Twin Cities and an M.L.S. from the University of Wisconsin-Madison. While working towards her M.L.S., she was a graduate assistant for information services at the Center for Instructional Materials and Computing for UW-Madison's School of Education. She now works as a librarian in Raleigh/Durham, North Carolina.

Bernie Foulk is an information services program assistant at the Center for Instructional Materials and Computing for the School of Education at the University of Wisconsin-Madison. He is currently working towards a M.L.S. at the University of Wisconsin-Madison and has enjoyed reference experience at a variety of academic libraries.

Harriet Hagenbruch received her M.L.S. from the Palmer School of Library and Information Science, Long Island University, C.W. Post Campus and her M.A. in elementary education from Hofstra University. Professor Hagenbruch has been an active member of the Greater New York Metropolitan Area Chapter of ACRL/NY and of the Long Island Division of ACRL/NY and in 2000 was elected to serve as its vice president/president elect. In addition, she founded and, until recently, chaired the Education/Curriculum Materials Center Librarians, a special interest group of ACRL/NY. She is the author of numerous articles on the instructional role of libraries.

Martha V. Henderson is a professor at Northwestern State University, Natchitoches, Louisiana. She holds a B.A. and an M.Ed. from Louisiana Tech University, an M.A.L.I.S. from the University of Oklahoma, and an Ed.D. from the University of Arkansas. She is a member of the graduate faculty of the College of Education and coordinates the library and information science certification program for school media specialists. In addition, she serves as the systems administrator and head of technical processes for Northwestern's libraries. She has published in the fields of information science, distance learning, and curriculum and instruction. She has an extensive record of service to educational associations, specifically AACTE and NCATE, having served on national boards for the past fourteen years.

John Hickok is the audiovisual and curriculum materials librarian at California State University Fullerton. He holds an M.L.I.S from UCLA and prior to that was a credentialled California secondary school teacher. His specialization is in both AV and CMC materials, using new technologies such as web-streamed video to enhance library access and orientation. John has been a member of three national CMC-related committees during the past four years.

Judith Miller Hildebrandt is the head of user services for Mason Library at Keene State College in New Hampshire. She holds a B.A. from Hiram College and an M.S.L.S. from Simmons College. Prior to assuming her current position, she was for many years director of Keene State College's Curriculum Materials Library, a federally-funded collection and service to New Hampshire educators with special emphasis on vocational–technical education. In that capacity, she served as state representative to the National Network for Curriculum Coordination and was active in the Vocational Instructional Materials section of the American Vocational Association.

Allison G. Kaplan is the assistant director of the Education Resource Center for the Delaware Center for Teacher Education and Coordinator of the School Library Media Specialist Program in the School of Education at the University of Delaware. She holds an M.L.S. from the University of California, Los Angeles. She has been involved in cataloging education materials since 1990 and currently has a book in press (Linworth Publishing, Inc.) on cataloging for school library media specialists.

Gary Lare is head of the Curriculum Resources Center at the University of Cincinnati. He holds a B.S. in education and an M.Ed, and a Ph.D. in curriculum and instruction from Kent State University. He has published books and articles in the areas of audiovisual media and curriculum materials centers. Dr. Lare has over twenty-five years experience in managing curriculum materials centers and providing service to the education and library fields.

Jeneen LaSee-Willemssen is information technology librarian and assistant professor of library science at the University of Wisconsin-Superior. She has published in the areas of education and children's literature. In addition to teaching courses in UW-Superior's Library Science program, she teaches the online children's literature class for the University of Wisconsin System School Library Education Consortium. Formerly, she was education librarian and curriculum materials center head at Kansas State University. She holds a B.A. and an M.A.L.S. from University of Wisconsin-Madison and is pursuing a Youth Literature and Technology certificate from Rutgers.

Patricia O'Brien Libutti is the social sciences/education librarian for Rutgers University Libraries. She has prepared instructional materials for the web on intellectual property and web production, as well as maintaining the web library of student-produced educational sites. She chaired the Education and Behavioral Sciences Section of ACRL in 1996. Dr. Libutti has held positions as a librarian and as an educator, teaching courses in K–12, gifted education, art, and human relations. Higher education experience has included teaching library science at Rutgers University and educational technology at Fordham University. Her publications and presentations over the last decade have focused on instructional roles of librarians in technology-rich scenarios. She has prepared instructional materials for the web on intellectual property and web production, as well as maintaining the web library of student-produced educational sites as a cybrarian.

Peggie Partello is director of the Curriculum Materials Library at Keene State College in Keene, New Hampshire. She holds a B.A. and an M.A. from Binghamton University, an M.L.S. from University at Albany, and will have completed the requirements for an M.B.A. from Plymouth State College by December 2001. She has been a contributor to *Library Journal, Magazines for Libraries,* and the *Film Literature Index,* for which she indexes Italian periodicals.

Adelaide Phelps is the coordinator of the Educational Resources Laboratory (ERL) for the School of Education and Human Services at Oakland University in Rochester, Michigan. She holds a B.A. in history from Oakland University and an M.L.I.S. with Archival Certification from Wayne State University in Detroit, Michigan. She is currently earning a second masters degree in English at Oakland University.

Lorene Sisson is the director of Learning Resources Display Center #34 at San Jose State University Library. She is the liaison librarian for the College of Education. She holds a B.A. and an M.L.S. from San Jose State University. She has published in the areas of teacher education and library science. She has a strong record of service to library associations including the California Library Association and the Education and Behavioral Sciences Section of ACRL.

Mike Tillman is the director of the Curriculum/Juvenile Library for the Henry Madden Library at California State University, Fresno. He holds a B.A. from Minnesota State University, Moorhead, an M.L.S. from the University of Arizona, and a B.S. from the State University of New York, Albany. He has published in the areas of bibliographic instruction, educational/information technology, and constructivist learning.

Judith Walker has been the curriculum materials librarian at the University of North Carolina, Charlotte, for over 14 years. She holds a B.A. in education from Montclair State University and an M.L.S. from Catholic University of America. She also was certified by Kutztown University in school library media and was a school media generalist in Harford County Public Schools in Maryland. Currently she is the secretary of the Education and Behavioral Sciences Section of ACRL and electronic list moderator for the section. As a member, and later chair, of the EBSS Curriculum Materials Committee, she was instrumental in the publication *Curriculum Materials Center Collection Development Policy* published by ACRL. Ms Walker works extensively with preservice and in-service educators and education faculty in the area of technology integration across the curriculum via summer institutes, workshops, and presentations.

Scott Walter is the head of the George B. Brain Education Library at Washington State University. He holds an M.A. in education from The American University and an M.L.S. from Indiana University, where he is currently a doctoral candidate in history of education. He has written on information literacy and education information systems and is an active member of the Education and Behavioral Sciences Section of ACRL and of the Education Division of the Special Libraries Association. He is currently a member of the editorial board of *Behavioral and Social Sciences Librarian* and the editor of *Education Libraries*.

Contributors of Profiles

As indicated in the introduction, staff members in twenty-six curriculum materials centers prepared extensive profiles of their centers to provide background information for this volume. These profiles will be included in a digital version of this publication that is currently under development. The authors wish to acknowledge the invaluable contribution that each of these CMCs has made to the development of this publication and to the development of CMCs that can meet the challenges and promise of the 21st century:

Boston College Educational Resource Center

Brock University

California State University Northridge Teacher Curriculum Center

Central Connecticut State College

Chicago State University

James Madison University

Kansas State University

Keen State College Curriculum Materials Library

Louisiana State University Education Resources

Midwestern State University

Montclair State University

Minnesota State University Moorhead Curriculum Materials Center

North Carolina State University Learning Resources Library

Ohio State University

Silver Lake College Curriculum Resource Center

Southern Adventist University

University of Cincinnati Curriculum Resource Center

University of Dayton

University of Delaware Education Resource Center

University of Illinois at Urbana Champaign Curriculum Collection

University of South Dakota

University of Tennessee at Martin Learning Resource Center

University of Wisconsin-Stout Education Materials Center

Washburn University of Topeka Curriculum Media Library

Western Kentucky University

Index

action research, 129, 130, 133–34, 178, 179
American Education Research Association, 15
American Library Association, 1, 125
American Association of Colleges for Teacher Education, 4, 133
American Association of School Libraries, 15
Appalachian State University, 71
audiovisual
  collection, 72, 104
  access, 79
  equipment, 49, 75

Baylor University 71
bibliographic instruction. *See* Instructional Services
Boston College, 36, 140, 146, 158, 192
Bridgewater State College, 71
Brock University, 36, 78, 119, 192
budget, 25–33, 36–37, 89
  definition 26
  staff 26, 30
  collections, 26, 27, 31

CRITO. *See* Center for Research on Informa-

tion Technology and Education
California Department of Education, 48
California Polytechnic State University, 71
California Learning Resources Display Centers, 48, 49, 50
California State University-Fresno, 89, 158
California State University-Fullerton, 71, 158
California State University-Northridge, 71, 78, 192
California State University-San Bernadino, 71
Center for Research on Information Technology and Education (CRITO), 148
Central Connecticut State University, 36, 71, 78, 140, 142, 192
Chadron State College, 71
Chicago State University, 192
children's literature, 4, 94, 145
  organization, 54
  selection, 106
Cleveland State University, 71
Coalition for Networked Information, 121, 122
collaboration, 10, 47–48, 101, 121, 122, 128–30, 138,141, 144, 177–80

194

collection development, 8–9, 27, 37–38 144, 155, 156, 171–75
   acquisition, 28, 44–48, 141, 173
   criteria, 59–66
   deselection, 29, 57–67, 91, 173, 174
   gifts, 29, 57–67
   policy, 58–59, 86–89, 102–3, 171
   selection, 57–67
collection management, 141
collection organization, 14–15, 69–77, 156
   audiovisual, 155
   cataloging, 28, 50–55, 78, 144, 172–73
   children's literature, 54
   Internet resources, 54–55
   processing, 28, 75–77, 99, 174
   shelving, 48–49, 70–75, 155
   textbooks, 48–49, 50–55
collections, 112
   access, 78–79
   audiovisual, 155
   children's literature, 27
   Internet resources, 25, 155
   reference, 101–8, 156
   software, 155
   tests, 104–6, 116
   textbooks, 31
Columbia University, 132
   Teachers College, 110, 140, 146
computers, 155–56, 160–61
   equipment, 89, 160–61
   services, 152–55
   See also Internet Resources
Concordia College, 71
Concordia University-St. Paul, 71
Consortium for Outstanding Achievement in Teaching with Technology, 123–24
cross-curricular instruction, 27
curriculum materials centers, 164–70
   administration, 37, 170–71
   definition, viii, 2, 12
   history, 3, 30, 109–12, 164, 165

librarian, education of, 2–7, 11–17, 169–70
librarians, 135, 138, 141
location, 27, 29, 77–78, 84, 137
mission, 34, 38
relationship to college of education, 27–28, 31
staffing, 77–78, 84–86, 88
users, 2, 5, 35–36, 113
curriculum trends, 135, 139

distance learning, 27, 121

EBSS. *See* Education and Behavioral Sciences Section
East Illinois State University, 71
Education and Behavioral Sciences Section, 17, 58, 70, 90, 115, 132, 138
educational technology, 4, 9, 15, 25, 144, 150, 152, 153, 180–85
Eisenhower National Clearinghouse, 48, 114
electronic resources. *See* computers; Internet resources

Framingham State University, 71
funding, 30–31, 36–37

Gonzaga University, 158
grants, 31, 36, 38–40, 85, 129–33, 177

Harvard University, 71
Hofstra University, 71, 138, 139, 142, 143, 144, 145

Illinois State University, 71
Indiana University, 71
information services, 29, 101, 112–14
information literacy. *See* instructional services
instructional services, 14, 88, 96, 98–100, 110, 114–25, 141, 142, 143, 144, 152–55, 175–77

instructional technology. See educational technology

interdisciplinary teaching. *See* cross-curricular instruction

interlibrary loan, 28, 79, 101

International Society for Technology in Education (ISTE), 150–53

Internet resources, 29, 81–92, 119, 120, 123–25, 149, 157–59, 160, 180

organization, 89, 124–25

selection, 26–89, 91–92

James Madison University, 71, 78, 192

Kansas State University, 36, 71, 117, 119, 120, 140, 142, 158, 192

Kansas University, 132

Keene State College, 34–41, 71, 193

Kutztown University, 36, 78, 158

library user education. *See* instructional services

Louisiana State University, 71, 78, 158, 193

MARC tags, 51–53, 79

Mansfield University, 71

Marshall University, 78

McNeese University, 71

media. *See* audiovisual

Midwestern State University, 36, 78, 158, 193

Minnesota State University-Mankato, 71

Minnesota State University-Moorhead 193

Mississippi College, 71

Montclair State University, 94, 159, 160

Moorhead State University, 71, 78, 119, 146

National Council for the Accreditation of Teacher Education (NCATE), 4, 26, 137, 139, 137, 149, 150, 152, 161

National Council of Teachers of Education, 15

National Library of Education, 3, 85, 110

New Jersey State University, 71

North Carolina State University, 78, 132, 193

Northern Michigan University, 71

Northwestern State University, 132

OCLC, 55

Oakland University, 117, 119

Office of Technology Assessment, 148

Ohio State University, The, 71, 140, 193

OhioLINK, 79

outreach, 137–45, 177–80

campus, 143–45

community, 40, 145

faculty, 138–41, 178

PK–12, 145–47

students, 141–43

See also collaboration

President's Committee of Advisors on Science and Technology, 151

public relations, 137

public services. *See* information services; instructional services; outreach; public relations

Quincy University, 71

Radford University, 71

reference collections, 101–8, 156

reference services. *See* information services

Regional Instructional Materials Review Center, 47–48

San Jose State University, 48–49, 71

scholarly activities, 128, 134

selection. *See* collection development

Shawnee State University, 71

Silver Lake College, 36, 193

Slippery Rock State University, 90, 159

software, 60, 72, 75, 96, 104, 123, 153–54, 156–57

Southern Adventist University, 193
Southern Illinois University, 71
surveys, 6, 7, 115, 129
State University of West Georgia, 71

technology, 121, 123, 148–63, 180–86
    standards, 150–52
Texas A&M University, 71, 159
textbooks, 9, 11, 31, 37, 42, 47, 53, 58, 59,
    60, 62, 70, 81–82, 113, 135, 155
    acquisitions, 44–48, 141
    definition, 43–44
    organization, 48–49, 50–55
    preview centers, 47–48
    selection, 95
trade books. *See* children's literature

United States Congress, 160
University of Akron, 71
University of Alabama, 120
University of Central Florida, 159
University of Cincinnati, 75, 78, 79, 90, 159,
    160, 193
University of Dayton, 78, 118, 140, 193
University of Delaware, 36, 144, 159, 193
University of Illinois-Chicago, 90, 132, 159
University of Illinois-Urbana Champaign, 134,
    193
University of Lethbridge, 159
University of Maine, 159
University of Nebraska Regional Instructional

Materials Review Center. *See* Regional Instructional Materials Review Center
University of Nebraska-Kearney, 47, 159
University of North Carolina-Charlotte, 119,
    120, 150, 153, 154, 159
University of South Dakota, 36, 78, 140,
    193
University of Tennessee-Martin, 36, 193
University of Vermont, 159
University of Wisconsin-Madison, 78, 119,
    120, 132, 142, 146, 159
University of Wisconsin-Oshkosh 159
University of Wisconsin-Stout, 36, 78, 142,
    146, 193
University of Southern Mississippi, 36, 78, 159
users, 35, 40
    campus, 143–45
    community, 40, 145
    faculty, 138–41, 178
    PK–12, 145–47
    students, 141–43

virtual collections. *See* Internet resources

Washburn University, 36, 159
Webliographies, 132
weeding. *See* collection development-deselection
Western Kentucky University, 78, 193
World Wide Web. *See* Internet